THE
REBIRTH OF
ORTHODOXY

THE
REBIRTH OF
ORTHODOXY

Signs of New Life in Christianity

THOMAS C. ODEN

HarperSanFrancisco
A Division of HarperCollins*Publishers*

FIRST EDITION

Translation indicated in each endnote.

Designed by Jessica Shatan

Library of Congress Cataloging-in-Publication Data
Oden, Thomas C.
   The rebirth of orthodoxy / Thomas C. Oden.
     p. cm.
   Includes bibliographical references and index.
   ISBN 0-06-009785-X (cloth : alk. paper)
     1. Theology. 2. Postmodernism—Religious aspects—Christianity. I. Title.
   BT28 .O34 2002
   230'.046—dc21   2002068531

03 04 05 06 07 ❖/RRD 10 9 8 7 6 5 4 3 2

To quiet heros of the New Ecumenism

John Leith (PCUSA)

Allan Churchill (UC Canada)

Diane Knippers (ECUSA)

William Rusch (ELCA)

James Heidinger (UMC)

CONTENTS

PREFACE

A reversal has occurred in our time. The faithful have in fact outlived the collapse of the foundations of secular society. Familiar dominant patterns of thought have lost their immune system for recuperation. The modern outlook is disintegrating. But communities of traditional faith flourish more than ever.

It is a fact: evangelical, Orthodox, and Catholic spirituality, scholarship, pastoral care, and institutional life have against all odds already weathered the waning winter of this modern decline. So has traditional Jewish life.

We are witnessing an emerging resolve in worldwide Christianity and Judaism to reclaim the familiar classic spiritual disciplines: close study of scripture, daily prayer, regular observance in a worshiping community, doctrinal integrity, and moral accountability. Even though my voice is Protestant, the arguments and evidences apply equally to Catholic, Orthodox, and Jewish life.

Turning from the illusions of modern life, the faithful are now quietly returning to the spiritual disciplines that have profoundly shaped their history, and in fact have enabled their survival. *This is the rebirth of orthodoxy.*

ACKNOWLEDGMENTS

Special thanks are due to Jewish partners in dialogue who have helped me over three decades to understand how efforts at the recovery of Christian orthodoxy have salient analogies with efforts to recover Judaic roots—especially Peter Ochs, David Novak, Fritz Rothschild, and the late Will Herberg. Blessed by a quarter-century of dialogue with esteemed Catholic colleagues, I am grateful especially to Avery Cardinal Dulles, Richard John Neuhaus, Robert P. George, and James M. O'Kane. Among friends who are building bridges between the Orthodox and evangelical traditions I especially thank George Dragas and David Ford. To colleagues in the Association for Church Renewal, and to my close associates in editing the *Ancient Christian Commentary on Scripture,* and to each of the editors of its twenty-eight volumes, I am profoundly grateful.

INTRODUCTION

Those made alive by the Spirit, grounded in sacred scripture, come to these times confidently. Laypeople whose lives have been quickened and stabilized by the emergent vitality of classic Christianity and Judaism are now living and breathing in a refreshing atmosphere. This century promises to be a pivotal period of opportunity, recovery, and rebuilding. Long-set-aside possibilities and aptitudes for spiritual deepening again have relevance and power, even though they are disdained by the knowledge elites and media managers.

MOVING CONFIDENTLY BEYOND THE MODERN FUTURE

The defenses of secularism are down. Its wasted opportunities are strewn about a stark landscape. However, amid this cultural death (as amid *any* cultural death) gracious gifts of providential guidance are being offered to human freedom and imagination. Human folly is always being quietly curbed by divine grace in history. Thus the demise of the underpinnings of the modern outlook offers worshiping communities an unparalleled opportunity.

The faithful who are healthy enough to have survived the collapse of the modern dream are no longer intimidated by the pretenses of its future durability. Recovering pilgrims of Catholic, evangelical, and Jewish spirituality have already paid their dues twice over to modern misjudgments. Now they are open to forgotten wisdom long ruled out by the narrow dogmas of post-Enlightenment naturalism.

This does not prevent the faithful from appreciating the technological achievements, economic benefits, political institutions, and social advantages of modern life. These can be celebrated precisely while soberly recognizing that modern thought faces a radical crisis.

ENTERING THE SIXTH MILLENNIUM OF HUMAN CULTURE

Human cultures extend three millennia before the birth of Jesus and two millennia after. Thus we are entering the sixth millennium of civilly ordered human societies:

Third millennium (3000–2000) BCE: Egyptian dynasties to written law, the wheel to writing

Second millennium BCE: Abraham to David, Neolithic period to Iron Age

First millennium BCE: David to John the Baptist, Iron Age to messianic age

The Pivot of History

First millennium CE: Paul to Anselm—classic Christianity

Second millennium CE: Anselm to John Paul II—medieval, Reformation, and modern times

Third millennium CE: The human prospect after the decline of modern times

The crisis of the new millennium is not political but rather spiritual and moral. It is a crisis of courage and, more profoundly, a crisis of faith. Can we effectively retrieve our faith-heritage for a meaningful human future?

Vexing parental and personal concerns stem from this dilemma: whether children can be nurtured, whether the madness of all-out war can be avoided, whether humanity can survive, whether life is worth living, whether the earth as we know it can be preserved, whether the human future is worth tackling.

A whole series of crises accompany this major watershed—crises involving the family, the environment, sexually transmitted diseases, the communications revolution, world poverty, the future of freedom and democracy. But none of these crises is more decisive than the crisis of meaning.

The gains of modern life have been accompanied by the loss of wonder. The achievements of the end of the previous millennium have left us with a deep sense of rootlessness and moral confusion. This, then, is a fitting moment to ponder who we are in relation to our human past.

The modern worldview is ebbing. Though perhaps not yet wholly extinct, it is low in emergent vitality, awaiting the lingering expiration of failed ideologies: individualism, narcissism, naturalism, and moral relativism. Others may term its death something other than the end of the modern way of knowing, but I have no better way of naming it.

PART I

THE GIFT OF
NEW LIFE

ONE

The Modern Impasse:
Living Without Roots

A spiritual crisis has followed in the wake of the modern scientific era. Many people question whether the wisdom of the human past can be recovered and whether that wisdom is necessary (or even valid) for the third millennium. This is the setting to which I respond in these chapters.

THE HIGH COST OF MODERN LIVING

The *modern period* spans the time from 1789 to 1989—that is, the time from the French Revolution to the fall of the Berlin Wall. It extends from the beginning of the Enlightenment to the collapse of the Enlightenment. That period characteristically embraced a secular worldview that once cast a long ideological spell—but has now fallen into irreversible decline. Some will take issue with the simplicity of my definition of the modern period, but it provides a window—from the Bastille to the Berlin Wall—through which a clear picture can be seen.

The Challenge of Modern Rootlessness

The naturalism of Freud is no longer marketable as a reliable therapy, because rigorous studies of its effectiveness have shown it to be terribly inefficient. The utopianism of Marx has collapsed from St. Petersburg to Havana. The narcissism of Nietzsche no longer has sufficient moral power to be taken seriously in Western culture, as it was before Hitler and Cambodia. The modern chauvinism typified by Feuerbach, Dewey, and Bultmann imagined that modern thought would continue to provide unquestioned cultural norms for judging all premodern texts and ideas. All that certitude is now gone, however, and we are left rootless.

Modern chauvinism has attempted a preemptive strike on all premodern wisdoms. The label *modern chauvinism* refers to the attitude of those who assume the intrinsic inferiority of all premodern ideas and texts, and the intrinsic superiority of all modern methods of investigation. Modern chauvinists, who long ago decided that no premodern voice said anything worth hearing, have carefully constructed inward defenses against taking seriously any ancient teaching. Though a serious handicap, this condition is not irreversible.

Under the tutelage of these once-confident ideologies still touted by secularizing elites, sex has been reduced to orgasm, persons to bodies, psychology to stimuli, economics to planning mechanisms, and politics to machinery. All these premature certitudes are being challenged. These assumptions are today everywhere in crisis, even while still being fawned over by the self-appointed gatekeepers, whether in popular culture, politics, the university, the media, or religion.

These illusions are woven together in an ideological temperament that still sentimentally shapes the liberal Catholic and mainline liberal Protestant leadership. They remain fixed especially in the politicized bureaucracies and academic professional organizations that remain unable to grasp either their own vulnerability or the possibilities embedded within this decisive historical opportunity.

Before modern science, human cultures were oriented toward maintaining and enhancing the received wisdom of the past. But within modern times, doubt has arisen as to whether any wisdom of any past is worth salvaging. Modern science and its technologies have left us cynical about the value of anything in the past tense.

The Death Throes of the Thought-Frame of Modern Times

What has happened to the Marxist-Freudian-Nietzschean-Bultmannian storm that once seemed so intellectually deafening? It passed over, like an angel of death. The Marxist-Leninism of the Soviet era is now diminished everywhere except in despairing pockets of totalitarianism—Cuba, North Korea, and half-heartedly in official China. The Freudian idealization of sexual liberation and the dream of freedom from limits have resulted in the realization that it is easier to make babies than parent them morally. Children reared on psychoanalysis are at peril. Nietzschean nihilism has spread a trail of genocide. Once-confident Bultmannians still await the modern form of certitude that has never materialized. The last fortress of modern ideology, ideological Darwinism, now being challenged by new evidence of intelligent design in the universe, is losing its vicelike grip on the biological sciences.

These once-unquestioned ideologies are now unmasked as dysfunctional and dated visions of the human possibility. None has succeeded in creating a viable intergenerational culture.

Each of these ideological programs has colluded to support the others, and they are now collapsing together like tottering dominoes:

The command economies

The backfiring therapeutic experiments

The fantastic speculations of demythology

The broken human remains of drug experimentation

The exploding splinters of private narcissism

This ideological conglomerate possesses a wholly owned subsidiary in the religious sphere. Knees buckle as the center fails to hold. The collapse is evident and far-reaching. If the Freudian project, the Marxist method, the Nietzschean experiment, the Bultmannian project, and the Darwinian enterprise are all spent, then the end-stage of the modern period has already passed. "Terminal modernity" is already dead; it can no longer regenerate itself intellectually or morally. In a despairing search for a humanistic utopia, the proponents of secularism have entombed themselves in a social and cultural black hole where nothing works, where even their own moral certainties cannot be sustained to the next generation; and their resources for climbing out of this tomb are exhausted.

What follows the collapse of the Enlightenment ideologies? Merely to name the evolving worldview "postmodern" does not illuminate its promise. Its promise is quite simply the recovery of religious depth.

In stark contrast with the impotence of exhausted secularism stands an emerging hope for deep spiritual roots—deep in history. This hope is now taking a surprising turn: everywhere we see the brightest of the emerging generation turning from the empty larders of secularism to find an inexhaustible store of nourishment in ancient Jewish and Christian wisdom.

The impotence of modern secularism—its inability to regenerate itself spiritually—contrasts with its own deflated and exaggerated hopes. Many had assumed that these ideas would stamp their genetic imprint on the next generation (and maybe on all future generations). Now we realize that the cool heads of the emerging generation are disavowing modern illusions.

THE HUNGER FOR ROOTS

The worshiping community does not view the death of modern thought-forms as an unrelieved tragedy. Rather, the faithful see this decline as a setting in which they can become increasingly aware of ever-renewing divine grace.

Seekers and Believers

Believers today are seeking to unpack and grasp the oldest layers of memory of God's history with humanity. This history cries out to be effectively re-appropriated today.

Seekers among Christians and Jews today passionately long for an accurate and plausible recollection of historical wisdom. Theirs is a passion for roots, a yearning for depth, an appetite for prudence, a longing for tradition. This is the rebirth that we know is already occurring.

Everything that follows in these pages speaks from within the framework of the classic consensus of biblical faith, attentive to two millennia of consensual teaching grounded in sacred scripture. The faith commonly held as a result is shared by a great cloud of witnesses crossing every worldwide ethnic barrier.

"Young fogeys" is the term that I affectionately give to young people who have been through the dark night of disillusionment of modern thought-forms and have joyously returned to classic Christianity. Young fogies are those who hold fast to "mere Christianity." Having entered in good faith into the disciplines of the modern academy and church—and having become disillusioned—they are again studying the texts of the ancient Christian tradition. These texts point to the Word of God revealed in history as attested by prophetic and apostolic witnesses whose testimonies have become authoritative scripture for a worldwide, multicultural, multigenerational community.

Young fogeys, determined to reshape institutions that have been bent out of shape, must constantly deflect mistaken epithets such as "reactionary" and "fundamentalist" thrown by those virtually ignorant of classic Christianity. They must learn to bear these burdens in a sound-bite world prone to misunderstand them. But they take heart in knowing that Polycarp, Athanasius, and Jerome must have felt similarly misperceived.

The young fogeys, who were feeling extremely lonely twenty years ago, are now in the forefront of emerging culture-formation. Today there are many high-profile Jewish and Christian voices that have expressed the need to return to classic moral reasoning—from Richard Neuhaus to Ellen Charry, David Novak to Thomas Sowell, Joseph Lieberman to Stephen Carter. These leaders do not all speak with one voice, but all express high respect for classic Christianity and Judaism.

The Least Likely Premise

Serious Jews and serious Christians are now being energized by this dawning realization that the past can teach the future. The living God of holy scripture is working powerfully amid these ironic circumstances. God the Spirit continues to bring life to the people of God.

Only under the old illusions of secularism could the false premises of the death of God and the decline of the faithful seem credible. If we step away from these illusions, it is easy to see that the demise of Western religion is the least likely premise in the Jewish and Christian understanding of history.

Those who willingly enslave themselves to passing idolatries should not be surprised when the gods of modern times are shown to have feet of clay. When idols die, the idolaters understandably mourn and rage. Meanwhile, the grace-enabled community freely celebrates its exodus through and beyond the waters of modernity. This community glories in the intricate providences of history. Each dying historical formation is giving birth to new forms and refreshing occasions for living responsively in relation to grace.

What is happening today is a profound rediscovery of the texts, methods, and pastoral wisdom of the long-neglected rabbinic and patristic traditions—that is, the traditions of the Talmud and Midrashim, and of the early fathers of the church of the first millennium. For Jews and Christians, this means a fresh investigation of scripture and its traditional interpreters. For Western Christians these new friends now include the Eastern church fathers of the first five Christian centuries. For Eastern Christians they belatedly include the Latin church fathers. The first millennium of Christianity and Judaism did not suffer as deeply as did medieval scholasticism from the moral distortions that required the Reformation.

What is happening amid this historical situation is a joyous return to the sacred texts of scripture and the consensual guides of the formative period of Judeo-Christian scripture interpretation. Meanwhile, modern ideologies persist in their compulsive preference for novelty. They make instant value judgments against whatever is old. But orthodoxy has an eye for those enduring truths more fully grasped in ancient than recent times.

The Fairness Revolution and Its Aftermath

In our lifetime many changes have occurred in our perception of fairness. The civil rights movement has awakened us to institutionalized racism and sought by legal and political remedies to overcome it. The women's movement has heightened our sensitivities to the oppression of women. The pope has apologized for the church's sins against the Jews and for the crusades. The Boy Scouts struggle with the question of scoutmasters with unconventional lifestyles. All these are among the signs of the "fairness revolution."

Much about this revolution is commendable. But it is not without its blind spots. The irony: initiatives intended to create greater equality have often resulted in unexpected consequences of deepening inequality. They have increased our proud temptation to think that we are the only generation that has ever sought justice or equality in a serious way. Thus the past itself has been inadvertently downgraded and often demeaned. Human worth itself is diminished when the whole human past is treated as worthless.

We who were born in this time of supposedly greater fairness now view dimly the courage and integrity of all who were born in former times of lesser fairness. This vast group includes, of course, the prophets, apostles, martyrs, and ancient teachers of scripture. Our fortuitous birth in this time has become our claim to absolute moral superiority. This claim is our modern version of announcing ourselves to be a chosen race, our way of saying that we are better. It is our version of justification by works: we are justified not by the rebirth of faith but by simply being born more recently!

God appears to be caught in the cross-fire. As one of Woody Allen's characters comments in *Everyone Says I Love You:* "Even if God exists, he's done such a terrible job, it's a wonder people don't get together and file a class-action suit against him."

The recent history of political remedies for unfairness are strewn with unintended consequences. A dependency population within a welfare state has become a fixed reality. Victimization has become a game. Women suffer more, not less, from divorce and economic instability. Family cohesion has diminished. The children of the fairness revolution are paying an extremely high price in family disorder, adolescent suicide rates, neuroses, and chronic anxiety. We struggle fairly to decide who will pay the bill for others, who will be taxed and who will live off of taxation, who will work and who is willing to be supported with loss of self-esteem.

Within the radical wing of the fairness revolution, any overarching attempt to explain the meaning of the whole is mistrusted as manipulative. So it is that religious understandings of any sort are immediately suspect as power moves. But this reactionary habit of dismissing any comprehensive human outlook is itself a narrow-minded view.

Orthodoxy as a Sociological Type

Our English word *orthodoxy* has a distinctly religious history. It is not one of those words that Western religions borrowed from the pagan environment. Rather, the very concept of orthodoxy emerged as early believers sought common clarity about what their canonical texts meant, based on their most trusted classic interpreters, in a way that could be received as generally plausible among believers of all cultures, times, and places.

Thus orthodoxy is a sociological artifact. It is a social process dedicated to the careful transmission of tradition. It makes truth-claims without apology. It seeks to guard and sustain those truth-claims through the hazards of time.

Orthodoxy is not a single view, of course. On the contrary, at any time there are many orthodoxies waxing and waning. The dying secular orthodoxies of modern times include the Darwinian philosophy, Keynesian economics, automatic progress in history, Communism, psychoanalysis, and defensive naturalism. These modern ideologies can be viewed as "orthodox" by analogy to the rules of tradition-transmission set by rabbinic writers and early Christian interpreters of sacred scripture. Each of these once-prevailing modern orthodoxies developed tradition transmitting strategies similar to those of the Judeo-Christian priestly tradition: apostolic succession, with constraints on association, hierarchic order, canon law, and the canonizing of particular texts by which truth-claims may be assessed. Each had a settled notion of historical succession, a canon of authoritative texts, and an authorized tradition of hagiography (meaning writings of and about the "saints" of the tradition—Sigmund Freud, Anna Freud, Oscar Pfister, Harry Stack Sullivan, Karl Marx, Friedrich Engels, Vladimir Lenin, Joseph Stalin).

Each of these modern orthodoxies is in trouble— vulnerable to demoralization and collapse. This crisis of the secular orthodoxies provides a wide opening for faith not seen for generations.

Why the Continuities in History Have Been Neglected

In the weakness of their waning ideologies, secular chauvinists have focused obsessively on how Christian teaching has changed over the years. They cannot get enough of the differences between Christians of various historical periods, gloating over these differences as if they were decisive. These chauvinists report every form of dissent while refusing to report on or listen for consensus. A huge literature exists on the conflicting varieties of Christian thought and on inconsistencies within Jewish and Christian history. But only a very small and pale scholarly literature is available on the sociology of tradition-transmission and the continuities of historical remembering.

This is evidence of a bias largely unrecognized—a bias that accounts for sociology's neglect of empirical inquiry into those ways in which orthodoxy has remained stable and centered. Stability is poorly understood and under-reported. Much more is known of the debates and reversals in religious teaching than of ongoing continuities within those developments. It is against the backdrop of that sort of academic myopia that today's actual rebirth of orthodoxy is occurring.

Why has this myopia persisted so long uncorrected? Modernization since the Enlightenment has had an insatiable fascination with change and has been bored by stability. Modern news media do not know how to report on continuities, only on changes. Modern ideologues are fixated on what disaster is likely to happen next, not on how human cultures will survive and thrive through whatever crisis. But they did not reckon with the regenerating power of ancient faith, which is the centerpiece of our story.

TWO

Serious Jews
Serious Christians

"The Orthodox renaissance stands as the most striking and unexpected phenomenon of modern American Jewish history," writes Samuel Freedman in his remarkable new book, *Jew vs. Jew*. There is much that divides Jew from Jew, as Freedman's book makes clear, but the center of Jewish identity is becoming ever more clear: "The portion of American Jewry that will flourish in the future . . . is the portion that has accepted the central premise of Orthodoxy—that religion defines Jewish identity."[1]

When I speak of the rebirth of orthodoxy within Judaism, I am not limiting my reference to the Union of Orthodox Jewish Congregations or Agudat Israel. The term *orthodox* is used here in a generic sense as a reference to a classic textual tradition. Similarly, in Christianity there is a classic Christian orthodoxy defined by texts that express the understanding reached by the early ecumenical councils—an orthodoxy that encompasses both Eastern and Western Christianity. Lowercase *orthodoxy* is a term not limited to any particular history of Greek, Antiochene, Syriac, Armenian, Mar Thoma, or Coptic Orthodoxy, although it certainly includes all of these. I speak of a lowercase orthodoxy as a sociological type, while greatly respecting the historical rootedness and durability of its capitalized forms.

COMPARING JEWISH ORTHODOXY AND CHRISTIAN ORTHODOXY
The most profound dilemma of modern life is the uprootedness caused by the failure of secular ideologies. To address that dilemma, Jews and Christians are striving to recover their religious roots, and each group is

learning from the other how to deepen and strengthen their own distinctive roots.

As we examine the evidences of a rebirth of orthodox Christian teaching, we note a similar struggle for Jewish orthodoxy. There is potential companionship in these parallel developments. They must not be viewed as antagonistic or adverse. On the contrary, their relationship points to the mystery of sovereign grace working in complementary ways.

The Shared History of Orthodox Jews and Orthodox Christians

Both Jews and Christians are people of the book, students of holy writ. My major focus in these chapters is on Christian orthodoxy, but our Jewish friends know, as we know, that no Christian orthodoxy whatsoever would exist without the actual history of Israel—a history recounted particularly in the Hebrew Bible. Judaism and Christianity both ground themselves in biblical history. In this way they stand together in stark contrast to all nonbiblical religions.

At the outset of this discussion about orthodoxy, we do well to examine the close relationship between these two correlated orthodoxies: Jewish and Christian. The orthodox life is drawn to the recovery not only of classic consensual *Christian* roots but also of classic consensual *Jewish* roots. These two root systems share a common taproot—God's revelation.

My purpose is to show that Jews have something decisive at stake in the recovery of classic Christianity, and vice versa. Both faith-groups experience the same cultural crisis and opportunity, both are heirs of similar spiritual disciplines, and both share the same psalms, prophets, Pentateuch, and Wisdom literature.

To claim that the sources quoted in this chapter represent a consensus of Jewish voices would be a gross exaggeration, but it cannot be denied that they are *significant* Jewish voices. A large body of Jewish literature exists, both ancient and modern, that seeks to assess the interface between Judaism and Christianity. For a review of this literature, see works by Fritz Rothschild, David Novak, Michael Wyschograd, Jacob Neusner, Jakob Petuchowski, Eugene Borowitz, Joachim Schoeps, James Parkes, Clemens Thoma, Franklin Littell, and Paul van Buren.

One of the earliest and most far-reaching ecumenical decisions made in the struggle of Christian doctrine against its counterfeits came in the challenge of Marcionism in the second century CE. This decision made clear that Christianity could never set aside the Torah or the writings of the prophets. Clemens Thoma rightly argues that a Christian who would "despise the Hebrew Scriptures would disclaim or abrogate his Christianity."[2]

At the heart of both Judaism and Christianity lies a particular history—that of Israel. Within both faith-traditions revelation occurs in a particular history, recounting events at particular times and places. Revelation in and through history is sometimes called the "scandal of particularity" since every historical event is particular to some location and moment. It often seems to be an offense against universal reasoning. God's word to humanity comes in and through a particular history of a people, a nation. Both Jews and Christians view all of history as the arena of revelation, but both see revelation through the lens of a *particular* history. They tell the story of salvation as a particular narrative, not as a general logical, scientific, or philosophical set of arguments.

Biblical faith itself not only *recounts* a history; it *is* a history. To separate faith from its history would be, as Will Herberg said, "like paraphrasing poetry."[3] Everything that gives faith power is understood and remembered in relation to a palpable history concerning what God has done in the history of Israel, and the story of people's responses to those events.

Christians have learned from Jews to reject idolatry. From the prophets they have learned to resist the elevation of nature as such into an object of worship. Together Christians and Jews reject any form of pantheism in which the human story is swallowed up in the cyclical rhythms of nature. It is alien to biblical faith to try to explain the meaning of life from within the assumptions of natural causes as such, as if apart from the history of God with humanity. Jews and Christians together differ sharply from Buddhism and Hinduism in this respect.

We Jews and Christians explain ourselves by explaining our history, which is irreducibly a history with the one God, Yahweh, Adonai, Elohim. We tell together the story of ourselves as a people. Some forms of Greek and pagan philosophy chose to speak of human existence without reference to any actual concrete history, preferring to focus on ideas or myths cast in a timeless eternity. Not so biblical religion, where human existence plays out in a particular chronicle of bondage and deliverance. From Tertullian's rejection of the anti-Jewish arguments of Marcion to Origen's rejection of the anti-historical arguments of Celsus, Christian teaching from its earliest stages has been irrevocably connected with the down-to-earth history of Abraham, Isaac, and Jacob, understood from the point of view of its alleged fulfillment.

What Already Unites Jews and Christians?

A great many issues unite Jews and Christians. Rabbi Abraham Heschel offers the following account: "A commitment to the Hebrew Bible as Holy Scripture. Faith in the Creator, the God of Abraham, commitment to many of His commandments, to justice and mercy, a sense of contrition, sensitivity to the sanctity of life and to the involvement of God in history."[4] Heschel noted that "the fate of the Jewish people and the fate of the Hebrew Bible are intertwined."[5] Jews and Christians "are all involved with one another," he added. "Spiritual betrayal on the part of one of us affects the faith of all of us. Views adopted in one community have an impact on other communities."[6]

In their sharing of the history of the covenant of God with Noah, Abraham, Moses, and the people of Israel, Jews and Christians together are guardians of the same memory of God's presence in the world. This contrasts with nonbiblical religions.

One is "no longer a true Jew," wrote Martin Buber, "who does not himself remember that God led him out of Egypt."[7] The history of Israel must become part of one's personal history. One's very self as a Jew or a Christian is revealed and decisively illumined by telling this particular story—of Israel, its election, its hopes, its failures, its destiny.

THERE IS *ONE* HISTORY OF ISRAEL, NOT *TWO*

The rebirth of Jewish orthodoxy is taking place alongside the rebirth of Christian orthodoxy. These rebirths are closely linked. Jews and Christians share not only the same uprooted world that follows after the demise of modern ideologies, but also the same sacred text and the same religious reality—the history of Israel.

Sharing the Same Sacred Text

Together with one voice Jews and Christians speak of God's making covenant first with all humanity in Noah and then with a particular family through Abraham, who was promised a land and a seed that would become a great nation and bear his blessing to all humanity. For both Jews and Christians, Abraham is the father of faith, a man who steadfastly trusted the promise of God. This happened through a particular family, a particular nation, who became the representative people of God.

Jews and Christians together understand that the One from whom all things come is the One who brings all things in history to a fitting end in the final judgment. In giving life to all, God calls all life to accountability. When the freedom God gives is twisted toward catastrophic paths of arbitrary self-will and rebellion, it is only through the mercy of God that reconciliation is possible. There is a profound realism in classical Judaism and Christianity that sees much of the human experiment as a failure, while at the same time affirming that God's grace continues to be offered to his covenant people despite their follies and infidelities.

Jews and Christians speak with one voice of God as giver and orderer of all nature and history, creator of man and woman in the image and likeness of God, creatures who when fallen are offered a way of atonement. Jews and Christians together view present history from the vantage point of Israel's salvation history: creation, covenant, disobedience, captivity, and expectation of redemption—all of this looking toward the final consummation of history. The memory of this history and the expectation of its final fulfillment binds Jews and Christians closely together, as distinguished from all contrary views.

This point was made recently by four leading Jewish scholars[8] in their declaration *Dabru Emet: A Jewish Statement on Christians and Christianity:* "It is time for Jews to learn about the efforts of Christians to honor Judaism. We believe it is time for Jews to reflect on what Judaism may now say about Christianity."[9] "Jews and Christians seek authority from the same book—the Bible (what Jews call 'Tanakh' and Christians call the 'Old Testament')." "Through Christianity hundreds of millions of people have entered into relationship with the God of Israel."[10] "The humanly irreconcilable difference between Jews and Christians will not be settled until God redeems the entire world as promised in Scripture." "A new relationship between Jews and Christians will not weaken Jewish practice."[11]

Jews and Christians together understand our present life in relation to both our memory of this covenant history and our expectation of its fulfillment in the future. Although we may differ on how that expectation is fulfilled, together we view history in relation to its end, its fulfillment, the last day of judgment and redemption. Judaism before Christianity expected God to make right the wrongs of history, even if only at the *end* of history. Judaism before Christianity placed all human actions under the divine requirement and looked to divine grace to bring divine-human reconciliation.

This perspective differs sharply from that of all nonbiblical religions, though Islam arguably resembles Judaism and Christianity more closely than do those religions that stand in a more remote relation to biblical history. The faith of Islam must be understood in relation to much the same Genesis narrative that Jews and Christians share, even if viewed differently. The relation of Islamic scriptures to the scriptures of Judaism and Christianity is itself a history of tragic ambivalence and conflict.

A Single Religious Reality: The Cohesion of Jewish and Christian History

Both Judaism and Christianity thus share a single religious reality, with Judaism facing inward toward a particular holy land and seed and Christianity facing outward toward the horizon of the world (the Gentiles), allowing all others who are not sons of Abraham ethnically to be brought into the covenant of God with Israel by faith. Judaism looks toward its promised land, while Christianity gratefully moves from Jerusalem to the ends of the earth, but not with a different Lord or creator. The same intent pervades both faiths: the reception of the kingdom of God.

Jewish and Christian perceptions of salvation history view the history of Israel as the decisive story for their self-understanding, but they see it differently in respect to its messianic fulfillment. Christians live through Christ, whereas Jews live through Israel. Jews view their participation in Israel from the vantage point of their election as people of God. Christians view their participation in Israel from the vantage point of the fulfillment of messianic hope in Jesus.

The key event of deliverance for Jews is the Exodus and the wilderness experience under Moses' leadership in the Sinai, while for Christians it is Exodus-Sinai viewed from the cross and resurrection. In their baptism, Christians participate in a new exodus, and in faith they receive a new life. Messianic fulfillment for Jews remains primarily in the future. For Christians this fulfillment is already happening in time, though it is also yet to be completed in the future.

Jews attest their faith simply by being Jews, by being the elect people of God through whom the world is to receive salvation. While Jews look toward the promise of a particular land, Christian are more like sojourners in history and strangers in every land, every social order. Although they may be citizens within various social orders and cultures, they do not see their fundamental identity before God as connected with land, place, or ethnicity, but with the faith of Abraham. One enters into the Jewish community by being born into it. One enters into the Christian community by being reborn by faith through baptism. The Jew is born a Jew. The Christian, born a Gentile or a Jew, becomes a Christian through faith.

Every reenactment in Jewish and Christian worship retells the history of God's covenant people. Jews have three liturgical feasts or seasons—Passover, Tabernacles, and Weeks (Pesach, Sukkot, Shabuoth)—that reflect the phases of revelation, redemption, and community-creation out of the Exodus-Sinai event that brought the people of Israel into being. Christians similarly reenact the analogous seasons of the cross, the resurrection, and the coming of the Holy Spirit (Good Friday, Easter, and Pentecost), reflecting the crucial moments of the decisive salvation-event that brought into being the Christian life.

These reenactments are more accurately remembered as *one* history, not *two*. The reappropriation of these events is experienced in the heart of the believer. In the Passover Haggadah prayer, the Jew says, "All this I do because of what God did for me in bringing me out of Egypt." The Christian believer participates in the same history viewed through the lens of the death and resurrection of Jesus.

In this sense orthodox Judaism and orthodox Christianity are best viewed not as two entirely different religions, but rather as a single religious tradition standing in a single history of covenant interpreted in two different ways—that is, as *promised* and as *fulfilled*. One interpretation awaits the Messiah as still expected, and the other celebrates the Messiah as having come (and as coming again). Although this difference is crucial, it does not overshadow the fact that the history Judaism and Christianity share is essential to understanding even their variances.

From Particular Covenant to Universal Covenant

The paradox in the history of Israel is this: the covenant with a particular people has universal significance for all people. The paradox of Christianity reverses that: Christianity transmutes the paradox of Judaism by bringing the God of Israel to the world, and the world to the same covenant of God with Israel. This is how the New Testament understands things: through Jesus, God brought the Gentiles into the faith of God's covenant with Israel. God's work in Israel thus became open to all humanity, meaning that covenant participation does not require circumcision or a change of ethnic status; it does not require becoming a part of a particular national identity, seed, or genealogy.

Paul the Jew wrote to his recent Gentile converts in Ephesus, "So remember that at that time when you were without Christ, you were aliens to the commonwealth of Israel and strangers to the covenants of promise. . . . But now through your union with Christ Jesus, you who were once far away have been brought near . . . so that you are no longer strangers and foreigners but fellow citizens of God's people and of the family of God."[12] To the Galatians he wrote, "If you are Christ's, then you are Abraham's seed, and heirs according to the promise."[13] All Gentiles who have become Christians embrace the history of Abraham as their own history, which they believe has come to a moment of fulfillment.

The new covenant in Christianity does not replace or supersede God's covenant with the people of Israel; rather, it enlarges and fulfills that covenant amid the Gentiles. Likewise, the New Testament does not supplant God's original covenant but extends, develops, and amplifies it. The election of Israel was implemented and brought into full effect through God's messianic coming, not annulled. God's faithfulness to Israel becomes now the proto-type and guarantee of God's faithfulness to all who repent and believe. In this way the covenant with Israel is intended for all and has become manifested for all.

This expansion of the covenant beyond Torah was made clear through the history of a particular Jew, Jesus of Nazareth, who did not renounce his Jew-ishness. Paul was himself a strict Jew, a Pharisee, a persecutor of Christians, who in taking the good news of Jesus Christ to the whole of the non-Jewish world, remained profoundly Jewish.

Rabbi Abraham Heschel captured the paradoxical relationship this way: "Leading Jewish authorities, such as Jehuda Halevi and Maimonides, ac-knowledge Christianity to be a *praeparatio messianica*, while the Church re-garded ancient Judaism to have been a *praeparatio evangelica*."[14] Heschel wrote ironically, "Judaism is the mother of the Christian faith. It has a stake in the destiny of Christianity. Should a mother ignore her child, even a way-ward, rebellious one?"[15] He also asked, of Jews and Christians, "Should we refuse to be on speaking terms with one another and hope for each other's failure? Or should we pray for each other's health, and help one another in preserving one's respective legacy, in preserving a common legacy?"[16]

AN INVITATION TO JEWS CONCERNING THE REBIRTH OF ORTHODOXY

David Novak noted, "In the present, Judaism and Christianity still have a common enemy. Secularism, by proclaiming its self-sufficiency, makes no place for either Judaism or Christianity."[17] Jews and Christians are drawn to-gether by their common response to the arrogance of secularism.

Shared Struggles with Modern Culture

Orthodox, Conservative, and Reform Judaism all stand in a potentially sig-nificant relation to the rebirth of Christian orthodoxy. Reformed Judaism seeks to open windows to the modern world, just as liberal Catholicism and Protestantism seek to open Christianity to modern ways; and both faith-forms have affinities with the secularizing world that is now in a crisis of moral impotence. Conservative Judaism sociologically resembles conserva-tive forms of Christianity in focusing on the maintenance of the community of faith through the hazardous seasons of time, faithfully persisting in the hallowing of time, the sanctifying of seasons. Orthodox Judaism resembles orthodox Christianity in receiving the sacred text as God's own address.

Tradition-transmission is crucial to both Jews and Christians. The Jewish theologian Franz Rosenzweig observed: "We experience our Judaism with immediacy in elders and children, . . . in the oldest and the youngest, in the elder who admonishes, in the lad who asks, in the ancestor who blesses and in the grandson who receives the blessing."[18] So in Christianity is the family the arena of transmission of the tradition.

Jewish orthodoxy rests on the teachings of the Torah, consisting of the Written Law as contained in the Pentateuch, and the Oral Law as represented by the Mishnah, the Gemara, the Responsa, and the Codes of Posekim. Orthodox Jews believe that the Torah was given to Moses by God on Mount Sinai as the only true guide to Jewish life and conduct. This belief is accompanied by an unswerving emphasis on loyalty to the covenant through dietary laws. Similarly, orthodox Christians believe that the Hebrew Bible and the New Testament were inspired by God the Spirit and reliably transmitted to the faithful, and are wholly reliable. Classic Jewish teaching set the pattern for the familiar practices of classic Christian orthodoxy: devoted study of the Bible, daily prayer, and strict observance of the sabbath.

Orthodox Jews have a different history within modernity than do Reformed Jews. Although this is not our subject here, it is useful to remember that there is a form of Orthodox Judaism that corresponds as a sociological type more clearly to Eastern Orthodoxy, or orthodoxy in Eastern Christianity.

Nonpracticing Jews, as well as Reformed and secularized Jews, are invited to be open to the developments in Christianity that are described in these chapters. The assumptions of such Jews may correspond more closely with liberal assumptions that prevail in modern culture, yet they may experience even more poignantly than orthodox Jews the uprootedness in culture that troubles modern Christians, and may have a heart for traditional Jewish practice and Halakhah, that seeks to embody Jewish faith in a way of life.

Even highly secularized Jews who have wandered far into nonobservance and know little about Judaism remain sons and daughters of Israel. The analogy among secularized Christians is those who are baptized but do not know clearly what their baptism means. The memory of the history of salvation presents the same challenges to both Jew and Christian alike, whether conservative or liberal. The same dilemmas of tradition-maintenance puzzle and disturb both. These are issues we share together with poignant intensity.

How Jewish and Christian Orthodoxies Interface and Complement Each Other

Christians need Jews to tell them the story of their election and to remind them of the persistence of God's love for Israel. Jews need Christians to take the story of Israel to the Gentiles, to retell the history of the salvation of Israel (and of *all* people *through* Israel).

Franz Rosenzweig asserted that "Israel can bring the world to God only through Christianity."[19] The service of Christianity to Judaism, then, is in its mission to bring the history of salvation to the Gentiles. The service of Judaism to Christianity is more obvious, as Rosenzweig has noted: "Christianity could not long remain a force for redemption without Israel in its midst."[20]

David Novak, in explaining Rosenzweig, clarifies this point:

> The necessity of Christianity for Judaism, then, is that it has the capacity to include all nations in the revealed relationship with God. Judaism cannot perform this redemptive function for itself. . . . It is not Judaism's task to engage in disputes with Christianity based on universalist criteria; it is Judaism's task to recognize the indispensable universalistic ministry of Christianity for the sake of the final redemption. By moving from paganism to the more immediate relationship with God, Christianity already contains the world within itself.[21]

Admittedly, not all Jews will recognize themselves in what has been said by great Jewish teachers such as Rosenzweig, Novak, and Heschel (quoted earlier). But many serious Jews will. The criterion for authenticity in our reflections on the analogies between Jewish orthodoxy and Christian orthodoxy is rigorous: each participant must be able to recognize him- or herself in any characterization by the other. Can the orthodox Jews recognize themselves in the Christian perception of Judaism, and can the orthodox Christians recognize themselves in the Jewish perception of Christianity? All of this must be asked with mutual respect and without diluting either voice.

My most important Jewish mentor, the late Will Herberg, wrote of Christianity, "Christ appears in early Christian thinking as, quite literally, an incarnate or one-man Israel, the Remnant-Man. Through union in faith with him, the Gentile believer becomes part of Israel; he therefore comes under the covenant and thereby becomes heir to the promises of God to Israel."[22] Paul could pray "that the blessing of Abraham might come on the Gentiles through Jesus Christ."[23] In Christ, Israel's history has become a history in which the world's peoples can share in the same faith by which Abraham believed in God's promise to Israel. In this way people of any race or culture can participate in the faith of Israel. By entering into the covenant, Gentiles vicariously become a part of that wandering people who have experienced the Exodus and have been tutored by the law and the prophets to expect the final fulfillment of history through God's own coming among us.

Even though Jews and Christians have different standpoints within the one history of God with humanity, both must stand by the truth of their own history. Only the wisdom of God can encompass both standpoints. For both this remains a mystery. In some ways each tends to correct the temptations and inadequacies of the other. Herberg wryly remarked, "The Christian who tends to be impatient with the Jew for refusing to see in Jesus the fulfillment and completion of God's redemptive work might pause a moment to consider whether this Jewish 'obstinacy' was not itself important as an indispensable reminder of the very incompleteness of this completion, of a redemption which may indeed have come but is nevertheless yet to come."[24]

If Jews are able to see in Christianity some providential role on behalf of the Jewish people, Christians are called to see in the history of the people of Israel God's election of a particular people in a particular time and place, through a particular family—Abraham, Isaac, and Jacob.

There can be no Christian faith without Abraham, Moses, David, and the prophets. It remains unlikely that worldwide recognition or actualization of the covenant of God with Israel will occur without something very much like Christianity. That is why this discussion of the rebirth of Christian orthodoxy has deep, even if hidden, resonances with the rebirth of Jewish orthodoxy.

How Contemporary Jewish Scholarship Seeks Classic Textual Regrounding

My closest Jewish partners in dialogue all have interests quite similar to those I am describing as the rebirth of orthodoxy. They seek the recovery of classic Jewish scriptural teaching amid and beyond the limitations and corruptions of modern living.

My former colleague at Drew University, Peter Ochs (now at the University of Virginia), provides leadership for a journal and a collegium of Jews and Christians on the postcritical study of scripture. Fritz Rothschild (at Jewish Theological Seminary, New York) has been my major mentor on Rosenzweig. David Novak (University of Toronto) has written the definitive Jewish study of Jewish-Christian dialogue, which significantly informs the position I have just stated above. My old friend Jacob Neusner has spent his entire professional life recovering the texts of the classic Jewish tradition, just as I have worked to recover patristic texts. The late blessed Rabbi Judah Goldin, with whom I did some memorable private rabbinic study, helped me more than anyone else to grasp a plausible role model of how the study of Talmud proceeds. The published conversations between Father Richard Neuhaus and Rabbi Leon Klenicki[25] ably demonstrate the spirit of this sort of respectful dialogue, which does not dilute or diminish either partner.[26]

In comparing the sources of classical Judaism and Christianity, it is useful to recall that the two Talmuds—the Babylonian (completed about 500 to 550 CE) and the Jerusalem (or Palestinian) Talmud (completed about 400 CE)—were written during the period of the zenith of Origen, John of Chrysostom, Jerome, and other classic Christian commentators on scripture, who were profoundly influenced by rabbinic ways of interpreting scripture. The Talmud consists of the Mishnah (implying repetition, teaching) and the Gemara (suggesting accomplishment or completion and containing discussions of the sages about the Mishnah). The Mishnah, the core of the talmudic tradition, was written during the first two centuries BCE and the first two centuries CE; the Gemara, written in response to the Mishnah, was finished a couple of centuries later. These writings, along with the Toseft, various midrashic (or interpretive) texts, the Targumim, and prayers, form the core of the rabbinic tradition.

The Jewish tradition of Midrash (meaning investigation, searching, or exegesis) formed the pattern for the Christian tradition of homily. At the synagogue, the rabbi would deliver a midrashic sermon that consisted of *pshat* (the literal meaning of the biblical text), and *drash* (actualization, symbolic interpretation, and appropriation of the meaning of the text). A similar distinction prevailed in most ancient Christian homilies, whether in Antioch or Alexandria.

Both rabbinic and patristic writers actively practiced *intra*textual exegesis, seeking to define and identify the exact wording of the text, its grammatical structure, and the interconnectedness of its parts. Simultaneously, they also practiced *extra*textual exegesis, seeking to discern the geographical, historical, or cultural context in which the text was written. Most important, they were also very well practiced in *inter*textual exegesis, seeking to discern the meaning of a text by comparing it with other texts.

The Limits of Dialogue: Good Fences Make Good Neighbors

These times present what Bernhard Casper calls "a situation for dialogue between Jews and Christians such as may perhaps not have existed since the beginnings of Christianity."[27] John Merkle also speaks of the need to reevaluate Jewish-Christian relations:

We are now living at a pivotal moment in the history of Jewish-Christian relations. For a little more than two decades, ever since the Second Vatican Council, the church has been in a process of reversing its perspective on Judaism and its nearly two millennia long relationship with the Jewish people. . . . Now that the church acknowledges the abiding validity of Judaism, it is imperative that we reevaluate the meaning of Christianity in relation to Judaism.[28]

Rabbi Abraham Heschel concurs, noting that Jews today have a unique opportunity "unprecedented in almost two thousand years" to dialogue with Christians who are "eager to hear the message of Jewish thought."[29]

Franz Rosenzweig argues that today the "synagogue and church are mutually dependent on one another."[30] Elsewhere he comments that "before God, then, Jew and Christian both labor at the same task. He cannot dispense with either. He has sent enmity between the two for all time, and withal has most intimately bound each to each."[31]

"To assume that the transformation of the Greco-Roman world into Christendom (and Islam) was a mere accident, and not part of God's redemptive plan, is difficult to believe for Jews who take history seriously," writes Fritz Rothschild.[32] Fellow Jew Jakob Petuchowski observes, "Neither Jews nor Christians can really afford to be isolationists. In this pagan world of ours, we together are the minority 'people of God.'"[33]

Christians must actively resist any attempt to diminish the importance of the Hebrew Bible for Christian faith. Such attempts have a long history, as Fritz Rothschild notes:

Attempts were made to exclude [the Hebrew Bible] from the canon by Marcion as early as the second century; its desanctification was advocated by Schleiermacher, the 'Church Father' of the nineteenth century; its rejection from the biblical canon was urged by Adolf von Harnack in 1921; its devaluation and avoidance by the 'German Christians' after 1933; and its irrelevance by the 'Death of God' theologians in the 1950's and 1960's.[34]

How Not to Reach Out

Orthodox Christians must not assume too much in reaching out for the solace of a conversation with orthodox Jewish traditions. We must remain aware of the fact that "Judaism is no mere appendix to Christianity, that it does not constitute an opponent to Christianity, nor does it consider Christianity a necessary partner," as Catholic theologian Clemens Thoma cautions. "Judaism ('the root') reaches deeply into Christian identity, while Christianity adds very little or nothing at all to Jewish self-understanding."[35]

Christians must not attempt to fabricate a Judaism that reflects their own latest interests or trends. Such an attempt will backfire if new anti-Jewish resentments are stirred up or old ones revived.

As Vatican II wisely stated:

> The Church, therefore, cannot forget that she received the revelation of the Old Testament through the people with whom God in his inexpressible mercy concluded the ancient covenant. Nor can she forget that she draws sustenance from the root of that well-cultivated olive tree onto which has been grafted the wild shoot, the Gentiles.[36]

THREE

Orthodox Remembering

I will build on the foundation of the first two chapters by first developing a working definition of the term *orthodoxy* and then taking a look at orthodoxy's major features.

WHAT IS ORTHODOXY?

By *orthodoxy* (in its lowercase form) I mean *integrated biblical teaching as interpreted in its most consensual classic period*. More simply put, orthodoxy (as defined by both Jews and Christians) is *ancient consensual scriptural teaching*. For Jews this means rabbinic and midrashic teaching; for Christians it means the doctrine taught during the period of ancient ecumenical Christianity—doctrine that is commonly called *classic* Christian teaching. For both faith-traditions the time-period for such teaching is generally assumed to be the first five centuries of the common era.

By "consensual," whether Jewish or Christian, I mean the teaching that has been duly confirmed by a process of general consent of the faithful over two millennia. For Jews this means the Talmud. For Christians this means the teaching of the same time-period—the creeds and early liturgies—confirmed by due process especially through the action of ecumenical councils that have been widely acknowledged and received as authoritative by the faithful worldwide.

The orthodox way adheres to the unified teaching that has remained faithful to the biblical witness as received by Christian believers of all cultures, languages, and times. It is ancient ecumenical teaching, as distinguished from modern ecumenical dialogue. Christian orthodoxy is that sustained tradition that has steadily centered the worldwide believing community in the earliest testimony to the coming of the Servant Messiah— testimony that has been consensually received and faithfully transmitted for two millennia.

Walking Within Boundaries

To walk in the orthodox way as a *Christian* means to think and live within the boundaries of the ancient Christian consensus of teaching from the prophetic and apostolic witness, applying that teaching contextually within ever-emergent cultural situations. To walk in the orthodox way as a *Jew* means to think and live within the boundaries of ancient rabbinic teaching on the law, the prophets, and the sages, especially regarding the seasons of feasts and celebrations, dietary and moral laws.

The New Testament is essentially a midrashic exposition on the Hebrew Bible's prophetic expectations,[1] showing how the life, death, and resurrection of Jesus fulfill those expectations. The first witnesses understood themselves as standing in a tradition of accurate and faithful remembering, which had been suddenly transformed by the coming of the Anointed One.

These boundaries enable freedom of inquiry and action by pointing to dangerous traps to avoid. No one is required to believe, but those who freely believe consent to live within these boundaries. Only by knowing where the boundaries lie is one free to move confidently within them.

Within these boundaries of free consent, anyone in a subsequent generation who comes to hear the scripture rightly and consensually attested can trust that the truth of the earliest witnesses has not been distorted.

By this means, believers are free to think with the earliest witnesses so as to be assured of receiving a reliable, and not a garbled, version of the original testimony of God's coming to humanity. Even the most recent converts to orthodox faith believe the very same truth that was attested by the earliest witnesses. They hold the same faith as that of the believing patriarchs, prophets, sages, apostles, saints, confessors, and martyrs. It is one faith variously received within a developing history.

Changing Culture, Unchanging Faith

The ancient consensual writers of Christianity warned hearers not to heed any theories (even their own!) that were in any way contrary to the earliest eyewitness testimony. They frequently cautioned believers not to follow any individual voice, especially if it distorted the revelation of God as expressed in the worship services where the Hebrew Bible[2] and the gospels and epistles were read as scripture; rather, believers were to turn to the earliest apostolic witnesses. These included Paul's own testimony of the risen Lord and the Lord's own revelation to Paul.

Orthodoxy in all its culturally varied forms, now as well as then, follows Paul's strict admonition to the Galatians:

> But even if we or an angel from heaven should preach a gospel other than *[heteran,* from which we derive our word *heterodoxy]* the one we preached to you, let him be anathema! As we had already said, so now I say again: If anybody is preaching to you a gospel other than what you accepted [that is, other than what you received from those to whom it was revealed], let him be anathema!"[3]

Creative revisionists are forewarned. Their revisions will not gain easy consent in the company of those who have been formed by the earliest attesters to the truth of God's coming in history.

Classic Christianity is most reliably defined textually by the New Testament itself. It is most *concisely* summed up in a primitive baptismal confession that was entirely derived from scripture as salvation history in a nutshell. This doctrinal core is recalled in the three prototype summaries of faith: the Apostles' Creed, the Nicene Creed, and the so-called Athanasian Creed (and their subsequent consensual confessions and interpretations). The faithful in Christ are baptized, according to scripture, in the name of the Father, Son, and Holy Spirit.[4] Amid myriad conflicts with false teachings, orthodox teaching became more precisely defined over the first millennium of Christianity through the deliberations of a series of ancient ecumenical councils that gained general lay consent. These and other consensually received findings of regional councils have held fast with general consent through the prodigious changes of medieval scholasticism, the Reformation, revivalism, and contemporary Christianity. This is orthodoxy. It is defined in these texts.

Tradition as Faithful Recollection of Scripture

Orthodoxy itself is nothing more or less than the ancient consensual tradition of Spirit-guided discernment of scripture. The church's book—the canon of holy writ received by believers of all times around the world—remains the crucial criterion for orthodox doctrine, polity, ethics, and social teaching. There is no way to validate the orthodox tradition, according to its own self-understanding, without constant reference to canonical scripture. The canon of scripture is merely the list of sacred texts read in services of worship. The four gospels and Paul's letters were in the list from the earliest Christian decades. The list was largely defined long before Athanasius, whose list was widely received after the fourth century. All that is meant by *tradition*, then, is the faithful handing down from generation to generation of scripture interpretation consensually received worldwide and cross-culturally through two millennia.

Classic Christianity never asserts either scripture against tradition or tradition against scripture. Rather, it understands itself as the right remembering of the earliest testimony of scripture to God's self-disclosure in history. In the phrase "right remembering," *right* has a social meaning—that which has been consensually received throughout all Christian ages and cultures. Nothing would be less orthodox than to assert a tradition that has no basis in scripture.

Scripture contains the received memory of God's action in history. For Jews this means the history of Israel; for Christians this means the fulfillment of Israel's history in Jesus.

The classic Jewish and Christian exegetes themselves always viewed the Spirit of God as working within the process of the recollection, accurate transmission, and interpretation of scripture. The Spirit works not merely in the inspiration of scripture, but also inwardly, within the hearing process. Thus the faithful are never abandoned to their own private, single-culture interpretations. They pray for the Spirit's presence in their reading of the sacred text in order that cultural biases be curbed.

Wherever one text of scripture may appear to contradict another, faithful Jews and Christians reason by analogy from clear passages to those less clear. They look for the spiritual message of a text, ruling out any reading that does not correspond with well-defined memory of historical revelation. The community of faith is "witness and keeper of holy Writ," as one ancient creed put it.[5] In classic Protestant confessions, those interpretations of scripture are judged "orthodox and genuine" that are "taken from the Scriptures themselves—that is, from the spirit of that tongue in which they were written, they being also weighed according to the circumstances and expounded according to the proportion of places" considered in their similarity and differences, and considered in accordance "with the rule of faith and charity."[6]

Even Basil the Great, who highly valued certain unwritten early traditions, nonetheless held even these oral traditions as authentic recollections of the earliest witnesses, rather than as later innovations or additions. He never pitted oral against written tradition.

Any teaching that polarizes tradition against scripture has already lost its orthodox equilibrium. The key balancing feature of classic ecumenical Christian tradition-transmission is this: tradition is itself a memory of scripture interpretation consensually received.

It is regrettable (and ironic) that some Protestant traditions appear dedicated to demeaning the work of the Holy Spirit in pre-Protestant (or non-Protestant or noncharismatic) periods of history. It is lamentable that some pre-Protestant traditions appear to be fixated upon downgrading every work of the Holy Spirit on any road that does not lead to Rome or Constantinople.

I respect the sensibilities of Orthodox believers who may feel that the concept of orthodoxy has been flattened in this argument, but I plea for time and empathy to make a fair case.

A RETURN TO THE FOUNTAIN

The rebirth of orthodoxy is not a nostalgia trip. It is not a religious form of antiquing. It rejects a sentimental view of past idealized social constructs. It is grounded in a much larger tradition than modern political conservatism. It towers above the strictures of Protestant fundamentalism.

The rebirth of orthodoxy stands in sharp contrast to all modern movements. It is not an innovative idea of religion; indeed, it rejects the cult of newness. Resisting idolatry within any particular worldview, orthodoxy reaches beyond relativistic multiculturalism to embrace a more profound multiculturalism that lives out of revelation.

Tested orthodoxy is always *critical* in the sense that it is constantly alert to discriminating truth from error. Seen in retrospect orthodoxy is postcritical in the sense that it is not captive to modern forms of criticism. Critical orthodoxy today seeks to regain analytical skills of discernment honed through centuries of testing.

Why We Cannot Call This Rebirth Neo-Orthodoxy

To avoid confusion it is best to distinguish the rebirth of orthodoxy from "neo-orthodoxy," a waning, once-self-assured school of religious thought and criticism that had its heyday in the 1950s. The difference is basic: unlike genuine orthodoxy, the once-conspicuous school of neo-orthodoxy showed less interest in ancient ecumenical teaching than in modern politics. It fantasized itself to be a fecund moral guide for almost all aspects of modern political life.

The neo-orthodoxy of Paul Tillich, Rudolf Bultmann, and Reinhold Niebuhr never grasped the central importance of the worshiping community. Prayer, discipline, life in Christ, and spiritual formation were not of central interest. Even elementary ideas of sacramental life, liturgy, and pastoral care were neglected. However intriguing their social criticism, proponents of neo-orthodoxy limped along with a diluted view of the Savior and of biblical authority. This neglect opened the door for naturalistic reductionists—that is, those who reduced all knowing to sensory knowing—to take over biblical criticism. This they did with a vengeance

An exception among neo-orthodox thinkers was Karl Barth, who was far more grounded in ancient ecumenical teaching than the others. Nonetheless, he remained always more indebted to Calvin than to Augustine, and more to Augustine than to the Eastern fathers.

Neo-orthodoxy reached its apex and began to slide in the mid-1960s—about the same time as the decline of modern thought. Mark well: neo-orthodoxy and modernity declined hand in hand. Far from a *correction* of modern consciousness, neo-orthodoxy was in most ways a bland *reflection* of modern consciousness.

It is misleading to connect neo-orthodoxy with ancient Christian orthodoxy. Neo-orthodoxy was not *orthodox* in any decisive sense, except in its attempt to teach the doctrine of original sin as a political reality. The core term *orthodoxy* has been spuriously taken over by the quintessentially modern tradition of Bultmann and Tillich—a tradition that never should have been called neo-orthodox in the first place. Since 1979 I have used the term *paleo-orthodoxy* for the orthodoxy that holds steadfast to classic consensual teaching, in order to make it clear that the ancient consensus of faith is starkly distinguishable from neo-orthodoxy. The "paleo" stratum of orthodoxy is its oldest layer. For Christians this means that which is apostolic and patristic. For Jews it means that which is rabbinic and midrashic. These two branches of the "paleo" stratum developed side by side during the same timeframe and within the same language world.[7]

Why Orthodoxy Does Not Take the World Too Seriously

The orthodox way seeks to understand how rightly to guard, reasonably vindicate, and wisely advocate the faith once delivered to the faithful. That way is discovered not by borrowing further from the concepts of the modern world, but by challenging them.

Meanwhile, the actual fallen world, the ongoing cosmos that runs on regular clock-time, is still the subject of God's concern. It is still in the process of being reconciled and having its sin overcome. To speak of an actual fallen world is to hold up for examination a penultimate prodigal history of sin that has not yet come to itself in repentance and faith. It remains a truncated world history that still despairs over its failure to come freely into the presence of God's mercy, as it can at any time by faith.

Classic Jewish and Christian teaching within that sort of posited world must carefully avoid taking the world's fallenness more seriously than it takes God's decisive redemption of this world. The search for truth within that sort of world (which is hypothesized as if it were still unmet by the living God, and as if it were still awaiting redemption) must take care not to be swallowed up by the power of the unredeemed imagination. That imagination is not the final word about the real world.

To *reify* an abstraction is to treat it as if it existed substantially—in other words, to attribute reality to it. The reification of the concept of the "non-Christian world" or "post-Christian culture" makes necessary the critical qualifier that the world is and remains God's. This world is already recipient of God's saving compassion. That gift, given for all, is ready to be received by all who repent and believe. Christian arguments amid the fallen world are forever tempted to overestimate the fleeting power of the fallen world.

Ancient Christian teaching does not speak to the human quandary merely out of humanity's skewed assumptions about itself. It has the privilege of speaking to the fallen world in reference to a thought-reversing assumption—that is, God's own assumption of humanity in the incarnate Lord, the event of divine-human reconciliation through the death and resurrection of the eternal Son.

This gospel is always declared within some particular time and place. It speaks not as an *echo* of the "spirit of the times" but in critical *response* to the times. The spirit of a given time cannot itself dictate the terms of salvation; it cannot redefine the vocabulary of scripture.

We must not concede to the spirit of the times the absolute truth of all its premises, for many of those premises are false. If we make that concession, we can then only seek despairingly to find some tiny aperture within the spirit of the times through which to speak. That is not the way to unveil the light of the truth that God reveals in history! The good news is abandoned already when we are cowed by the spirit of the times. Christian teaching, like personal caregiving, has the empathic task of reaching out for the fallen and hungry precisely where they are fallen and hungry, yet without encouraging the demonic pretense that this fallenness is the last word.

Due to its specific commission to communicate with the fallen world in hearable language, Christianity is continually tempted to be overly awed by the very vitality of the fallen world which the mercy of God has decisively overcome. When this happens, it is the world as such, not God, that is inordinately magnified.

In being overawed by the transient power of the fallen world, one may easily lose sight of the majesty of the incomparable One from whom all things come and into whom all things return, in whose constant love there is no shadow of change or turning. Under the noble fantasy of taking the world absolutely seriously, sovereign grace becomes inadvertently trivialized.

Faith encounters that conjectured world with the real world as God's gift, valuing the real world more than its conjectured counterpart. The apostolic testimony within that real world does better to offer its own gifts to the world than to borrow hungrily from the world's despairing aspirations. This requires Christian teachers to attend to their own sacred texts and allow them a full voice. Faith need not be thrown off track by the presumed vitality of a dying world or the imagined power of an evanescent subculture.

The "Non-Christian World" Understood Within the Orthodox Consensus

It has often been said that today we live in a "post-Christian" or "non-Christian" world, labels that the laity find confusing. In so characterizing the world, scholars imply that the world given by God now exists *without* God, that the history of sin has totally eclipsed the work of the Spirit (when in fact the Spirit has been willfully neglected), that Christian testimony has been permanently silenced. They imply that the world lacks both the governance of the all-wise God and the accompaniment of the crucified and risen Son by the power of the Spirit.

And yet those implications are wrong. To call the world "non-Christian" is in fact to state that the world has defiantly decided to proceed as if the Word of God had not been spoken in history, as if the alleged coming of God in time had no abiding relevance for the world. The idea of a "post-Christian" society can only mean, for classic Christianity, a world falsely posited by unbelievers that lacks the grace of God, a view of the world falsely conceived as if still unmet by the living God, as if still awaiting God's decisive self-disclosure.

The term "non-Christian world" points to a world that insists on living in despair, not realizing that it has been given the gift of forgiving, atoning love. The "non-Christian world" lives already under the judgment of the Holy One whose judgment will be made complete on the last day. In such an environment, the people of God must take care not to be swallowed up by the power of the unredeemed imagination, which fantasizes the durability of its own idolatry. This world remains a place in which the sanctifying fruits of the Spirit are continuously offered, even when spurned and rejected.

Is Orthodoxy Merely the Skewed Memory of Winners?

Is the orthodox way merely a case of political "winners" eliminating "losers"—a survivor game on a grand scale? If so, the faithful have a right to know how they have been deluded by a series of cynical power plays.

Critical orthodoxy has repeatedly examined this important question. Not a new issue, it has a history of serious inquiry from Justin Martyr, Irenaeus, and Eusebius through John Chrysostom, Augustine, and Vincent of Lérins.

Here is the issue in a nutshell: Suppose that the only thing that various heretics through the ages lacked was clout. Suppose that Montanus and Marcion, for example, were just as right apostolically and doctrinally as their "orthodox" opponents but lacked the muscle—no army, no police—with which to coerce their position. Suppose that the winners were by definition labeled as orthodox and the losers by definition as heretics. If that were the case, the history of orthodoxy would be nothing more than the history of a powerful majority; it would not be the history of truth.[8]

The above suppositions reflect a standard sophomore classroom objection to orthodoxy. The most familiar form of that argument is the Marxist or social-location argument, which challenges religious judgments on the premise that they can always be shown to come from some particular social location or vested interest within the economic order. The Marxist explanation of orthodoxy was simple: economic interests prevailed. Ideological winners imposed their views on ideological losers coercively—a matter of power. Though Marxism is now in disrepute, dreary echoes of the Marxist explanation of orthodoxy still linger—oddly enough, in university departments of religious studies, of all places.

Vincent of Lérins, a fifth-century monk about whom much will be told in later chapters, provided the classic answer to the social-location argument: the argument from martyrdom. As Vincent noted, it is self-evident that the martyrs had no economic interest. Their very willingness to give their lives for the truth showed their contempt for all economic interests. Most had already given their fortune to the poor, so they had no material wealth to risk.

It is sad that the witness of the defenseless Christian martyrs has been clouded in our time by Islamicist activists who choose brutally to kill others while themselves dying. These are not analogous cases. On the contrary, the former case dies to attest the truth; the latter dies intentionally to hurt and kill. Islamicist suicide killers are not adequate or faithful representatives of the faith of historic Islam. Christian martyrs, on the other hand, profoundly attest the deep faith of Christianity.

What is so conspicuously wrong with the "orthodoxy as winners" premise? Vincent explained the error as follows:

During the height of Arianism (an early heresy that questioned the divinity of Jesus), many orthodox believers were hunted and persecuted by their more powerful opponents. There was no economic sense in which they could be described as winners. In fact, it offends their memory to consider them under the metaphor of worldly "winners." Vincent likened them to the faith-heroes of the book of Hebrews.

> They were tortured, refusing to accept release in order to obtain a better resurrection. Others suffered mocking and flogging, and even chains and imprisonment. They were stoned to death, they were sawed in two, they were killed by the sword; they went about in skins of sheep and goats, destitute, persecuted, tormented—of whom the world was not worthy. They wandered in deserts and mountains, and in caves and holes in the ground.[9]

The fourth-century Arians lived by collusion with political oppressors. They had plenty of intellectuals and power manipulators on their side, while orthodoxy had to be defended largely by nonscholars and laypeople, by modest men and women of no means, by lowly persons who had no training or special expertise but understood their lives in Christ.[10] The power of numbers and votes in those days was clearly on the side of the Arians, who insisted on reinterpreting scriptural texts on the Son of God in a new and diluted sense. In response God put in his A-team: not scholars, but saints; not elite agents of power, but poor, uneducated, ordinary men—and a great many women—willing to die for their faith. Many Christian wives and widows and daughters suffered during the Arian persecutions. By these ironic means God worked to renew the community of believers.

Similarly, in Soviet times the faithful were not the powerful but the poor, the dispossessed, those who were forced to keep the scripture hidden in a closet. The heterodox, on the other hand, included people of ingenuity backed by streams of money, an eloquent mastery of language, and hordes of bullies.

It is absurd to think of the martyrs of the Decian persecution (CE 249–251) as winners—those men and women who were tortured and died because they refused to offer sacrifice to the Emperor. Nor is Athanasius justly pigeonholed as a winner—exiled a half-dozen times and chased all over the Mediterranean world during the Arian times. John Chrysostom suffered exile and death in political oblivion. Jerome lost his position in Rome and went to the far country of Palestine to live the monastic life. Augustine died in the midst of an invasion by the barbarians. None of these orthodox believers "won" in the secular power moves of their day. Only the slowly un-folding process of intergenerational lay consent in time would recognize them as the great "doctors of the church" they were. The faithful laity had to discover and confirm the authenticity and wisdom of Athanasius and Jerome before they could become ecumenical teachers.

In what conceivable economic or political sense was Anthony of the Desert a winner? He ate wild grains and berries and insects. Or Mother Theodora? Or blind Didymus? How did Polycarp or Felicitas or Perpetua or Cyprian or Ignatius "win"? They died horribly for their faith. Those who imagine that the consensus-bearers of those earlier centuries were upper-class, comfort-able elitists know nothing of the biographies of Justin Martyr, Benedict, or Lawrence of Rome. Nor do they know of John of Damascus, who sought refuge in the isolated location of San Sabbas in Palestine after the Islamic conquest. Think of Dame Julian of Norwich, who literally lived in a hole in the wall of a church; or Francis of Assisi, who lived in a mud hut or slept out-doors. Winners? Not in worldly terms. That would be a gross misreading.

Indeed, some few were born to wealth, Gregory the Great among them; but in his case he voluntarily gave away all his wealth to the poor and en-tered monastic life, as did Ambrose, who resigned his office of governance when baptized and gave everything to the poor. Augustine and Jerome, who were arguably the most learned of the Western fathers, lived most of their lives under conditions that most today would regard as extreme poverty and ascetic deprivation beyond description. Many early Christian writers spent more time in jail or exile or being hunted and hounded than they did living comfortable lives.

Consensuality does not imply that everyone got an equal vote, as if the making of dogma might correspond to the taking of a popular straw-poll. (After all, it was the Holy Spirit who formed the consensus.) Rather, the premise is that all who stand at the Lord's table have freely consented to the apostolic testimony. That is why they are standing there. Their voices of con-sent have been factored into the *general* consent, which has been received in a constrained way so as to resist false and perfidious teachings.

The "winner-loser" oversimplification wrongly applies a competitive sports metaphor to complex historical processes. Fair-minded people will look deeper before allowing such a demeaning generalization to dismiss classic Christian wisdom.

Some modern criticism focuses tendentiously on women who never got to speak, on slaves who never had a say, on classes and nations and cultures alienated from centers of power. But that criticism ignores how important in the ecumenical lay consensus were women and slaves and the dispossessed.

The Spirit found ways of hearing and making known the voices of the underclass, of women, of slaves, and of the oppressed in the deliberative process leading to the ecumenical councils. The Spirit opened ways to awaken general lay consent, even when worldly power or hierarchical organization seemed to override it.[11] Such councils could not have happened (or their conclusions been accepted) without the consent of the poor, of women, of slaves, of bonded servants, and of third-class citizens of the world. These were the very citizens that populated the city of God, a city manifesting itself already through Word and sacrament. They constituted the decisive jury for ecumenical teaching.

FOUR

Why Orthodoxy Persists

There are some surprising reasons why orthodoxy is such a canny survivor.

WHY ORTHODOXY IS SURVIVING THE FAILURES OF MODERN LIFE

Not long ago it seemed certain to everyone that orthodoxy would fail. It was thought to be the least likely candidate to survive the overwhelming creativity and power of modernity. Those who scaled the walls of the Bastille expected orthodoxy to disappear with the old regime. Those who stormed the heights of psychoanalytic theory expected the traditional forms of pastoral care to pass away.

And yet, despite all challenges and negative predictions, orthodoxy has survived. Why? The multifaceted answer is surprising.

Because It Is Cross-Culturally Agile

The most salient feature of orthodoxy is not its rigidity but its flexibility. Since orthodoxy is centered in life in the eternal Word, it is free to enter willingly into infinitely varied cultural settings on behalf of its all-embracing vision of the truth.

Orthodoxy has the reputation of being suspicious of other cultures, forever imprisoned in particular ethnic groups—Greek Orthodoxy looks too Greek, for example, Serbian orthodoxy too Serb, and so on. This is a bad rap. What a poor concept orthodoxy would be if it occurred only in one culture! Orthodoxy is deeply invested not in *one* culture but in *many* (and in principle in *all*)—Greek, Serbian, Coptic, etc.

The orthodox life glories precisely in this readiness to reach out deeply to meet, confront, engage, and dialogue with different cultures, to become all things to all peoples on behalf of God's own coming.[1] Orthodoxy's history shows that it has been uncommonly capable of relating to emergent cultural formations.

Classic Christianity has not survived twenty centuries by being un-resourceful or unable to make adroit responses. Rather, it has been freed to make variable cultural responses precisely by being firmly centered in the revelation of God in history. The people of God live by penetrating and embracing each new culture and language and symbol-system as God's special providential gift.

Cultures and languages change constantly. The same ancient memory of revelation must be attested in ever-new cultures and languages. It is a necessary feature of tradition-transmission that it both guards the original testimony and communicates that testimony effectively within dawning cultures. To fail either task is to default on right remembering. Far from implying unbending immobility, reliable remembering requires constant and mobile connectivity of the primitive testimony to new historical challenges and languages, without altering or diluting the original witness.

Because God's Sovereign Grace Is Sure

Will the community of faith survive whatever cultural formations succeed current culture? The community's answer cannot be based on some clever calculus of social power or predictability. Rather, it must be based on the premise of the intention of God to become known in the future. Without this premise, Jews and Christians have neither a distinctive grasp of the future nor a self-evident right to speculate on probabilities.

Current culture seems capable of undermining any claim to truth. Hence a decisive spiritual issue for Christians is whether the truth of Christianity can be preserved through time. Classically, this is known as *the question of the perseverance of the elect people of God amid proximate temporary apostasies.*

The one holy catholic and apostolic church the world over is promised imperishable continuance, even if particular associations and groupings of apostate believers languish, falter, or atrophy. The covenant of God with Israel is not threatened by human faithlessness. It is an *eternal* covenant, not limited to any particular time or ethos. It is held together by God's own sovereign will.

This is a standard teaching within orthodoxy, whether Jewish or Christian. Yet the neglect of this teaching has deeply affected our moral courage and our ability to relate to our unique cultural opportunities. The modern world is inexactly described as a "post-Christian world" (as we saw in the previous chapter). From the viewpoint of faith, it would be more accurate to describe the world as "post-secular." Meanwhile, faith sees beyond secularization.

The task of adhering to the teaching of God's eternal faithfulness is an urgent one for orthodox remembering in our time. Once again we must learn to speak clearly of the long-range assurance of survival of the community of faith that lives by the Word of God and the power of the Spirit. This confidence rests not on empirical certainty, but rather on the certainty of faith in God's sovereign will. This theme, brilliantly articulated by Justin Martyr, Augustine, Thomas Aquinas, and John Calvin, now begs rediscovery by the faithful. Both Jews and Christians look to Deuteronomy 14:2: "You are a people holy to the Lord your God; it is you the Lord has chosen out of all the peoples on earth to be his people, his treasured possession" [using NRSV]. God calls Jewish and Christian reasoning once again to reclaim the orthodox teaching of the perpetuity, imperishability, and essential durability of the elect people of God.

Although the people of God in some times and places may appear virtually extinct, we always find to our surprise that there are "seven thousand who have not bowed the knee to Baal."[2] Although their vitality may become "so obscured and defaced that the Church seems almost quite razed out," "yet, in the meantime, the Lord has in this world, even in this darkness, his true worshipers."[3] The foundation is standing sure, and the Lord knows who are his.[4]

This faith is seen clearly in the relentless, persistent community of believers in China following the Cultural Revolution. Look also at the heroic faithful in Cuba hanging on to their beliefs even amid the disintegration of Fidelismo. Jews and Christians in the former Soviet Union showed us many examples of the tenacity and courage of faith. These real-life patterns offer us a new opportunity to discover and learn from the eternal remnant to which we belong. But remember: the remnant's continuity is guaranteed not by our cleverness but by sovereign grace.

Because God Does Not Leave Himself Without Witness

The future of belief is left not to chance or human will, but to the electing love and grace of God. God *wills* to be known by rational creatures. That divine will does not depend on our receptivity.

Many branches of the seasonally changing vine may drop off in the varied storms and seasons of passing cultures. Once-vital ideas and institutions may become dysfunctional and atrophy. But God will preserve his people till the end of time. That is a biblical promise, first to Israel and then to the ingrafted Israel.

This is a sure tenet of faith commonly shared by Lutherans, Calvinists, Anglicans, Wesleyans, and Baptists: the ultimate destiny of the believing community of faith is eternally secure. Those who treat this tenet as a distinctively Reformed doctrine do well to read Wesley on election.

Faith alone remains the crucial condition of participating in this secure promise. And where faith is weak, grace continues to awaken and sustain it. The Holy Spirit is determined to prevail over idolatry and disbelief in God's own time. But this assurance is not to be held in such a way as to diminish faithful good works or neglect the responsibilities of human freedom.

This teaching cannot be grasped within the short timeframe of only a few generations. Rather, it can best be seen within the long-range historical and social frame of reference, reaching from the beginning to the end of history. Though individual believers may come to shipwreck, and centuries of emerging and deteriorating traditions may lose their bearings during periods of confusion and crisis, the people of God who are being guided by the Holy Spirit will be sustained by grace until the end.[5]

God will not be left without witness in the world.[6] The "one holy Christian church will be and remain forever."[7] In my own Wesleyan tradition the Order for Confirmation and Reception into the Church states, "The Church is of God, and will be preserved to the end of time, for the conduct of worship and the due administration of his Word and Sacraments, the maintenance of Christian fellowship and discipline, the edification of believers, and the conversion of the world. All, of every age and station, stand in need of the means of grace which it alone supplies."[8] This is a phrase I learned by heart when ordained, and even in the days when I did not adequately understand it, it helped to keep my soul more steady and serene.

Here is the heart of the doctrine: God supplies that grace of perseverance by which the faithful are sustained while being challenged by infirmities, forgetfulness, apostasies, persecutions, and schisms. As the community of faith sails on the turbulent seas of history and continues to be vulnerable to all those hazards that accompany historical existence generally, it is preserved to "proclaim the Lord's death until he comes."[9] The Holy Spirit does not abandon the ever-forming, ever-renewing community of faith amid its earthly struggles.

Against the faithful "the gates of hell shall not prevail," Jesus declared.[10] The people of God will never decline into total forgetfulness. The Spirit guides them and promises always to accompany them,[11] even when all the short-term audits do not add up. The community of faith, insofar as it is guided by the Spirit, never falls entirely away from the central truth of faith or plummets into irretrievable error. It is preserved by grace, not by human craft or numbers or political skill.[12]

Because the Divine Will Transcends Temporary Apostasies

Despite temporary apostasies, though real and devastating, it is unthinkable that God would allow the community of faith finally to become absolutely and continuously apostate or to lose all touch with the righteousness that the Redeemer has once for all bestowed upon the bride of Christ. "For you have been born again," we are told in 1 Peter, "not of perishable seed, but of imperishable, through the living and enduring word of God. For 'All men are like grass, . . . but the word of the Lord stands forever.' And this is the word that was preached to you."[13]

The promise of the ultimate durability of the people of God is offered not with regard to a particular congregation or polity or denomination or generation or period of history, but rather to the whole community of faith viewed from beginning to end. God promises to preserve his people from fundamental error in the long course of history—in fact, to the last day.[14] Insofar as the faithful are sustained by pure Word and sacrament, adhering to the "faith once delivered,"[15] God receives their eucharistic sacrifice—Christ's own self-giving to redeem sin—as faultless.

The Second Helvetic Confession saliently captures this affirmation for Reformed believers, asserting that the community of faith "does not err, so long as it relies upon the rock Christ, and upon the foundation of the prophets and apostles."[16] Though particular assemblies may lapse, the elect people of God will not fall away irrecoverably from salvation, due to the Spirit's guidance.

The Spirit will not allow all those called and elected to err completely and simultaneously. While grace does not coerce belief, neither does it ever bat zero in any given ecclesial season. We know from the history of God's care-giving that providence does not work that way. God did not create the community of faith at such great cost only to let it fall finally into irremediable error. This is not a conclusion of an optimistic anthropology; it is a doctrine grounded in the utter reliability of the divine will to accomplish God's purpose.

Jesus promised the faithful of each generation and of all cultures that the Holy Spirit will "teach you all things and will remind you of everything I have said to you."[17] The Holy Spirit has a perfect memory of the truth, even when we remember imperfectly. Always some seeds of faith sprout from the ashes of the believing remnant. Sometimes such seeds may seem to struggle as semi-endangered species, scattered all too thinly throughout a particular weed-infested culture, as relics of previous covenant communities. Yet wherever Word and sacrament are being faithfully offered, they are not without effect, for "my word" shall "not return to me empty, but will accomplish what I desire,"[18] says the Lord.

Thus the Spirit protects the continuity of the Word in history, ensuring that the whole church does not at any given time completely err, and that it does not err in the foundation, even if in temporary and nonessential ways it may.[19] This is a defining ecumenical doctrine: the community of faith, enabled by the Spirit, is ultimately sure and certain *(asphales)* insofar as it clings to the revealed Word.

Because Human Weakness Highlights Divine Power

The ultimate faithfulness of God's people, with the help of the Holy Spirit, does not diminish the recognition that, amid the history of sin, the vulnerable, visible, local assemblies of the faithful are ever prone to forgetfulness and fallibility. Nor does it imply that the community of faith is saved from making strategic mistakes and errors of judgment and lapses of memory that may have multigenerational echoes. The fallibility of the church is an empirical fact.

Nonetheless, as we have seen, the Holy Spirit promises to uphold faith from an irrecoverable fall into apostasy. Unbelievers do not have the power to prevent subsequent generations from hearing the gospel. The acknowledged limitations of the pilgrim community—and there are many—cannot quench the gospel; on the contrary, they highlight God's determination to transcend and correct human failings. Thus the statement that the church is only one generation away from extinction is short-sighted: it forgets about the Spirit's faithfulness through time.

As long as the community of faith exists within the conditions of the history of sin, it will be prone to being corrupted and distorted. It will remain vulnerable to those who wish to use it for their own self-interest. Until the consummation of history, when the incurably wicked will be cut off from the living vine, a mixture of wheat and tares will remain among the people of God.

Trying to flee altogether from this scene of human corruption is not the answer. That would require abandoning the community of faith's distinctive arena of servant ministry. Following the pattern of the incarnate Lord, the church does not seek to escape embodiment in the world, but rather lives through embodying the Word.

The consequences of the history of sin continue to plague the community of faith and limit its full growth. This community continues to battle the partisan spirit that would divide it, the heretical spirit that would change it, the antinomian spirit that would turn liberty into license, and the legalistic spirit that would turn grace into law. Despite these continuing infirmities, the body of Christ lives on, strengthened by a kind providence. The vine sends forth new shoots. The Spirit enlivens and heals. The Head continues to guide and order the whole organism.[20]

Those who prefer clean hands to a servant heart tend to hold aloof from the incarnational life. Not so with Jesus. He mixed with sinners, eating and drinking with those who were most despicable and rejected. Without sin himself, he chose to identify with sinners, most notably in his baptism and on the cross.

The living community of believers continues to struggle against corruptions—against ubiquitous personal sin, lapsed ministry, overzealous rigorism, and a host of other human failings. But clean hands do not a believer make; only a contrite heart that trusts in God can do that.

Because the Spirit Works to Enable Consent from Generation to Generation

The history of the people of God is not one of uninterrupted progress or sustained ecstasy without challenge or chastisement. Pascal, in the *Pensées,* pictured Christianity as having appeared a thousand times to be "on the point of universal destruction," and he noted that "every time that it has been in this condition, God has raised it up by some extraordinary stroke of his power."[21] Each seeming defeat readies the community for some deeper level of potential understanding. Each apparent victory readies the community for a deeper level of conflict.

The general consent of the people of God, measured over very long stretches of time and space, provides concrete empirical and historical evidence of the durability and unity of the community of faith. The central feature of this unity is alignment with this universal consent.

The Holy Spirit is the vital center of the historical confidence enjoyed in faith. The Spirit acts to illuminate and guard from error the original prophetic and apostolic witness. This occurs not mechanically (as if impersonally manipulated by the Spirit apart from human freedom), but rather deliberately: the Spirit works through human debate, inquiry, parliamentary deliberation, voting, and the apparatus of policy formation.

The community of faith has deep wellsprings of vitality, even where it seems to have been totally undone. This is an amazing story that is recounted in actual human histories, featuring startling recoveries after deadly periods of malaise.

The worst days of martyrdom have been characteristically accompanied by the most profound movements of the Spirit. Correctives such as those of Benedict of Nursia, Bernard of Clairvaux, Francis of Assisi, Luther, Calvin, Teresa of Avila, Jonathan Edwards, and John Wesley have often followed deep sloughs of demoralization. To the present, God's promise has held, even against great odds: the gates of hell have not prevailed against the community of believers.

Because Consent Is Divinely Guarded

The faithful have found that they can rely on the Spirit over time to bring the truth to light, to remember the truth rightly, and to guide the whole community of believers toward the truth, in its entirety.

A crucial premise underlies the durability of faith: God intends, through the Spirit, to awaken the same fullness of faith in the whole communion of saints throughout the world. The Spirit works relentlessly (in the patient way that only God knows) to offer noncoercive resistance to false teachings, striving for unity of the faithful and valid transmission of the apostolic tradition.

A simple historical fact stands as evidence of the durable assent of the whole community of faith: the history of reception of the ecumenical councils. It is astonishing that councils convened between 325 and 787 CE have been accurately remembered and honored as the work of the Spirit. This history shows that the Spirit is ever working to center the community in scriptural truth.

It is this universal consent that the faithful of all times find perennially reliable. It is the stunning durability of this consent that engenders historical confidence. The longer such consent persists, the more clearly it attests the ultimate survivability of the community of faith as a gift of grace.[22]

Because the Faithful Are Given Patience

The victory of general lay consent will ultimately be vindicated only on the last day. Then wheat and tares will be separated. Then the unity, holiness, catholicity, and apostolicity of the faithful will shine forth, though we now see through a glass darkly. This is a conviction of faith made sure by looking at the history of providence.

Countless are the temporary lapses in Christian memory. But all of them, taken together, have not led the witnessing community to despair over the truth of revelation. Rather, they have paradoxically revealed the meekness and vulnerability of the remembering faithful. Through this vulnerability the faithful are trained and disciplined (with a patience supplied by grace) to rely on God's promise, aware of their egocentric temptations, social location, racism, sexism, and nationalism. Even the best expressions of the living community of believers in history continue to net a mixed catch of good and bad fish.

The faithful rightly doubt any alleged consensus formed only in a single generation. Having lived patiently through many trials (and having seen the blemishes of past consensus), they have a healthy respect for the slow but sure test of time.

Because the Orthodox Heart Has the Advantage of Long-Term Memory

Any particular assertion of Christian truth must stand under the constant corrective of the cumulative consent of the faithful over a wide range of time. The long memory of tested Christian truth tends eventually to override the shorter memory of error. The advantage of a very long memory is that it has more levels of applicability, more occasions to learn, and more possible nuances. The more durable the consensual memory, the more likely it is to be trustworthy and blessed by One who remembers rightly, the Holy Spirit. A durable memory has had many more chances to be corrected than a memory lasting only one generation.

Why does orthodoxy persist? Because of all the above reasons—but especially because orthodoxy possesses an extremely long memory. In fact, orthodoxy precisely *is* this long memory. The long memory of the community of faith works always to overcome the shortsighted forms of distorted memory in particular situations. The modern project is trapped in short-term memory, with long-term memory deficiency.

History abounds with regrettable illustrations of errors temporarily held. Even though many such errors have been corrected, the remedies have often been either insufficient or excessive. In the short term we frequently *over-correct*. The medieval indulgence preachers needed the corrective of the Reformation. The Reformation and Counter-Reformation then needed a different counter-corrective through the remedies of the Enlightenment, which themselves are now in need of an even greater correction. And so it goes.

In each of these cases the faithful over time sought a reconciling ground to mediate the best aspects of each potential remedy and to complement those with other misplaced aspects of classic consensual memory. But these correctives took time. Only a very long historical memory could provide critical balance for the journey through unpredictable hazards.

How often the fleeting popular consensus has been temporarily ill-formed or misunderstood. How deeply the unity of the community of faith has been severed. How often imbalance has paraded as balance.

All the lasting advantages for survival lie on the side of the longer, more nuanced, more refined forms of historical memory. Thus orthodoxy's extensive memory is its special gift to the faithful.

In sum, these are the reasons that orthodoxy is surviving the failures of modern times: it is cross-culturally agile; God's sovereign grace is sure; God does not leave himself without witness; the divine will transcends temporary apostasies; human weaknesses illuminate the divine power; the Spirit works to enable consent from generation to generation; consent is divinely guarded; the faithful are given patience; and the orthodox heart has the advantages of long-term memory. But there is more.

GOING DEEPER: THE KERNEL OF TENACITY

Modern narcissism stands amazed at the tenacity of orthodoxy. What is the source of its durability? Where is the ground of its courage and toughness? Why so confident and unintimidated? From where does its resilience come? There is one more, still deeper reason that orthodoxy's faithful witnesses persist: they are willing to suffer for the truth.

Why the Faithful Are Willing to Suffer for Truth

The faithful throughout history have always been willing to suffer for the truth. God raises up, in every age, witnesses ready to deny themselves and bear the cross, rock solid confessors who view that offering as an inestimable privilege.

A readiness to suffer for the sake of the truth permeates the whole fabric of biblical teaching. It is not an *optional* part of the curriculum for equipping the faithful.[23] Rather, it is what is meant by taking up the cross and following Jesus.

To speak of truth without a willingness to suffer for the truth is backhandedly to debase that truth. No teacher can be taken seriously who refuses to be inconvenienced for the truth he or she teaches. Legitimacy is quickly self-canceling if one is unwilling to tolerate anguish on its behalf.

Any truth that is not worth suffering for cannot possibly be the truth of Christianity.[24] The very concept of truth in classic Christianity depends on the willingness to put one's body on the line for the truth.

Jesus made it clear to his disciples that they must be prepared to "be handed over for punishment and execution." He further cautioned: "[M]en of all nations will hate you for your allegiance to me."[25] Paul set the pattern for the apostolic witness. His teaching was personally validated in the most costly way—by his unhesitating willingness to be "exposed to hardship, even to the point of being shut up like a common criminal," always remembering that "the Word of God is not shut up."[26]

Why the Blood of the Christian Martyrs Constitutes a Unique Form of Argument

As noted in the previous chapter, Vincent of Lérins recognized the unique role of the martyrs in defense of the apostolic faith.[27] He saw that they constituted a persuasive form of validation much more credible and convincing than any conceptual argument. In making that case, he pointed to the synods of Sirium and Rimini in 359, at which the emperor attempted to compel all bishops and laity to deny the orthodox faith and subscribe to Arian teaching. Those who refused were denied permission to return to their congregations, and many of the orthodox believers were tortured. They willingly gave up their lives rather than collapse before state-led heretical persecution.

The argument from martyrdom—this special form of evidentiary reasoning—arises from the real experience of those willing to die rather than disavow the truth. That willingness to suffer dearly for the truth was integral to the testimony of the early Christians.[28] Their readiness to die for the truth helps to explain the durability of the orthodox way.

A martyr is a believer who has borne witness to Christ by shedding his or her blood. Though that definition is straightforward, martyrdom resists simplistic explanations. It cannot be explained simply by the premise of a death wish, for example, or by political courage or the desire for recognition. Such interpretations cannot account for the orthodox confessors. They cannot fathom Lawrence, who was burned on a griddle, or the martyrs of Vienne, or Perpetua or Felicitas, "whom no force could keep from defending the faith, . . . no threats, no blandishments, neither life nor death, not the palace, not the courtiers, not the emperor, not the empire, not men, not demons."[29]

Providence worked powerfully through these martyrs and confessors, and "because of their tenacious attachment to the ancient faith," many of the lapsed were restored to belief. Through these martyrs, God "restored battered churches and brought to life peoples that were spiritually dead."[30] Martyrdom itself became the supreme evangelizer under the challenge of persecution.

By their faithfulness God recalled the world "from the new perfidy to the old faith, from modern unreasonableness to ancient sanity, from the blindness of novelty to the ancient light."[31] The special power of the confessors lay in their dauntless stand against accommodation to cheap grace, worldliness, popular opinion, and in their appeal to the ancient faith universally received prior to contemporary novelties.

If it were only a few confessors or martyrs who had stood up for their faith, they might have been overlooked; but there were far too many to ignore. During the Arian persecution large numbers of people over the known world were willing to die rather than confess what they knew to be a diminution of the truth. Vincent knew and referred to many narratives describing these faithful ones, and quite likely he had known some martyrs personally. "They preferred to surrender themselves rather than the faith universally held from the beginning."[32]

The courage, sanctity, and goodwill of the martyrs and confessors showed forth luminously in their unwillingness to yield even amid torture and death—an overpowering witness, hard to refute. The best analogies in our time are found in the numberless Christian martyrs of Communist Russia and Asia, and those of the Middle East and Africa. The spiritual authority of Sudanese, Iranian, and Vietnamese confessors, for example, testifies powerfully to faith that stands against an almost universal prevailing opinion.

What deconstructionist is willing to die for his or her teachings? Name the postmodern critics who are laying their lives on the line. The very idea is laughable, because martyrdom would be entirely inconsistent with such critics' commitment to absolute cultural relativism.

Orthodoxy cannot be exhaustively explained either sociologically (as merely an appeal to oppressive authoritarianism) or psychologically (as a phobic resistance to any kind of change or an erotic fixation). Likewise, it is implausible to argue that Christian confessors, in the name of salvation, were lusting simply for whatever is old, familiar, and conventional: orthodoxy is not merely a reactionary nostalgia enamored with power. On the basis of these various naturalistic explanations, there would be no way reasonably to explain the faith of confessors, in chains or in prison, who over the centuries have been prepared to die for apostolic faith in Christ.[33]

Why Suicide Is Not Martyrdom

Given our current world situation, ideologically motivated suicide is often confused with martyrdom, as I noted in the previous chapter. The two are very different, however. Suicide is the intentional taking of one's own life; it is self-destruction (for whatever reason). Martyrdom, on the other hand, neither desires nor intends the taking of one's own (or any other) life; it desires only to witness to faith, whatever the cost. The martyr is destroyed for the *faith,* not for the sake of ending life.

How utterly different is the Christian martyr from the modern suicide bomber, yet the two continue to be perversely compared. The former dies for the integrity of life in Christ without taking another's life, while the latter murders for a desperate cause.

Those who intentionally kill are not worthy to be compared to those who die for their faith. It is absurd and willfully wrongheaded to link the issue of Christian martyrdom with suicide killing. Wherever hinted at, this false correlation should be protested. Yet some are ready to dismiss or demean the history of Christian martyrdom by stereotyping it in the same breath with modern suicide bombing.

The actual story of martyrdom among the people of God is galvanizing: "They were stoned; they were sawed in two; they were put to death by the sword. They went about in sheepskins and goatskins, destitute, persecuted and mistreated—the world was not worthy of them. They wandered in deserts and mountains, and in caves and holes in the ground."[34] Far from killing others, Jewish and Christian martyrs were (and continue to be) willing to die rather than fail to attest the truth.

Sadly, there are many more Christian martyrs in our century than in any previous one. Their imprisonment, torture, and death is just as appalling as the ancient persecutions.

Why Truth Risks Becoming Embodied

The truth risks becoming embodied because truth *embodied* is greater than truth merely *conceived*. Stated another way, embodied truth is truer than truth without embodiment. This is a simple, easy-to-understand argument: Consider two expressions of truth—one embodied, the other spoken but not embodied. Which is truer?

The truth risks becoming embodied because God has shown the way, and because its enactment comes naturally to it. What is the truth, for Jews and Christians? That question cannot be answered without looking through the lens of those particular events in history in which God has been revealed. For Jews the truth centers in events: God chooses Israel, covenants with Israel, delivers Israel, and remains faithful to Israel. For Christians the truth likewise centers in particular historical events: a lowly birth, a suffering death, and an unexpected resurrection. By "truth" the New Testament means God's own personal coming to us in mercy and grace. In this truth a Word is spoken through a personal life lived.

The truth has become an *event* in Jesus—an event in which we are individually called to participate. God has become personally known in human history, insofar as God is knowable. God has become human, having entered our fleshly sphere—having been born as we are born, having been tempted as we are tempted, having died as we die, and having risen to attest who it was who died. Faith participates in this personally-lived-out truth by personally living it out in daily life.

The truth risks becoming embodied because its hope *exceeds* all risks. To tell the truth rightly is to follow the One who *is* truth. The truth embodied in the One who was "nailed to the cross" still appears to many to be a "stone of stumbling" and "folly."[35] But for the faithful it has become the chief cornerstone.

Because truth that is lived is evidence of truth that is spoken, truth thought and told must be embodied to be taken with full seriousness. The fact that Jews and Christians have a three-thousand-year history of being willing to take the truth seriously is stunning and shattering and puzzling to modern narcissism. Ours is an *imperfect* history, but it is nonetheless an *actual* history.

FIVE

The New Ecumenism

The twentieth century saw a burst of modern ecumenical dialogue. That dialogue is weary and aging. Yet a new ecumenism, quite different in form and spirit, is taking shape. The irony of the new ecumenism is that it is much older (by a millennium, in fact) than what I will refer to here as the old ecumenism. Paradoxically, then, by *old* I mean old-modern and by *new* I mean new-classic. Modernity is old. What is new in relation to modernity is classic Christianity.

The new ecumenism has ancient ecumenical roots that are still deep and vital. The old ecumenism, now moribund, has decaying modern roots. As that old ecumenism withers, a new post–Lambeth Conference, post–National Council of Churches[1] ecumenism is taking form in the womb of current history. In short, we are witnessing a basic reconfiguration of ecumenism. Interpreting this emerging situation is an ironic exercise.

OLD AND NEW ECUMENISMS CONTRASTED

The *old ecumenism* is decisively identified with Geneva and the 475 Riverside establishments—that is, the World Council of Churches (WCC) and the National Council of Churches (NCC). This is the ecumenical movement that everybody involved in church life has known for fifty years.

But few are yet aware of the emerging *new ecumenism,* a movement that, though embryonic, is sufficiently developed to be recognizable in its main features. These two ecumenisms do not differ absolutely, but they represent distinguishable tendencies and have quite different manifestations. Table 1 offers a brief glimpse of the differences.

TABLE 1
COMPARING THE OLD AND NEW ECUMENISMS

Old	New
Distrustful of ancient ecumenism	Deliberately grounded in ancient ecumenism
Uncritically accommodating toward modernity	Critical of failed modern ideas
Oriented mainly toward Enlightenment assumptions and the Reformation's left wing	Oriented mainly toward classic Christianity and teaching grounded in the consensus of the ecumenical councils
Characterized by revolutionary pretenses	Partial to an organic view of historical change
Preoccupied with ushering in rapid social change	Keenly aware of the recalcitrance of sin
Ideologically drawn to the heirs of Marx, Freud, and Nietzsche	Mindful of the tragic consequences of Marx, Freud, and Nietzsche
Chronically activist	Patient amid historical turbulence
Bureaucratic	Suspicious of top-heavy administration
Favoring left-leaning state planning strategies	Supportive of a free and democratic society
Utopian	Realistic
Interested in negotiated inter-institutional unity	Committed to unity based on classic Christian truth
Declining in favor and support	Emerging
Analogous to hierarchical business organizations	Analogous to web-network
Financially vexed, troubled by loss of nerve	Confident, resourceful
Seeking unity in shifting political alliances	Based on unity already found in Christ

Old	New
Begun with the founding of the wcc, 1948 (Amsterdam)	Begun in the Council of Jerusalem, 46 CE
Peaked at the Geneva Conference, 1966	Peaked in the seven ecumenical councils, 325–787 CE
Dying by the time of the Harare "Padare" (the eighth assembly of the wcc), 1998	Still alive and strong

This list of paired characteristics points to tendencies, not absolute distinctions, and the categories overlap to some extent. Still, it serves to point to distinct differences of tone, orientation, and trajectory.

The old ecumenism has been focused on negotiating structures of organic unity. The new ecumenism seeks to restore classic Christian verities within and despite the old divisions. It is not headquartered in any particular bureaucracy or establishment but is as diffuse as is the uniting work of the Holy Spirit.

What is happening in this new ecumenism? God is at work in grassroots Christianity, awakening a groundswell of longing for classic ecumenical teaching in all communions. There are many local and lay manifestations of this unity. Though some are calling it an *alternative* ecumenical movement, my own view is that it is not alternative, but the original and genuine *oecumene*, in fertile continuity with the communion of saints.

Evidences of the New Ecumenism

The Holy Spirit is creating forms of unity in the church far beyond our poor human attempts. Because the promise of the Spirit is to guide the church into all truth, the Spirit enables accurate memory of the apostolic testimony. The Spirit is even today reliably reminding the faithful of the good news of the kingdom. The Spirit is at work to transcend ecumenical bureaucracies, provide a critique of blatantly politicized ecumenism, and restore confidence in classic ecumenical teaching.

This uniting work of the Holy Spirit is taking form on a breathtaking world scale, and yet it is manifested primarily in quiet and inconspicuous ways in local churches, parachurch ministries, and unobtrusive grassroots missions. The Spirit is working in diverse arenas ranging from urgent food relief to long-term scholarly projects to collaborative evangelization. This ecumenism is not just a matter of pragmatic cooperation; rather, it is a living embodiment of the body of Christ.

There is an internet analogy here, imperfect but suggestive. Think of the new ecumenism as analogous to the worldwide information web: it is dispersed, decisions are made mainly through local initiatives, and there is minimal need for central integrative control. The old ecumenism is more like defensive proprietary hardware, while the new ecumenism is like public-domain software: the old guard wants to keep control. In the new ecumenism there is no desire to control the work of the Holy Spirit. The faithful want to reflect and celebrate that work, not capture and can it institutionally.

The terminal illness of the old ecumenism was triggered by the entrenched habit of believing that the embodiment of the body of Christ depends largely upon deft organizational management, human ingenuity, equivocal rhetoric, and bland humanistic goodwill that gives no offense. It remains fixated on negotiation of special interests that coalesce especially around idealistic "causes" of political action. It imagines that visible unity will be accomplished by getting institutions and groups to agree with each other, verbally and formally, even if reduced to the lowest common nondoctrinal denominator, especially in supposed political acts that give the appearance of great prophetic courage (though they are carried out with a steady eye toward favorable journalistic reporting).[2]

The old ecumenism brought institutions together to agree on high-sounding documents and bold-sounding revolutionary public-policy proposals. The new ecumenism sees the Holy Spirit as doing something far more unexpected, diffuse, and magnificent than paper proclamations or the building of a new bureaucracy. God the Spirit is not sentimentally attached to a socialist vision of economic order at a time when that vision has already collapsed. The new ecumenism long ago survived the collapse of control economies, and it is grateful to God that this collapse came to pass.

The new ecumenism is already widely dispersed among Protestant, Catholic, and Orthodox believers, not as an organizational expression of institutional union, but as a movement of the Spirit already gradually dawning. The old ecumenism was largely a liberal Protestant artifact, with Eastern Orthodoxy included as a frustrated minority partner, while in the new ecumenism, both lowercase orthodoxy and uppercase Orthodoxy are central features.

The new ecumenism is above all committed unapologetically to ancient classic ecumenical teaching. That means that it has a high doctrine of scripture, a long-term view of cumulative historical consensus, and a classic ecumenical view of God the Father, God the Son, and God the Holy Spirit that makes no concession to political correctness. It adheres to the classic consensual doctrines of incarnation, atonement and resurrection, and the return of the Lord. These are fixed boundary stones in the ancient ecumenical tradition—stones that we are commanded not to move or attempt to refashion.

In the old ecumenism of the hot-house God-box in New York,[3] these classic doctrines were largely submerged under the provocative rhetoric of supposedly radical social transformation. The old ecumenism became intensely embarrassed by allegedly sexist language about God the Father and God the Son—so much so that some of its leaders were quite willing to give up classic trinitarian language in favor of more "correct" formulations such as God the Parent, God the Child, and God the Spirit of Love. The old ecumenism appealed constantly to social-location analysis and psychoanalytic theories of religion. It looked desperately for alternative humanistic explanations of the mystery of the incarnation, the resurrection, and the Trinity.

From Amsterdam to Harare

The old ecumenism began with the launching of the World Council of Churches at Amsterdam in 1948 (the same year that the United Nations was created) and functionally expired at Harare, Zimbabwe, fifty years later, in 1998. In its early years it was in sound continuity with international missionary societies and the earlier evangelical alliances for Christian unity, all well grounded in classic Christian teaching. But in its later years it disintegrated.

What began with Amsterdam's bold vision ended with Harare's pathetic "Padare" (in the eighth assembly of the wcc), named for the Shona word for "a meeting place for talking it out." At the Padare, a broad platform of absolute toleration was provided, allowing anyone to speak of any faith-feeling or trendy take on social process. Under the rubric of "talking it out," anything at all could be baptized as "ecumenical," whether shamanism or syncretism or clog-dancing or group-think experiences or amateur photography or mercurial political advocacy. The once-serious ecumenical movement had become captive to fads.

I attended the second assembly of the World Council of Churches at Evanston in 1954 (as a youth observer), then the Geneva Conference in 1966, and finally the Harare Padare in 1998. Thus I have personally beheld the old ecumenism in its earlier, middle, and waning phases. I have seen it move from adolescent idealism to overconfident middle-age bureaucratic activism to senile introversion, all in one lifetime. I can attest that a radical turn had occurred by the mid-sixties—a turn toward revolutionary rhetoric, social engineering, and regulatory politics.

1966 and All That

It was not until 1966 that the old ecumenism took its radical turn toward an imagined revolution. Although a transformation occurred gradually during the sixties, it was at the World Conference on Church and Society, held in Geneva in 1966, that the radical turn became public and irreversible.

The engine of utopianism that was revved up in 1966 persists today in the Geneva bureaucracy. Its major designers at the outset were James Pike, Paul Abrecht, Eugene Carson Blake, and Patriarch Alesky (Ridiger) II, who was later identified as a willing agent of the Soviet KGB. The middle managers of the ecumenical takeover in the mid-sixties ranged from Margaret Mead to Stephen Rose, from Janet Lacey to Robert W. Spike, from Arend van Leeuwen to Metropolitan Nicodim of Leningrad, from Betty Thompson to Albert van den Heuvel, and from Richard Shaull to Konrad Raiser. The ideological echoes of these sixties dreamers can still be heard today.

The apogee of the old ecumenism was reached at that 1966 conference—a conference that occasioned Paul Ramsey's brilliant response: *Who Speaks for the Church?*[4] Thereafter, the momentum of the old ecumenism turned decisively in the direction of faddism and utopianism. Barely two decades old, ecumenism began to decline, losing its theological equilibrium and spinning out into a frenetic accommodation to outdated ideological programs. It collapsed into desperate syndromes of self-justification that bore bitter fruit in the Canberra (1990) and Harare (1998) General Assemblies.

What happened at Harare in 1998 was a final shift from Christian truth to a bland interfaith, world-religions dialogue. The ecumenical frame of reference was changed from the apostolic deposit of faith to a group-think conversational quest in which Shirley MacLaine would have felt right at home. The search was not for truth but for self-expression—a search that followed tempting paths toward neo-paganism, shamanism, and animistic primitivism as alternatives for ecumenical rejuvenation. By 1998 the old ecumenism had disintegrated into a cacophony of politicized voices.[5]

The Rise and Fall of the Old Ecumenical Movement

The old ecumenism has suffered the shock of wave after wave of ideological excess. It has become habituated to viewing current public-policy issues through the eyes of liberation theology (of one sort or another), run-amok egalitarianism, defensive feminism, and sexual liberation advocacy. All of these patterns are focused on one central, absolute commitment: accommodation to modernity.

In the old ecumenism the institutional manipulators tried to create unity by negotiation, force-feeding church-union schemes while ignoring grassroots sentiments that hungered for classic ecumenical teaching. In the new ecumenism territorial claims are less relevant and proprietary ownership concerns are subordinated. Within the old ecumenism, Christian unity appeared to be based more on calculation, deliberation skills, tolerant expression of feelings, and the sharing of political goals than on truth-claims. In the emerging new ecumenism, Christian unity is based expressly upon Christian truth.

When I attended the world ecumenical conferences in Evanston and Geneva, I thought of myself as a dedicated ecumenist. It took me a long time to realize that what I was committed to in those days was *oecumene*-lite. My 1960s ecumenical enthusiasm, with its hunger to accommodate to modern ideologies and its stubborn aversion to ancient ecumenism, now seems cheap and phony, especially in relation to the bloody and hard-won testimony of the actual martyrs, saints, confessors, and classical exegetes.

Desperate attempts to resuscitate the old ecumenism have withered. The Council on Christian Unity (COCU), the old guard of the old ecumenism, was closed down at the turn of the millennium for lack of interest. The COCU was then replaced by Churches Uniting in Christ (CUIC), with a new round of paper proposals but no constituency. No wonder the CUIC has become known as the "shot heard round the closet." (The CUIC proposals, following the obvious hint of the anagram, are commonly referred to as "Quickies.")

Meanwhile, the emerging new ecumenism, with its classical grounding, survived not only the sixties but the millennium with a growing confidence in an incremental (rather than revolutionary) view of social change and in equity judgments shaped by classic Christian moral reasoning.

The Rediscovery of Ancient Ecumenism

While the old ecumenism has been waning, the new ecumenism has been quietly rediscovering ancient Christian ecumenism, without press notice, without fanfare. It is silently reclaiming the courage of the martyrs and the faith of the confessors, the resolve of the early councils, and the wisdom of the church fathers. It is engaged in rediscovering the truth as revealed, once for all, in Jesus Christ. The work of the Holy Spirit is deepening the spiritual unity of the community of baptized believers worldwide without being locked into denominationalism.

The new ecumenism is not a rhetorical ploy. It exists already as a fact of our time, as a palpable movement of confession and renewal within the churches, and as a deep-felt hunger within modern culture. Though still emerging, it is a global reality, as much or more alive in Singapore than Geneva.

THE PRESENT CRISIS OF ECUMENISM

The crisis of the two ecumenisms is a crisis of legitimacy. The very notion of *oecumene* implies a claim to *wholeness,* an appeal to classic catholicity.[6] The old ecumenism presumes that it has a proprietary right to shape with its modernist ideology every potential expression of the unity of the church. Meanwhile, the very modernity to which it is seeking to adapt the church is dying.

Now, however, the old ecumenism's presumed proprietary right must be tested. Is the World Council of Churches the sole legitimate heir of the office of bringing unity to the body of Christ? This obviously circumvents North American evangelicals in the mainline, Roman Catholics, and most Orthodox. The old NCC ecumenism makes an implicit claim of truth and universality. Yet its very claim is corrupted by its own radical relativism. It is that corruption that has required the Holy Spirit to raise up a new ecumenism.

The old ecumenism wholeheartedly accepts the canons of modern consciousness as a permanent feature of every conceivable future. The new ecumenism, on the other hand, is not intimidated by dying modernity. It does not permit modern assumptions to stand as absolute judge of apostolic truth. Modernity has miserably failed to create viable, stable, humane conditions for living. As a result, apostolic truth has now become the forceful critic of modernity.[7]

The crisis comes down to the question of whether God in time will bless one or the other—the modern institutional form or the classic ecumenical form. There is increasing evidence that God is already blessing the renewal of classic Christian ecumenism, regrounded in the ancient consensual tradition of scriptural study.

The Divisiveness of the Old Ecumenical Movement

It is only now that we can clearly see how damaging the old ecumenism has been to the very cause of Christian unity, how it has in fact fostered the *disunity* of the church. Arguably, nothing has been more divisive in contemporary Christianity than the social witness of modern ecumenists who have forgotten the ancient ecumenical consensus. They have been most divisive just at those points at which they have offended against ancient ecumenical boundaries: permissive sexuality, power politics, and schismatic utopianism. Meanwhile, the new ecumenism has grasped a vision of the unity of the body of Christ, based on ancient ecumenism, but it is not yet able to actualize it or manifest it institutionally within its own emergent networks and memories of confession.

Those of us working toward this new ecumenism must continue to hone an accurate and truth-telling form of advocacy journalism. Why? Because each mainline bureaucracy has a wholly owned publishing operation whose slanted reportage is funded and designed to prop up the old infrastructure.

Denominational organizations maintain vast closed-shop publication resources that remain largely in the hands of the tired denominational apologists for the old elitist ecumenism. In order to break through this defensive gridlock, new ecumenists must strive, through accurate investigative journalism, to challenge just those points of the old ecumenism that are inconsistent with classic Christian teaching.[8]

The Institutional Instruments of the New Ecumenism

Since Canberra, the Holy Spirit has been teaching Orthodox, Catholic, and evangelical Christians that they are closer to each other than they are to modern liberal accommodative assumptions. The Holy Spirit is at work to elicit an apostolic unity that has not yet been manifested fully but is in the process of being created.[9] What configuration promises to emerge out of the old alphabet soup of WCC, NAE, NCC, ACR, and NCCB? Clearly, the old ecumenism is already overly burdened with institutionalism! My own view is that the Holy Spirit will show us the way in God's own time. We already have corporate manifestations of parachurch movements and embryonic unity movements (such as the Lausanne Movement and the World Evangelical Alliance) that are in their own ways working to bring greater unity to the body of Christ.

The instruments of this unity all over the world are seen in believing Christians in every communion, but also in international ministries that express Christian unity concretely and pragmatically, transcending denominational boundaries—such vital ministries as Prison Fellowship, World Relief, World Vision, the Billy Graham Evangelistic Association, and Samaritan's Purse. These ministries must be nurtured in our prayers and hopes for unity.

The old ecumenism has collapsed through boredom and neglect. It cannot raise money for its programs. It has lost its historical identity. The Holy Spirit is acting concretely and tangibly the world over, but it is hard for us to see the unity in all this diversity. It is there, though: the unity lies in the One who unites—God the Holy Spirit, who can work precisely through antinomies, historical developments, signs of contradiction, and paradox. The major challenge of the new ecumenism is to grasp the incredible abundance of gifts that the Holy Spirit is bringing to the faithful community.

The new ecumenism has not clearly decided whether or how it might engender or manifest new post-WCC expressions of the unity of the body of Christ. It may decide not to seek any structure at all at this time, but to allow the regenerating work of the Holy Spirit to shape whatever structures are required. This debate is only beginning. Among the journals giving voice to its substantive issue are *First Things, Pro Ecclesia, Touchstone,* and *Faith and Freedom.*

Old Ecumenism and the Neglect of Classic Christianity

Why is the old ecumenism in such difficulties? The short answer: it has neglected classic ecumenism.

The ecumenism of the twentieth century is based on negotiations between bureaucrats; ancient ecumenism is based on apostolic testimony that has gained worldwide consent. The ecumenism of the twentieth century remains bound by modern culture; ancient ecumenism owes no such debt. The ecumenism of the twentieth century has shown itself to be easily distractible; ancient ecumenism, more patient and less prone to abrupt turns and temptations, trusts in the testimony of the whole *sanctorum communio* over time, rather than bowing to the particular negotiated settlements of recent claimants.

For these reasons, Christians of many diverse forms of ethnicity and culture are turning to Christianity's ancient witnesses to the truth. This rebirth of classic Christianity has occurred in our time.

Christians whose traditions have long distanced themselves from each other through separate and often competing church memories are now finding their unity in the classic consensus. The early Christian commentators on scripture most clearly express this classic consensus in a way that can be trusted by those who might otherwise be partisans. Classic Christianity, with its texts of many cultures and epochs, is a wide and welcoming umbrella. On this ecumenical ship gather conservative Protestants alongside Eastern Orthodox, Baptists with Catholics, Reformed with Wesleyans and charismatics, Anglicans with Pentecostals, high- with low-church adherents, and premodern traditionalists with postmodern classicists.

How do such varied Christians find inspiration and common faith within this joint effort? By affirming together that the texts on which classic Christianity is grounded are intrinsically and obviously ecumenical, undeniably catholic in their cultural range. All of the above-named traditions have an equal right to appeal to the earliest Spirit-led history of Christianity. All of these traditions can, without compromising intellect or conscience, come together under the authority of the ancient ecumenical texts that are common to them all.

These early consensual texts decisively shaped the entire subsequent history of scripture interpretation. Protestants have as much right to the councils and church fathers as do the Antiochenes. Augustine and Athanasius are not owned by the Africans; they belong to all. The Turks do not possess Polycarp or Gregory of Nyssa. The Syrians do not possess Ephraim. Rome does not own Leo or Gregory the Great. As the common heritage of all Christians, they may be equally received and celebrated and enjoyed by all.

Believers everywhere may lay equal claim to this vast patrimony—and they are doing so in ever greater numbers. People of vastly different cultures are recognizing in these witnesses their own unity as the people of God, despite different cultural memories, foods, garments, and habits of piety.

Rediscovering Evangelical Roots in Classic Christian Orthodoxy

After centuries of separation, the orthodox way is at long last discovering its evangelical partners. For too long, evangelicals have remained distanced from many of the classic themes of orthodoxy. Their congregational polity, free liturgical patterns, voluntarism, and enthusiasm have made them seem culturally "unorthodox." Often evangelicals have ruled themselves out of orthodoxy because of a distrust of its alleged ethnic captivity, superstitiousness, and hierarchy. Much of this distance is now being closed by increased interaction between evangelicals and Eastern Orthodox, and between evangelicals and Catholics, especially through biblical exegesis.

But why just now is this rediscovery of classic Christian wisdom occurring *among evangelicals?* What is drawing evangelicals toward ancient Christian writers and their way of reading scripture? What accounts for this rapid and basic reversal of mood among the inheritors of the traditions of Protestant revivalism?

In their desire to have no text but scripture, evangelicals have tended to lose sight of the ways the Spirit has worked through the history of exegesis to bring the Word of scripture to reception. Prematurely assuming that ancient patristic sources must be anti-scriptural rather than confirming of scripture, they have eschewed patristic nourishment, leaving unsatisfied their hunger for roots—a hunger that has grown since the days of Luther, Calvin, and Wesley, who knew the writings of the church fathers well.

Evangelicals have also been hampered by both Protestant pietism and the French Enlightenment. Both of these traditions expressed disdain for classic forms of scripture interpretation, though for opposite reasons, offering up personal existential storytelling (pietism) and historical-critical work (Enlightenment) as the key to scripture. Evangelicals are now eager to break free of the constrictions of these traditions.

Today the world of orthodoxy is intriguing to evangelicals worldwide. They realize that they have missed out on something in their isolation. Meanwhile evangelicals have been burgeoning out of a history of revivalism that has often been wrongly caricatured as philosophically naive or historically lobotomized. Evangelicals have often been dismissed by the uppercase Orthodoxies as simplistic and fundamentalist. But now the evangelical and charismatic and Baptist and Pentecostal traditions are beginning to notice the actual history of the Holy Spirit. Among the children of the Great Awakening an orthodox *re*awakening is emerging, itself arguably a work of the Holy Spirit. As these evangelical and charismatic traditions continue to mature and deepen, recognizing their need for biblical wisdom far beyond those made available to them in both the pietistic and historical-critical traditions. They are turning toward the scriptural reasoning of classic Christianity.

THE SURPRISING WORK OF THE SPIRIT IN OUR TIME

There is much that we do not know of what the Holy Spirit is doing on our behalf, both as individuals and as a church, although we can and do know some things. This work is happening all about us, often without our recognition.

What the Holy Spirit Is Doing Among Us

We do have some preliminary clues as to the workings of the Holy Spirit:

- The Holy Spirit is encouraging the growth of evangelical and confessing movements within mainline denominations—movements that are calling their churches back to classic Christianity as the source of renewal and unity.

- The Holy Spirit is giving encouragement to the martyrs and confessors of many different ecclesial memories worldwide, under appalling conditions of state persecution.[10]

- The Holy Spirit is hedging and undercutting the false teachings of narcissistic hedonism, autonomous individualism, and oppressive totalitarianism in our time.

- The Holy Spirit is mending conflicts that have stood for over a thousand years, such as those that have long separated Chalcedonian and non-Chalcedonian churches.[11]

- The Holy Spirit is engendering liturgical renewal in all branches of the vine.

- The Holy Spirit is working to recover the history of scriptural exegesis.

Every reader of scripture has a right to the texts of classic scriptural interpretation. In the early Christian centuries this rich history of interpretation was ecumenically informed by a decisive attentiveness to the unity of the body of Christ. Christians are now reclaiming these ancient texts and returning to classic understandings of scriptural wisdom.

These are just samplings of what the Holy Spirit is doing in our time, with much left unsaid. Our oneness in Christ is not a matter of our searching to discover a way to some negotiated settlement. It is rather a matter of recognizing and expressing what is already present in our actual life in Christ, in the Spirit's leading, and in our intercessions, hymns, and hopes.

We cannot rightly confess the unity of the church without regrounding that unity in the apostolic teaching that was hammered out on the anvil of martyrdom and defined by the early conciliar process (that is, in the ecumenical councils of the first millennium), when heresies were rejected and the ancient consensus defined. The unified church—constituted by those who repent and believe, who live in faith in this real but imperfect communion, whose lives are shaped by their participation in the living Christ— seeks to mirror the holiness of God in their lives in the world. This community reaches out to all cultures, all classes, in all languages. We behold this one church most fully alive when we see believers ready to put their lives on the line for its truth.

It is time to call the mainline churches, which are subsidizing the prolonged malingering of the old ecumenism, to withdraw their financial support altogether and seek a new ecumenism grounded in classic ecumenical teaching. This has powerful implications for the future of the mainline.

The Timeliness of the Orthodox Mind

The orthodox way of reasoning listens to the most representative voices that best reflect the consenting mind of the people of God viewed within the maximum range of times and cultures. It is not mesmerized by speculative brilliance or erratic innovation. It is intent on listening to consensual strains of understanding of holy writ. What the consensual tradition trusts least is individualistic innovation that has not yet learned what the worshiping communities already know.

Classic textual resources, now available for Jewish and Christian lay readers, have remained largely inaccessible during the last two secularizing centuries, while historical-critical issues have been extensively explored. Without neglecting these issues, the orthodox mind now seeks to understand and reappropriate the multicultural, transgenerational, multilingual wisdom of the classic religious tradition. As a result, a growing, hungry, diverse, and robust community of orthodox faith is awakening.

Such an endeavor is especially poignant and timely now. Increasing numbers of Jews and Christians are discovering dimensions of commonality not recognized until recently. Jews, whether Orthodox, Conservative, or Reformed, are recognizing their common heritage, just as are evangelical, Orthodox, and Catholic Christians. The study of the church fathers and the study of the rabbinic tradition go hand in hand, because both traditions focus on holy writ. These initiatives promise further interactions between Protestants, Catholics, and Jews on issues that have troubled them for centuries: grace, law, messianic hope, sanctification, and eschatology. Believers of these distinctive faiths are finding in rabbinic and patristic texts many aspects of a common faith to which they can together appeal. This is the specific arena in which Protestants feel most at home: biblical authority and interpretation.

Reprise

Before moving on to Part 2, where we will examine multiple evidences of the rebirth of orthodoxy, I briefly review the findings of Part 1.

Worshiping communities are reframing their priorities as they enter into the sixth millennium of human culture, to enable them to venture confidently beyond the constricted future of modern failures. The children of the sexual revolution have suffered through the high costs of modern living, which include rootlessness, costly social experimentation, and political delusions.

Amid these conditions, the classic religious tradition is being rediscovered by both Jews and Christians, who together possess the memory of God's revelation in history—a memory that has been denied by modern chauvinism. Jews and Christians together remember Israel's salvation history as a *single* history of Israel, not *two* histories.

Although orthodoxy as a sociological type has many modern examples, its prototype remains ancient ecumenical Christianity. That ancient faith argues for faithfully recollecting scripture, giving scripture primacy over tradition, and thinking critically out of a consensual reading of each sacred text. Orthodoxy, which views the modern world with proximate (not ultimate) seriousness, provides the freedom to walk within reliable boundaries. The history of martyrdom disproves the argument that orthodoxy is merely the skewed memory of winners.

Orthodoxy persists, despite all contrary predictions, because it is more cross-culturally agile than modern multiculturalism, because God's sovereign grace provides the basis of its durability, because God does not leave himself without witness in the world, because the weakness of the pilgrim community in time attests the surpassing power of the Holy Spirit, and because the consent of the communion of saints over generations is divinely guarded and guaranteed.

The faithful are called to patience as they look toward vindication on the Last Day. And that patience bears fruit, because orthodoxy has advantages of long-term memory that are unavailable to modern consciousness.

The faithful are willing to suffer for truth. The blood of martyrdom, past and present, constitutes a valid and persuasive form of argument.

Classic Christianity is more ecumenical than the ecumenism of the twentieth century, opening doors for wider intellectual freedom than is available within modern prejudices.

PART II

SIGNS OF
NEW LIFE

As if finding a lost child, we are now looking gratefully into the eyes of a re-discovered cultural reality: the orthodox way. As if discovering jewels buried underneath historical debris, we are rediscovering cultural assets long buried.

This discovery is now happening. It is a demonstrable fact of our time. And it is happening not just in one isolated location, or in a few, but world-wide. It is changing lives, including my own.

EVIDENCES OF THE REBIRTH OF ORTHODOXY

In Part 2 I will set forth six layers of evidence to show that there is indeed a widespread rekindling of the orthodox spirit:

1. *Personal transformation.* The clearest evidence of the rebirth of orthodoxy is that ordinary lives are being transformed. I begin by offering evidence from my own experience, but beyond my own story, a whole genre of recent literature extends this experiential proof. In dozens of narratives, regenerated people talk about coming forth as traditional believers out of the ruins of modern life.

2. *Faithful scriptural interpretation.* Orthodoxy is being reborn because its classic texts are being rediscovered not only by the Orthodox but by chastened liberals and awakening Pentecostals. Those texts are not only being read but believed; and because they inspire belief, they are being applied to social criticism and ordinary life. I will set forth evidence that the academic study of historic orthodoxy is receiving more intensive scrutiny now than at any time during the previous century. The study of ancient Christian scriptural interpretation is rapidly becoming a core concern of biblical studies today.

3. *Ancient ecumenical multiculturalism.* I will show how orthodoxy connects with and contributes to the fairness revolution by strengthening and deepening multicultural consensus. No modern multiculturalism is as deep or as fertile as historical ecumenical multiculturalism. The cross-cultural richness of the church catholic is becoming more evident today.

4. *Well-established boundaries.* After many decades of uncritical permissiveness, we are now witnessing a bold new level of energy being given to clearer boundary-definition in questions of religious truth. I will demonstrate that the faithful are relearning how to say no together on behalf of a greater yes, and how to mark boundaries established for centuries. They are experiencing the blessed freedom that comes from dwelling within more secure boundaries.

5. *Ecumenical roots reclaimed.* I will show the many ways in which confessing and renewing movements are currently changing local congregations and whole denominations. They are confessing the ancient faith, and renewing the communities of the faith confessed. The heirs of modern ecumenism are rediscovering their ancient ecumenical roots.

6. *Consensual ecumenical discernment.* I will show evidence that there is a revival of classic consensual ecumenical method, as first clearly set forth by Vincent of Lérins in his great *Commonitory,* or "act of remembrance." Laypersons can easily grasp and celebrate what has been believed everywhere, always, and by common consent.

We cannot dismiss these conjoined vectors of evidence as simply an incidental fad of passing interest. Though there are other forms of evidence, these six arenas are sufficient to show that the rebirth of orthodoxy is occurring in our time. Extending far beyond the long-standing communions of Eastern Orthodoxy, nonethnic forms of orthodoxy are developing in new configurations. They affect worshiping communities that we care about, and the institutions that serve them.

These forms of evidence span a range whose scale and breadth are surprising. The rebirth described in these chapters is appearing not simply in a few isolated pockets, but throughout the culture. It can be seen in the way prayers are offered, curricula are organized, teaching is focused, and ethical issues are argued. Not only personal lives, but also institutions are being courageously reshaped.

Forty years ago many of us assumed that the German lexicographer Walter Baur had said the last word on orthodoxy and heresy. We thought that we could dismiss the possibility of a renewed orthodoxy and go on to better things. Now, however, all the same basic issues have resurfaced. History has caught up with us. We have been overtaken by the great gift of orthodox remembering. These issues are on the lips of rabbis and pastors, clergy and laity, students and teachers, evangelicals and Catholics. Most of the evidence presented here for a rebirth of the orthodox way comes from the Christian side of the Jewish-Christian interface, but there is plenty of evidence to be had in both faiths. Another book begs to be written on the rebirth of orthodox sensibilities within Conservative, Reform, and Orthodox Judaism.

In summary, here are the evidences for the rebirth of orthodoxy: they are *personal,* as seen in autobiographies; they are *academic,* as seen in the study of the history of exegesis; they are *cross-cultural,* as seen in the intrinsically multicultural nature of orthodoxy; they are *critical,* as seen in the new interest in boundary-definition; they are *institutional,* as seen in renewing and confessing movements within the religious communities; and they are *ecumenical,* as seen in the new ecumenism based on ancient ecumenical method.

Table 2 helps trace the rebirth of orthodoxy, showing what evidence of that rebirth can be found, where the rebirth is taking place, how it came about, and who is involved in leadership roles. Please note, though, that the categories shown are not mutually exclusive; they overlap frequently. Some writers belong in more than one category.[1]

TABLE 2: EVIDENCES OF THE REBIRTH OF ORTHODOXY

Chapter 6: Transforming Character

What is happening?	Where is it happening?	How is it happening (by what means)?	Who are the key leaders and writers?
Lives are being changed	In individual lives, vocational life, and personal existence as seen in narrative stories on the road to Canterbury, Rome, Antioch, Wittenberg, and Geneva	Through prayer, scripture study, liturgy, religious observance, and works of mercy	A. Solzhenitsyn, M. Muggeridge, G. Weigel, L. Newbigin, T. Howard, P. Toon, D. Willard, A. Walker, W. Willimon, K. Fournier, P. Vitz, J. Hahn, C. Colson, P. Gilquist

Chapter 7: Rediscovering the Earliest Biblical Interpreters

What is happening?	Where is it happening?	How is it happening (by what means)?	Who are the key leaders and writers?
Ancient Christian writers are being reexamined	In universities, faculties, curricula, academic societies, and the biblical guild	Through academic inquiries mining ancient textual wisdom found in neglected commentaries, hymnody, homilies, and liturgies	H. Urs von Balthasar, R. Wilken, A. McGrath, M. Simonetti, A. Louth, S. Ashbrook-Harvey, R. Bondi, S. Harakas, F. Norris, K. Froehlich, Kwami Bediako, B. Childs, S. Sykes, R. Williams, O. O'Donovan, R. Greer, B. Daley, D. Balac, S. Brock, S. Griffith, G. Bray, M. Edwards, R. Wright, C. Gunton, J. Lienhard, R. Heine, J. Breck, S. Burgess, P. Gorday, C. Kannengieser, H. Hollerweger, A. Palmer, D. H. Williams, J. Trigg,

D. Dockery, T. M. Moore, R. Webber, W. Weinrich, P. Krey, A. Just, A. Berquist, R. Taft, B. Witherington

Chapter 8: Strengthening the Multicultural Nature of Orthodoxy

What *is happening*?	Where *is it happening*?	How *is it happening (by what means)*?	Who *are the key leaders and writers*?
Historical cultures worldwide are interpenetrating and cross-fertilizing	In the world of nations and religions viewed as global, multicultural phenomena	Through undertaking cross-cultural ecumenical social analysis, listening to diversity, and grasping orthodoxy as a vast and varied social achievement and intergenerational sociological type	E. Charry, J. Pelikan, N. Hatch, J. B. Elshtain, J. D. Roberts, A. Ugolnik, T. Hopko, G. Dragas, T. Tiennou. L. Kishkovsky, V. Samuel, P. Marshall, E. Wan, K. Ng, V. Thampu, S. Lingenfelter, C. Henry, G. Tinder, J. Stout, J. Stackhouse, R. Wuthnow, N. Wolterstorff, C. Robeck, R. Spittler, S. Grenz

Chapter 9: Learning to Say No

What *is happening*?	Where *is it happening*?	How *is it happening (by what means)*?	Who *are the key leaders and writers*?
Religious communities are rediscovering classic doctrinal and moral boundaries	In critical literature and in documents of renewing and confessing movements	Through orthodox cultural criticism in journals and organizations: *First Things, Touchstone, Pro Ecclesia, Books and Culture, Modern Reformation, New Oxford Review;* Association for Church Renewal, L'Abri, SEAD, EPPC	G. W. Rutler, C. F. Allison, G. Grisez, S. Hauerwas, T. Weinandy, J. Ratzinger, R. George, M. Noll, G. Marsden, M. Horton, R. C. Sproul, O. Guinness, A. MacIntyre, D. Wells, Eleanore Stump, D. D'Souza, H. Ross, P. Kreeft, P. Johnson, J. Woodbridge, D. Carson,

Chapter 9: Learning to Say No (cont.)

What is happening?	Where is it happening?	How is it happening (by what means)?	Who are the key leaders and writers?
			R. Zacharias, A. Mohler, H.O.J. Brown, E. Hindson, J. MacArthur, R. Nash, M. Novak, B. Hebblethwaite, D. Yeago, R. Reno, A. Sell, R. Land, M. Cromartie, H. Blocher, E. M. Jones, W. L. Craig, MD. Levin, C. Lasch, M. Welker, M. Bauman, P. J. Griffiths, J. Hitchcock, P. Mankowski, R. Hittinger, J.P. Moreland, G. Habermas, G. Lewis, N. Maloney, M. Erikson, T. George

Chapter 10: Recentering the Mainline

What is happening?	Where is it happening?	How is it happening (by what means)?	Who are the key leaders and writers?
Lapsed religious institutions are being reclaimed	In churches, boards, agencies, seminaries, curricula, trustees, faculties, endowments, and accountability to donors	Through proactive efforts at institutional renovation and through renewing and confessing movements	J. Leith, V. Guroian, G. Jones, W. Placher, W. Abraham, M. Achtemeier, C. Sugden, J. Rodgers, J. Heidinger, E. Radner, P. Williamson, D. Knippers, A. Carlson, R. Foster, P. Turner, E. Achtemeier, D. Browning T. Campbell, R. Gagnon

Chapter 11: Rediscovering the Classic Ecumenical Method

What is happening?	Where is it happening?	How is it happening (by what means)?	Who are the key leaders and writers?
Classic ecumenism is being rediscovered	In Catholic, evangelical, and Orthodox bilateral conversations, formal and informal	By means of the ancient orthodox ecumenical method of recovering consensual doctrinal integrity	John Paul II, A. Dulles, J. Stott, W. Pannenberg, W. Kasper, T. Torrance, R. Neuhaus, K. Kantzer, E. Storkey, D. Hardy, R. Jenson, G. Wainwright, C. Braaten, G. Lindbeck, W. Rusch, J. Sparks, D. Steinmetz, S. Coakley, M. Lamb, W. Lazareth, R. Hays, M. Stackhouse, D. Allen, R. Sider, J. Stamoolis, P. Henry, T. George, K. Vanhoozer, J. Packer, R. Mouw, G. Fackre, J. A. DiNoia, J. Buckley, P. Hinlicky, J. Wicks, G. O'Collins, D. Bloesch, M. Scanlan, T. Rausch, T. Stransky, E. Oakes, Francis Cardinal George, P. Stuhlmacher, R. Royal, J. Polkinghorne, T. Phillips, C. Seitz

I have previously noted informal lists of "fellow pilgrims"—in 1979 (*Agenda for Theology*), 1990 (*After Modernity What?*), and 1995 (*Requiem* and an essay in *The Challenge of Postmodernism*). I was attempting in those cases to indicate those whom I at those times regarded as the most typical representatives of postcritical or postmodern orthodoxy. This lengthier list (in Table 2) now includes many others who are today clearly working with the methods and premises of orthodoxy. A discernible movement has by now emerged that was not so clearly seen before. The import of Table 2 is this: *an ever-extending body of literature exists today that did not exist in 1979—literature that is widely ecumenical and strongly oriented toward classic Jewish and Christian teaching*. The many diverse authors and leaders listed share one thing in common: all are thoughtfully examining the ancient consensual Jewish and Christian texts as normative for contemporary reflection.

The Timeframe

Part 2 is a cusp-of-the-millennium report. It is news, an update reporting on what has been happening in six decisive arenas as the millennium has turned.

Why the cusp? Though much pertinent literature came before 1989, I have chosen to focus largely on the period after that date. Only in that latter timeframe can we delineate a vast cultural movement, a clear shift of consciousness, including a readiness to think boldly out of orthodox premises among people who are located far beyond the formal bounds of the Eastern Orthodox and Roman Catholic traditions.

Marxism bedeviled us for a long time, and for a few brief years before 1989 it seemed to be threatening to take over, casting itself as legitimate heir to the human future. But by 1989 that illusion had been irreparably shattered. Since the 1990s we have seen increasing evidence of the rebirth of orthodoxy, especially with the firm and certain collapse of the Soviet Union. After that event, the orthodox cowered no more under the mystique of modernity.

The twentieth century was in one sense already over by 1989.[2] We have been rebuilding a new consensus since then, in which the voices of Jewish and Christian orthodoxy are key partners. We are swimming in the stream of a vast, palpable cultural and literary movement.

Most orthodox writers lived long before modernity. The main twentieth-century prototypes, G. K. Chesterton and C. S. Lewis, follow the classic prototypes: John Chrysostom, Augustine, Vincent, Isidore, Cassiodorus, John of Damascus, Bede, and Alcuin. But it is those whose influence has survived modernity, especially since 1989, that constitute the subject of this discussion.

Just before this manuscript went to press, an article appeared in *The American Enterprise* entitled "Back Toward Orthodoxy: A Conservative Resurgence Sweeps American religion."[3] Its theme: "Many Americans know that in recent decades the nation's more conservative and evangelical churches have been growing much faster than mainline faiths. What you may not know is that even within major liberal denominations of Methodism and Presbyterianism—not to mention American Judaism— there has been a backlash against theological laxity." In that series Jeff Jacoby wrote "Traditional Judaism Roars Back" and Richard Cimino wrote "The Church of Hillary Clinton and George W. Bush Takes a Step Away from Liberalism."

The last half of this book tells the story of these religious developments in more detail and provides extended evidence for the reversal from religious liberalism toward orthodoxy.

SIX

Transforming Character

The real significance of the rebirth of orthodoxy lies in how it is transforming lives. Thus I will begin Part 2—a review of the evidences of that rebirth—with a chapter focusing on the inner arena.

There is nothing new about the life-changing properties of orthodoxy. Although orthodoxy has been touching increasing numbers of people in recent years, it has been changing lives for two millennia. Not surprisingly, then, autobiographical narrative is a familiar genre within historical orthodoxy.[1] Many twentieth-century believers have also written narratives of transformation, detailing how orthodoxy has changed their life and faith. Noble voices such as those of Aleksandr Solzhenitsyn, Lesslie Newbigin, Malcolm Muggeridge, and Richard John Neuhaus epitomize the genre.[2] They tell the story of the power of classic Christianity to transform modern lives.[3]

A PERSONAL ODYSSEY

My life, too, has been changed by orthodoxy. I would like to tell my story here as representative of the myriad stories of ordinary people whose lives have been transformed by the orthodox experience. I would like to recall for you the basic reversal of my life, which all hinges on orthodox remembering.

Evidence at the Personal Level

I want to show, in these pages, how orthodoxy unexpectedly transformed the course of my life. This is not a retreat to a quaint form of sentimental pietism, however. Quite the opposite: I hope to show how my life has become entirely intertwined with the lives of the ancient consensual interpreters of scripture.

Although orthodoxy typically resists focusing inordinately upon personal narrative,[4] it permits autobiography in order to show how ecumenical consensus transcends and reshapes personal existence. Autobiography in this tradition is not primarily an act of pure self-expression, as in Proust or Thomas Wolfe, but of God's own coming within personal life, as in Augustine's *Confessions*. Christian autobiography is valued as a means to show how grace transcends and reshapes personal identity.

As we have seen, classic Christianity lives out of a history of *consensual* ecumenical worship. It depends not upon any particular individual's view but upon how the classic consensus molds a particular person's daily life. It is never out of bounds for a believer to report accurately upon how the Spirit is working to change his or her life. But it is presumptuous to assume that one's own life provides a normative pattern for others. Thus I offer my story simply as living evidence of how one life has been radically reversed by meeting the saints of classic Christianity.

Because I doubted the authenticity of many of the religious experiences I heard reported as a young man, I became wary of recounting my own personal experience. In my tradition, personal conversion testimony had become so warped and devolved by the time of my young adulthood that I intuitively resisted focusing any religious arguments on my own story. Rather, I preferred to appeal to history, morality, and empirical evidence. Despite these resistances, my own personal odyssey presents a kind of evidence of the rebirth of orthodoxy (even though it has occurred in an improbable academic setting). Although my own personal vocational struggle is inconsequential in relation to the classic consensus, I have belatedly realized that my story has edified others when I have shared pieces of it. Here I present that story in a fuller form than before.

Liberal Roots, Revolutionary Mentors

I grew up in the flat southwestern corner of Oklahoma, only twelve miles from the Texas border, where the distant hills roll gently, the purple Quartz Mountains rise from the prairie, and the fields are green with wheat in February and white with cotton in August. In that part of the world the milk of human kindness often flows generously. Door are left unlocked. A neighbor's word is his bond.

Because my parents were incredibly caring and godly, I avoided the adolescent pitfall of rebelling against them. But they themselves were highly

independent mavericks—pious, quiet radicals. My attorney father was politically progressive at a time when Oklahoma was tending toward a rural
populist socialism in the tradition of the Wisconsin Farmer-Labor Party
(quite different from the radical politics of Huey Long).[5] Mother taught
piano to Anglos, African Americans, and Hispanics in our small town.

In college days I learned my agnosticism from Nietzsche, my social views
from radical Methodists and existentialists, and my theology (God help me,
I confess) from Alan Watts.[6] The further I moved into the underground
maze of the left wing of the academy, the more I became socialized to speak
as little as possible from my personal religious experience.

After Ph.D. studies at Yale and ordination, I taught in two seminaries.[7] Although it was assumed that I was teaching theology, my heart was focused
on radical visions of social change and on the blatant politicizing of the mission of the church.[8] I was narrowly modern, only pretending to be a theologian. My motivation for entering the ministry had been nine-tenths
political. I saw the church as a potential instrument for rapid social change.
My interest in theology lay primarily in how the revolution might take religion captive to political idealism. I was one of those little men with big ideas
but not the vaguest notion of how those ideas might be implemented.[9]

Comparative Trajectories of Two Methodist Radicals

Not until I recently explained to younger friends how closely my path had
followed the same trajectory as that of Hillary Rodham Clinton did they
grasp what I was saying about my history. It seems odd now, but Hillary was
working out of precisely the same sources and moving in the same circles as
I in our formative years. In fact, our two trajectories almost mirrored one
another until the early seventies. I fell much harder for Marxist ideology
than she ever did, but we made many of the same ideological stops along the
way.[10]

Why do I mention this? Because Hillary's pattern clarifies where I once
squarely located myself ideologically, only later to reverse myself and disavow previous opinions. My education paralleled hers (Yale, Methodist activism, moving ever leftward), both in the ideas we held and the people by
whom we were mentored. We were both avid followers of Saul Alinsky, a
pragmatic urban organizer and unprincipled amoralist. Hillary became in-
trigued by situation ethics, the subject on which I wrote my dissertation. She
learned her tough amoral activism from Alinsky and her view of history
from quasi-Marxists, just as I did. She once revealed that she had saved every
copy of *motive* magazine, the progenitor of much of her religious and political radicalism, and so have I. That magazine fueled me intellectually during

my heady years as a pacifist, existentialist, Tillichian, and aspiring Marxist, and its editors (Roger Ortmayer and B. J. Styles) were old friends of mine. In those days I trusted completely the Methodist radicalism of *motive*. It set the leftist momentum of all my thinking, as it did Hillary's.

Hillary's chief mentors in Chicago included dear friends of mine, Joseph and Lynn Mathews, and their associates in the Ecumenical Institute of Austin, Texas (later to become the Ecumenical Institute of Chicago), where some of my writings were embedded in their standard curriculum. I went to Yale more than a decade before Hillary did, but we had many threads of mutual friends and almost a total congruence of values in those early days. Her former pastor and mentor, Professor Don Jones, remains my close colleague in ethics at Drew University. During her years in the White House, she belonged to one of the most politically radical local congregations among United Methodists.

When I look now at Hillary's persistent situational ethics, political messianism, statist social idealism, and pragmatic toughness, I see mirrored the self I was a few decades ago. Methodist social liberalism taught me how to advocate liberalized abortion and early feminism almost a decade before the works of Germaine Greer and Rosemary Radford Ruether further raised my consciousness.

Once Completely at Home with Modernity

I left seminary having learned to treat scripture selectively, according to how it well it might serve my political idealism. I adapted the Bible to my ideology—an ideology of social and political change largely shaped by soft Marxist premises about history and a romanticized vision of the emerging power and virtue of the underclass. Though during this time it was largely knowledge elites (professors, writers, movement leaders) rather than the underclass that shaped my views, I nursed an inordinate confidence in my own ability to define the interests of the poor.

Like all broad-minded clergy I knew, I tried hard to reason out of modern naturalistic premises, employing biblical narratives narrowly and selectively. I could plead for social change and teach hearers to take pride in their good intentions and works; but I was not prepared to communicate the saving grace of God on the cross, which I experienced only at some vague and diffuse level and would never have thought of personally attesting publicly.

For years I tried to read the New Testament entirely without the premises of incarnation and resurrection—something that is very hard to do.[11] I habitually assumed that truth in religion would be finally reducible to economics (with Marx), or psychosexual factors (with Freud), or power dynamics (with Nietzsche). I was uncritically accommodating to the very modernity that pretended to be prophetic, yet I did not recognize modernity's captivity to secular humanistic assumptions. That accommodation lasted until I personally experienced the collapse of modern values.

THE REVERSAL

I do not commend my experience as normative for anyone else, but only invite others to see what God has done through it. Only in retrospect can I now see how thorough going was the reversal.

An Unexpected Journey

In the early 1970s I went through what seemed to me a lonely, almost solitary pilgrimage—lonely because I was the only one I knew who was traveling this backroad, which took me from obsessive spiritual faddism to stable classic Christian teaching. This journey resulted in the publication of *Agenda for Theology* (1979), *Classical Pastoral Care* (four volumes, 1986–1989), *Pastoral Theology* (1983), three volumes of *Systematic Theology* (1987–1992), and *Ancient Christian Commentary on Scripture* (1995–present). Yet for years I have resisted telling more than the bare outline of how that journey came about.

Why did I so long resist telling my own personal testimony? It seemed too self-referential.[12] Yet on those occasions when I *have* told my story, people have said to me, "Tell me more of your own personal reversal. Recall the path that God took you upon. Map out your own spiritual journey. How did it happen that you, once a situation ethicist, once a socialist, once a human-potential movement camp-follower, became a traditional Christian, an advocate of postmodern paleo-orthodoxy?" When reluctantly I have shared even bits of my story, I have heard listeners breathe from deep within and say, "God is great."

And God is great, as I came to understand—greater than I grasped midstream in this process. I am sometimes asked when I became a Christian. My parents taught me: when I was baptized.[13] But I took a detoured route to confirming my baptism. Oddly, that confirmation came only long after my ordination, after years of theological teaching, and after many wrong turns![14]

The Meandering Path of a Movement Theologian

I was a "movement" theologian in my early years. I assumed that some vast social revolution was impending. With paradigms in constant motion, I made my bed with one movement after another, whether political, therapeutic, or philosophical.

It is amusing now to contrast the concerns I had then with the vocation I have undertaken since the ancient Christian writers have become my constant companions. If I now am tempted to exaggerate differences between the before and after, my intent is to offer an accurate description of this decisive reversal, without allowing it to die the death of a thousand qualifications. I do not disavow the providence of God working within my former (Freudian-Marxist-existentialist-demythologizing) past, or fail to see grace leading me through and beyond it. Rather, I celebrate that history as having been taken up into a more inclusive understanding of history and divine-human encounter.

Did I say "inclusive"? That word remains the key shibboleth of my hyper-liberated generation. We sought to be inclusive but managed to be so only within the strict limits of modern ideologies trapped in secular premises. In this captivity we systematically excluded most premodern wisdom. Now I experience a gracious sense of multigenerational inclusion in the communion of saints. Those saints precede and transcend modern life and will survive its death. The faithful belong to a much more inclusive communion than is even conceivable within the limits of modern ideologies.

Triggering the Turnaround

The reversal occurred when Will Herberg, my irascible, endearing Jewish mentor and my elder colleague at Drew, held me accountable to my religious heritage. He told me straightforwardly that I would remain theologically uneducated until I had studied carefully Athanasius, Ambrose, Basil, and Cyril of Alexandria. In his usual gruff voice he said, "Tom, you have not yet met the great minds of your own tradition. Just as I, after my Communist days, found it decisive to read the Talmud and the Midrashim carefully to discover who I was as a Jew, you will have to sit at the feet of the ancient Christian writers to discover who you are as a possible person of faith. Without solid textual grounding, you will become lost in supposed relevance. If you are going to deepen to become a working theologian instead of a know-it-all contemporary pundit, you had best get at it—and until you do, you are not a theologian except in name, even if remunerated as one." I was stunned. He had nailed me.

If you had asked me then what my life might look like now, I would have guessed dead wrong. Grace and providence were nudging my life toward far more surprising outcomes than I would ever have imagined. At that time I never dreamed that I would someday grant to scripture its own distinctive premises: divine sovereignty, revelation, incarnation, resurrection, and final judgment. I had been taught that these premises were precisely what had to be transcended, reworded, circumvented, and danced around in order to communicate with the modern mind. I had been taught that the scripture interpreter exists to *protect* the modern hearer from the text and to provide an alternative explanation of the text that fits neatly into modern assumptions. Now I revel in the very premises I once carefully learned to set aside: the triune mystery, the preexistent Logos, the radical depth of sin passing through the generations, the risen Lord, the grace of baptism.

As, heeding Herberg's injunction, I worked my way through the beautiful, long-hidden texts of classic Christianity, the deeper perennial questions resurfaced. I reemerged out of the secularizing maze to once again delight in the holy mysteries of the faith and in the recurrent puzzles of human existence. Rather than interpreting the texts, I found the texts interpreting me. They freed me to ask a broader range of questions: How can God have become truly human without ceasing to be God? How can human freedom, when so distorted by the history of sin, have been radically atoned in the cross? If God is almighty and all good, how can God allow sin to have such a persistent hold on human social processes? How can the incomprehensible God make himself sufficiently known to finite human minds? If God is Father, God is Son, and God is Holy Spirit, how is God *one*? How can the faithful mirror the holiness of God within the history of sin? Not a new question in the list, nor a dull one.

I had earlier learned to understand my pastoral task as that of finding the best fad therapy or popular political strategy and baptizing it. Long after receiving my Ph.D. in theology, after pretending for years to be a theologian, after publishing books on theology, and after teaching theology for years, something happened. What was it? A reversal, a conversion, a repentance? However it is named, that something occurred only incrementally, like a mustard seed growing.

The Abiding Conversation

The radical reversal that I experienced took place mostly through quiet reading in early mornings and through long conversations with the faithful (especially my Orthodox, Catholic, and evangelical students). My immersion in classic orthodox writings yielded what to me was surprising fruit:

- While reading John of Damascus on the economy (*oikonomia*, or arranging providence) of God in *The Orthodox Faith*, I belatedly realized that the reordering of theological ideas I fondly imagined I was just then inventing had been well understood as a received tradition in the eighth century.

- While reading John Chrysostom on voluntary poverty, I discovered that Peter Berger's sociological theory of knowledge elites had long ago been accurately described.

- While reading Cyril of Jerusalem's catechetical lecture on evidences for the resurrection, I became persuaded that Pannenberg had provided a more accurate account than Bultmann of that event.

- While reading fourth-century Sister Macrina and learning of the women surrounding Jerome, I began to recognize the profound influences of women on the earliest and richest traditions of spiritual formation, especially in monastic and ascetic disciplines.

- While reading Augustine's *City of God* on the ironic providences of history, I finally grasped how right Solzhenitsyn had been about the spiritual promise of Russia.

And so it went. Every question that I thought was new and unprecedented I found had been already much investigated, and had in fact left a profound textual residue. I was on the threshold of the intergenerational wisdom of the ancient community of faith, which I found was still persisting as a living, caring community.

Earlier, during my years as a movement theologian, I had focused intently upon psychological analysis, putting great trust in psychological methods (primarily psychoanalysis, behavioral engineering, and client-centered therapy). As I conversed with the ancient ecumenical teachers, I gradually came to behold interpersonal transactions and personal dynamics in the light of God's becoming fully human in the incarnation. My despairing freedom could then be seen in the light of the theandric (or divine-human) One in whom human personhood is most fully actualized and understood. This incarnational revolution invaded every corner of my psychological research.

Once blown by every wind of doctrine and preoccupied with therapeutic fads amid the spirit of hypertoleration, I came to grasp the consensual reasoning that occurs so effortlessly within classic Christianity. I became fascinated with the social dynamics of orthodoxy, the process of apostolic tradition-transmission, and the received canons of classic consensual teaching. Those who adored absolute toleration began to notice that I was suffering fools a little less gladly.

An Enlarged Freedom of Inquiry
I was moving away from culture-bound experience and toward the publicly shared texts of scripture and ecumenical tradition. I was learning to appreciate

the hard work of developing durable habits of moral excellence in a covenant community. I was moving away from trust in regulatory power and rationalistic planning and toward reasoning out of the concrete histories of suffering persons, some of whom had been damaged by my own idealism.

I now stand within the blessed presence of the communion of saints of all generations. In that company I experience greater, not diminished, cross-cultural freedom of inquiry. Subjects previously blocked from investigation are now open: creation and providence, divine foreknowledge, revelation in history, demonic temptation, the lives of saints, angelic succor—anything. Scripture and the classic texts have become my daily bread: I am now steeped in inquiry into the vast chorus of rabbinic and patristic interpretations of the sacred text.

I have glimpsed the centered teaching of the classic witnesses who penned these interpretations. I am grateful to have been liberated to orthodoxy. These long-ago believers, who personify and embody a Spirit-led organic equilibrium, have helped to free me from narrow modern dogmatisms. I delight in their gracious flexibility.

This orthodox matrix now melds and unites all that I do. The orthodox mind that came to reside in my mind finds itself at home in every conceivable cultural and intellectual environment.

It is not a fabrication or projection that I once was a militant pacifist, a psychotherapeutic camp-follower, a sober existentialist, and a zealous advocate of women's liberation. I have served my time in all those liberation armies. That period of my life left an extensive record of activity and writing. But I am now squeezing myself out of the dogmatic modern cocoon.

My youthful form of bureaucratic ecumenism, viewed from the standpoint of the ancient ecumenical tradition, now seems anti-ecumenical. I am not demonizing these forsaken ideologies so much as recognizing the demonic in my own history. Following in the curious steps of my once Communist, later conservative Jewish mentor Will Herberg, I am recognizing a fair amount of self-delusion and demonic deception in ideologies that once appeared to me seductive.

The Pivot of the Reversal

What changed the course of my life? A simple reversal that hung on a single pivot: attentiveness to the text of scripture, especially as viewed by its early consensual interpreters. Before my reversal, all of my questions about theology and the modern world had been premised on key value assumptions of modern consciousness—assumptions such as absolute moral relativism.[15] After meeting new friends in the writings of antiquity, I had a new grounding for those questions: each current issue was now transformed by the counter-premises of the most trusted ancient scriptural interpreters of classic Christianity. Those interpreters taught me how to accept redemptive sacrifice, know through a worshiping community, refuse idolatries, and listen for intergenerational consensus. Collectively they lived through deeper crises and dilemmas than are imaginable within the narrow premises of modern living.

The history of Christianity is a history of scriptural discernment by interpreters who sought in their day only to give voice to the already coherent mind of the believing community that had preceded them in attesting the history of revelation. They lived in grateful recollection of the earliest witnesses to God's own coming in the flesh.

The names of these major consensual interpreters of scripture are no secret: Athanasius, Basil, Gregory of Nazianzus, and Chrysostom in the East; Ambrose, Jerome, Augustine, and Gregory the Great in the West. These mentors, who weaned me away from modern biases, were widely respected East and West in the formation of ancient ecumenism.

Then and Now

Then I distrusted even the faint smell of orthodoxy. I was in love with heresy—the wilder, the more seductive.

Now I have come to trust the very consensus I once dismissed and distrusted. Generations of double-checking confirm it as a reliable body of scriptural interpretation. I now relish studying the diverse rainbow of orthodox voices from varied cultures spanning all continents over two thousand years.

Now I embrace the term *orthodoxy*. I esteem nothing higher than the written word as ecumenically received and consensually explicated. My classes focus textually on meeting classic minds who have freely consented in varied cultures and times to the apostolic testimony. That consensual seed always bears fruit in its own time and season. That apostolic word will address modern hearers directly in its own distinctive way as long as it is not accompanied by too much static from contemporary prejudices.

THE REVERSAL BECOMES A METAMORPHOSIS

By the McGovern campaign of 1972 the main factors of reversal were in place, but I was not yet fully committed, heart and soul, to orthodoxy. The turn had been decisive, but the timeframe for change was sluggish; the birth was labored.

A decisive moment in my development occurred while I was reading Vincent of Lérins's fifth-century aid to remembering—a work called *Commonitory*.

There I gained an essential foothold in defining ecumenical teaching under the threefold test of classic Christianity: that which "has been believed everywhere, always, and by all."[16] (See Chapter 11 for further discussion of that threefold test.) From that moment on my reasoning about religious truth gradually became a straightforward matter of searching modestly to identify those baptismal teachings that believers in all places and times have, with one voice, confessed and believed and been willing to die for.

I do not mean that I have ceased being a modern man or have become bored with what the Holy Spirit is doing now. This creation I see around me is being redeemed. This world is becoming ever more alive, viewed from the coming glory of the end of history. The seed of the Word is everywhere being planted precisely within the fertilized soil of a waning culture.

No boredom can linger where mystery abounds. Everywhere there is wonder: the creation itself, time, providence in history, the interpenetration of grace and freedom, sin in believers, and radical judgment at the end of history. The lamp of scripture illuminates all and makes all new.

Originality Versus Consensus

I have been searched out and found by ancient wisdoms. They have forced me to retreat from all pretenses to originality. Modern life feigns always to be original, yet its originality is tired and jaded. What is lively and not jaded is the new light that shines radiantly upon our pretenses.

Grasping the deceptiveness of originality, I can now listen intently to those who attest a well-grounded tradition of general consent rather than a narrow contemporary bias. I listen to voices that echo what has been affirmed by the community of saints of all times and places.

That was not always the case, however. My final research project before my orthodox metamorphosis became complete dealt with interpersonal transactional analysis. I had given Eric Berne's Transactional Analysis a theological spin and a favorable nod in *Game-Free*. My second round of conclusions were published in a book titled *TAG: The Transactional Awareness Game*.[17] My chief mentor in this transactional study was none other than the famous Timothy Leary, during a period in which he was just beginning his tragic idealizations of drug experimentation. I thank God that I was never tempted to any illicit drug usage, but I had put myself in a position where I easily could have been.

In my revision of Leary's view of interpersonal analysis, I fantasized that I was creating an original pattern for understanding interpersonal transactions. Later, the more deeply I explored the classic Christian analysts of interpersonal relationships (Basil, John Chrysostom, Augustine, and Gregory the Great, as seen in their letters and homilies), the more I realized that these same analytical processes had been understood long before the modern period.

Since Leary I have remained committed to unoriginality. This imperative appears in everything I have written since the mid-seventies: a commitment to offer nothing original. That is not a joke but a solemn pledge. I am trying to curb any pretense at "improving" upon the apostles and fathers.

In my commitment to that early chorus of consensual voices, I have come to a new ecumenical union with hearts and voices in the present. Now I enjoy a rich colloquy with orthodox believers far different from myself. This is a great gift that the modern academic ghetto was never able to give me. I have often felt like a translator between remote dialects, conflicting historical vocabularies, moral languages, and cultural memories, and sometimes like a lonely bridge-builder between continents of separated religious traditions. But many have joined me on what once seemed a lonely journey.

The Councils Showed the Way

It was while reading the texts of the canons of the ecumenical councils in 1972 that I first grasped the social dynamics of orthodoxy. I read through the fourteenth volume of the *Nicene and Post-Nicene Fathers,* an unadorned report of the definitive canons (including pastoral judgments, not merely the dogmatic decrees) of the ecumenical councils and significant regional councils that fed into the great general councils of the first millennium. I read the volume straight through in a few days of engrossed concentration and have not been the same since. That reading affected literally everything I would touch as a teacher, writer, and editor for the rest of my life.

As I turned page after page on those crucial days, I learned how conciliar boundaries were marked, how ecumenical decisions were rendered, and how the Spirit nurtured and enabled unity—things that my graduate education had never thought important enough to mention to me. Many clues embedded in these texts revealed the main assumptions of the ancient decision-making process. About the same time I found my way back to the *Commonitory* of Vincent of Lérins. There I saw explicated for the first time in a clear and systematic way the ecumenical way of truth that I already knew to be operating in the ecumenical councils.

THE NEW VOCATION

The question of personal vocation asks poignantly: Who am I? What distinctive mission am I called to undertake? Each of us must ask these questions and prayerfully seek to answer them.

The Emergence of Vocation Out of Personal Suffering

I have come to a deeply held conviction that it is only from one's unique history of suffering that one can define accurately one's own calling. Only from a particular history of special anguish and personal travail can one come to know how God is calling one to be present to the suffering world even as God the Son has become present to it. This has a social analog: it is only out of a social or institutional history of distress that the special vocation and mission of a culture, nation, or institution is rightly understood.

Even though I did not know it clearly in my earlier days, I now think that my vocation has been from the beginning to become an advocate of classic Christian orthodoxy. My decision to advocate for orthodoxy evolved against the almost unanimous advice of my friends and university colleagues. I do not think that I would have learned the depth of this vocation had I not traveled this circuitous path. My vocation has grown directly from my own hunger for roots, my failed search for roots in modernity, my thirst for historical grounding beyond my former world of compulsive faddism, my native radicalism. It is perhaps an exaggeration to call this a history of *suffering,* but it was certainly an anguished trajectory. My early striving was essentially a moral search for virtue, goodness, and social justice. Only later did it become a recognition of God's search for me.

A keen awareness of final judgment gives me an entirely different frame of reference for accountability. As an example of that shift in perspective, the single most decisive reversal that my new vocation required of me came in a sudden but overwhelming wave of moral revulsion against the very abortion-on-demand laws that I once advocated. In the sixties, teaching seminary ethics classes, I showed young pastors step-by-step arguments for the legitimacy of abortion. After 1973 those arguments backfired upon me as I disavowed the situation ethics on which they were based. Now my conscience calls me to be pro-choice before conception and pro-life thereafter.

The Constancy of God in a Changing World

Some old friends still wonder why I changed my mind. I suspect that they will never get it. The irony is that I changed only by moving closer to that which is unchanging. I plod steadily toward that which alters in no way, the still point of the turning world. The one-time change in my vocation centered in the steady, slow growth toward orthodoxy, toward consensual classic Christianity with its steady refractions of continuity, catholicity, and apostolicity. I had to find the depths and dregs of faddism before I could come to that centered equilibrium, which implies a growing distaste for novelty, heresy, anarchy, pretensions of discontinuity, revolutionary talk, and nonhistorical idealism.

When the Lord tore the kingdom of Israel from Saul, Samuel declared: "He who is the Glory of Israel does not lie or change his mind; for he is not a man, that he should change his mind."[18] God's constant, attentive, holy love is eternally unchanging. It is my stance toward God that has changed, in my slow awakening to the bright immutability of God's responsive covenant love. Yahweh must have laughed in addressing the heirs of the old rascal Jacob with this ironic word: "I the Lord do not change. So you, O descendants of Jacob, are not destroyed."[19] If God's purposes were constantly revisable, how could the faithful rely upon them? Still it is so: "Every good and perfect gift is from above, coming down from the Father of the heavenly lights, who does not change like shifting shadows."[20] The change in my personal history rests on recognition of the unchanging character of God, making every season sweet.

One who walks in this way bends to Coleridge's winter benediction:

Therefore all seasons shall be sweet to thee,
Whether the summer clothe the general earth
With greenness, or the redbreast sit and sing
Betwixt the tufts of snow on the bare branch
Of mossy apple-tree, while the nigh thatch
Smokes in the sun-thaw; whether the eave-drops fall
Heard only in the trances of the blast,
Or if the secret ministry of frost
Shall hang them up in silent icicles,
Quietly shining to the quiet Moon.[21]

The Sheer Joy of the Study of God

Some might counter that what happened to me is just the usual result of ordinary psychogenetic development. That is a polite way of reminding me that I am growing older, which I am grateful not to have to deny.

My vocation has become clearer as the years go by: to study the unchanging God without something else to do, some pragmatic reason or result. This is what I feel most called to do: simply enjoy the study of God — not write about it, not view it in relation to its political residue or imagine that my opinions will have some visible social effect. The joy of inquiry into God is a sufficient end in itself, not only a means to some practical consequence.

Dear old friends keep asking: Why are you merely studying God? Why aren't you out there with "our side" on the streets making "significant changes" (which usually means imagined revolutions)? I explain to them that I am now repenting a lot of the changes for which I earlier labored. I *am* in fact out there on the street in the most serious way I know: by staying close to books and texts. Those who see no connection have not understood the vocation to the life of learning. I do not love the suffering poor less by offering them what they need more.

Plain theology delights in its very acts of thinking, reading, praying, and communing—not for the effects, written artifacts, or social consequences of those acts (though they have profound social consequences), but for the beauty of their subject. Spirit-blessed theology seeks One who is more than a means to an end for social change, although I can think of no act that has more enduring political significance than life with God. The study of God is to be simply enjoyed for its own unique subject: the One most beautiful of all, most worthy to be praised.

Her Dying

To the courageous and gracious woman who accompanied me for forty-six years of my earthly journey, I am incalculably grateful. Edrita brought abundant glory and splendor into my life, sharing every step along my curious path. She has gone on (though I feel her beside me even yet), and I look to join her. It would seem incomplete to leave unspoken the towering fact of her illness, given that I lived with her dying during much of the time of the preparation of this manuscript. She fought a rare type of cancer in a declining spiral that ended in January 1998. She faced with courage the difficult summons of slow death and the singular gracious work of giving up her soul to God.

Why mention this? Her struggle was closely interwoven with the writing of early drafts of this manuscript. As I shaped these chapters, I found it impossible to look at the issues of the death of modernity and the resurrection of orthodoxy without seeing them in this highly personal context of her loss and our shared confidence in the resurrection.

William Butler Yeats wrote:

All through the years of our youth,
Neither could have known their own thought from the other's,
We were so much at one.[22]

So it was with us.

In her final crisis, she was uncowed by death and literally full of life. She showed me how to face severe liabilities and growing limitations without complaint and with good humor, and how finally to yield quietly to death, so as to embody Job's confession: "The Lord gives and the Lord takes away; blessed be the name of the Lord."[23]

SEVEN

Rediscovering the Earliest Biblical Interpreters

We began our pursuit of evidence of the rebirth of orthodoxy with a look at how individual lives are being transformed in today's world. Now, in this chapter, we look to a renewed interest in the earliest orthodox believers and their writings.

THE COMMUNION OF SAINTS IN BIBLE STUDY

This second layer of evidence of an orthodox rebirth is found in the universities—that is, in the academic study of orthodoxy. It is not only religion departments that are turning their attention to orthodoxy, however. In the field of sociology, for example, tradition-maintenance has become a serious inquiry. In literature, the impact of religious teaching on poetry and prose is being examined more intently than ever. In political science, an understanding of the ancient religious fault-lines of the clash of civilizations has become essential to an understanding of international and social conflicts. But most of all, orthodoxy is being reborn as an academic inquiry because its earliest texts are being rediscovered, retranslated, and made available. The texts have their own persuasive power.

Recovering the History of Scriptural Interpretation: The Leading Indicator of Rebirth in the Academy

Within the academy, the most lively arena for the recovery of orthodoxy is the translation and interpretation of early readings of scripture (a field technically called *the history of exegesis*). An unprecedented effort is under way to recover the earliest Christian interpretations of scripture and to understand their parallels with rabbinic interpretations. The study of the early church fathers is becoming a dynamic factor in contemporary biblical and historical inquiries.

One part of this scholarly effort is the project for which I am personally responsible as general editor: the *Ancient Christian Commentary on Scripture* (ACCS). It is the work of an ecumenical team of translators and editors who are reconstructing for the first time in centuries a massive (twenty-eight-volume) patristic commentary on the whole of scripture. This vast effort stands as primary scholarly evidence of the rebirth of orthodoxy. This commentary makes available powerful primary scripture texts as they were ecumenically viewed during the patristic period, spanning the era from Clement of Rome (fl. c. 95) to John of Damascus (c. 645–c. 749). The observations, reflections, debates, and deliberations of early Christian leaders, are ordered verse by verse through the whole range of scripture. This project, which shows evidence of an emerging orthodox mode of the study of scripture, is accessible to anyone (layperson or scholar) who wishes to think with the early church about the sacred text.

No profound recovery of orthodoxy can occur apart from the recovery of its classic texts. Thus serious readers of scripture have long wished that these early commentaries might be accurately recovered, translated, and thoughtfully examined and compared. This longing has largely been ignored by two hundred years of active biblical scholarship, which has instead elected to focus on post-Enlightenment historical analysis and literary and critical methods. Now, for the first time in recent centuries, these earliest layers of classic Christian readings of biblical texts are being made available for lay reflection.

Many other scholarly projects are currently ongoing to recover, in reliable critical editions, definitive translations of classic Christian texts. In English alone we have the *Fathers of the Church* series (Catholic University of America Press), *Ancient Christian Writers* (Paulist Press), *Cistercian Studies* (Cistercian Publications), *The Message of the Fathers of the Church* (Liturgical Press), and *Texts and Studies* (Cambridge).[1] However, none of the above series aims primarily at comprehensive commenting on particular texts of the Bible, showing the varieties of wisdom about each of those texts in earliest Christian teaching. The ACCS, however—like the chains of references assembled by medieval monks—reorders definitive selections from these writings in a string or chain *(catena)* of classic arguments arranged in their canonical order. More closely aligned with classic methods than with typical modern efforts, the ACCS focuses on scripture interpretation in its earliest authoritative layers; it seeks out the mind of the believing church and attempts to express it; it sets forth textual selections in a comparative way; and it thus serves the worshiping community.

We now know that virtually no portion of the early Christian scripture—Old or New Testament—eluded the scrutiny of meaningful comment by the ancient Christian teachers. They studied the Bible thoroughly, with deep discernment, carefully comparing text with text. They often memorized large portions of holy writ, the better to understand and communicate it.

In vastly differing cultural settings, contemporary lay readers are asking how they might grasp the meaning of sacred texts under the instruction of the great minds of the ancient tradition of scripture interpretation. The Talmud and Midrashim have long offered such instruction to Jewish readers; now Christian readers of scripture are seeking the earliest layers of classic consensual wisdom regarding their sacred texts. The major goals are the renewal of Christian preaching based on classic Christian exegesis, the intensified study of scripture by laypeople who wish to think with the early church about canonical texts, and the stimulation of Christian scholarship in the direction of further inquiry into the biblical understandings of the ancient Christian writers.

These ancient Christian writers were viewed by John Wesley as "the most authentic commentators on Scripture, as being both nearest the fountain, and eminently endued with the Spirit by whom all Scripture was given. . . . I speak chiefly of those who wrote before the Council of Nice. But who would not likewise desire to have some acquaintance with those that followed them? with St. Chrysostom, Basil, Jerome, Austin [Augustine]; and above all, the man of a broken heart, Ephraim Syrus?"[2] Wesley thought that the ancient Christian writers were especially useful for "the *explication* of a doctrine that is not sufficiently explained, or for *confirmation* of a doctrine generally received."[3]

The Holy Spirit has a history. When that history, embodied in the writings of those who have wrestled thoughtfully and prayerfully with scripture, is systematically forgotten, the faithful must recover it—and do so accurately. This requires a rigorous effort to restore idioms and meanings misplaced over time.

Countering Modern Excesses in Biblical Studies: The Orthodox Critique of Reductionist Criticism

Vital Bible study stands in urgent need of deeper grounding beyond the scope of historical-critical orientations (with their often blatant philosophical bias toward naturalism and relativism) that have cyclically dominated

biblical studies in our time. We have lived through literally dozens of itera-
tions of cycles of literary and historical criticism, as students of scripture
have sought earnestly to expound and interpret texts out of ever-narrowing
empiricist premises.

The wisdom of the ancient exegetes remains shockingly unfamiliar even
to otherwise highly literate biblical scholars, trained exhaustively in the
methods of criticism. As we have seen, the ancient Christian exegetes have
seldom been revisited in the last two hundred years, and then only margin-
ally and tendentiously. Clear and indisputable evidence of the prevailing
modern neglect of classic exegesis is seen in this bare fact: many of the once-
authoritative classic commentaries on scripture to this day remain still un-
translated into modern languages—much of the exegesis of Origen,
Theodoret of Cyr, and Cyril of Alexandria, for example. Even classic Bud-
dhist and Confucian commentaries in modern China have not suffered this
ugly fate of utter neglect.

In recent years, however, a deep hunger for classic Christian exegesis has
been growing as the theological community has become increasingly skepti-
cal about the usefulness of post-Enlightenment criticism. There is a burgeoning recognition, in the academy and in the pulpit, that such criticism
has succumbed often and deeply to speculative excesses. As a result, the
faithful are turning to the classic Christian writers for grounding.

It is not only theologians who are recognizing the merits of orthodoxy.
Students entering graduate schools and seminaries today are eager to learn
from the patristic texts and resources, as are many of their teachers (though
all too few biblical and historical professors are prepared to show students
the way into the history of exegesis). Lay readers of scripture are also gravi-
tating steadily toward classic sources for meditation on scripture and examining moral choices. Communities of prayer and service, crisis ministries,
counseling ministries, retreat settings, monasteries, and ministries of compassion are searching out these illuminating and authoritative early texts for
spiritual formation. Because the ancient Christian exegetes addressed lay
worshipers primarily, it is only right that their audience today extend beyond scholars to laity eager to hear the reasoned arguments that have sustained Christian textual interpretation and spiritual formation through
many previous modernities.

RECLAIMING THE SACRED TEXTS

The orthodox life has nothing to fear from unbiased historical inquiry. The
faithful are looking forward to improving historical inquiry, not diminishing it; they hope to bring it ever closer to the truth of God's own revelation

in history. The Holy Spirit, who has promised to help each faithful reader of scripture remember rightly, will not allow a defective testimony to be transmitted permanently or irreversibly to the community of faith.

God's own coming in history in human form is for Christians a question of historical evidences that are subject to the usual tests of accurate historical reporting. For example, faith is free to investigate whether the incarnation is history, whether the resurrection occurred, and whether the providential work of the Holy Spirit can be traced historically.

The remembering people of God savor the inspired words of patriarchs, prophets, and apostles. Hearing these blessed voices is like relishing a beautiful symphony echoing through the fragile documents of human memory. It is hard to believe that the Holy Spirit would leave such an important matter as the intergenerational transmission of truth to the jaded imagination of tenured radicals speculating about oral tradition criticism. That premise holds less force for the faithful than that the witness of the sacred text is Spirit-guided.

As contemporary readers, we are not asked to "creatively decide" or imagine what is truly apostolic. A determination of apostolicity was made centuries ago by the apostles themselves. God blesses contemporary witnesses who are faithful to the apostles and believe in the truth of their testimony, and who honor the varied cultural embodiments in the transmission of their words. Contemporary witnesses are called to take every thought (their own and others') captive to God's Word, to appraise any hypothesis by its correspondence with the consensually received testimony of the writers of scripture. Only the original eyewitnesses can attest the truth of God's own coming in history, in the flesh. From them we learn directly the truth of the apostolic testimony.

Listening to Scripture Through the Community of Believers

Anyone schooled in orthodox exegesis can easily spot the limitations of typical biblical commentaries: overspeculation, philosophical partisanship, polemical slanting, and aggressive control of the text by a biased interpreter. Each ancient text surveyed comes under the power of the values, assumptions, predispositions, and ideological biases of the modern interpreter.

These interpretive habits spring from the modern belief that recent interpreters are presumptively superior to classic interpreters. Because of this prejudice, contemporary readers tend to view every biblical text exclusively through whatever historical-critical lens is au courant or appears useful. Within orthodoxy, however, any text's assumptions about itself supersede modern assumptions about it.

Any secondary source or interpreter who presumes to lord it over holy writ so as to become the arbiter of scripture's authenticity—and such interpreters are in the majority today—has ceased being a faithful steward of Jewish and Christian teaching. It is time to demand of guild scholars who see themselves as gatekeepers of the New Testament text, *Give us back our canon!* They found the canon in the worshiping community. Now the worshiping community wants it back. Amid persecution Tertullian warned that the scriptures belong to the church and should not be yielded to secular authorities for common abuse.

The faithful reader contributes not creative imagination, but obedient listening. That is not an easy assignment in today's world. Modern individualism habitually romanticizes the creative imagination of the individual reader. And yet creative imagination is dangerous, even deadly, viewed from within the frame of orthodox listening. The right reading of scripture is not an act of supposed value-free historical analysis. The right reading of scripture must be an act of obedience, praise, worship, and glory in the mystery of God revealed.

The faithful hear scripture as the address of God, communicated with an earnest desire that their faith may become active in love. Orthodox believers strive to make the written Word an enlivened word embodied in their lives, consonant with the prophetic and apostolic testimony as received by classic consensual teachers.

The most exquisite consensual reasoning (such as that found in Rabbi Nachman or Gregory of Nazianzus) comes as a work of sanctifying grace, not merely of clever scholarly research, nor of convicting and prevenient grace, and surely not of autonomous freedom alone. It is a mature work of the Spirit. It seeks to articulate what can only be spoken after much prayer, study, and historical listening. Even then the patient listener for consensus can only exclaim, with the father of the convulsive child, "Lord, I believe; help my unbelief,"[4] and with the publican, "God, have mercy on me, a sinner."[5]

Cross-Referencing and Contextualizing Scripture Texts

From rabbinic and apostolic times the privilege of citing scriptural references has always belonged to the worshiping community; in fact, one cannot even begin to attest Jewish or Christian truth without reference to scripture. But the ancients followed rigorous guidelines regarding the right hearing of scripture.

First, the classic exegetes developed a highly refined pattern of scriptural cross-referencing. It rests on the assumption that no scripture text stands alone, apart from the whole story of revelation. Because each scripture text is rightly understood in relation to the whole of scripture, the comparison of texts is essential to orthodox scripture teaching. (This has nothing to do with fundamentalism, I might add—a movement that did not emerge until the late nineteenth century.)

Second, the classic exegetes looked at scripture not only in relation to other texts but also in relation to the broader context of its culture, history, and language—but never to the extent that the context or language analysis threatened the primacy of the text. Peter at Pentecost did not divert his sermon into historical inquiry into the root word for *repent,* for example; he, like other early believers, made reference to texts of holy writ unapologetically. Yet it has become a modern habit to assume that for each scriptural reference extensive contextual inquiry is required.

The orthodox rule: a text may be quoted *apart* from its context, but not *against* its context. The interpreter is not free to exploit the sacred text in any way contrary to that which is required by its context. Even when a passage is quoted without extensive attention to context, external determinants—the social, economic, psychological, and political factors, for example—always remain open for further inquiry.

This rule of orthodoxy protects Jewish and Christian teaching from being reduced simply to a detached historical investigation of the language and related contexts of holy writ. Contextual study remains a valuable exercise, but not when cut off from the divine address in scripture. The rule also protects orthodox teaching from applying a text apart from its context anywhere and everywhere, uncritically, without attentiveness to the inspired author's intention and meaning.

Classical Judaism and Christianity invite rigorous study of particular texts of scripture that seek to grasp the flow of events within which the revelation of God became known, spoken, written, and transmitted. They welcome serious philological and historical investigation but do not ever regard these as a substitute for listening to the living Word of God. Clergy are given free time and are supported by the laity in order to study these matters in sufficient detail to edify the whole people of God. This is the purpose for which the rabbi or minister is released from other burdens. The laity love to give clergy this freedom, as long as it is not abused or distorted into a political agenda or a cause separate from the gospel. But when clergy forget the direct divine address and remember only the historical ambiguities—a common error in recent centuries—a corrective is required. This corrective is occurring today with the rebirth of orthodoxy.

Respecting Both the Plain Sense and the Spiritual Sense of Scripture

Orthodoxy requires that no scripture text be stretched symbolically beyond recognition or restricted to its most obvious sense. It was assumed by the classic exegetes that the Holy Spirit had veiled the outward expression of some texts whose meaning would be revealed in God's own time. As the person has body, soul, and spirit in union, so does the interpretation of scripture have not only literal, historical, and moral meanings, but also a spiritual or mystical meaning.[6]

Scripture must be allowed to speak for itself without our vested interests overbearing. Where a text has multiple meanings and layers of potential interpretation, both its plain sense and its spiritual meaning are open to investigation. When a spiritual meaning is itself embedded in the text, then constrained spiritual exegesis is not only possible but required, especially when that spiritual meaning is repeatedly confirmed by the leading classic consensual interpreters. However, when a spiritual meaning is invented apart from a text and *imposed* upon it, the written word is not rightly honored.

The umbrella of orthodoxy provides ample room for varied spiritual interpretations, provided they arise out of the text itself. This variety is seen even in the earliest major interpreters in widely varied locations—Irenaeus in southern France, Origen in Lower Egypt, and Tertullian in North Africa. In the early centuries of Christianity, the faithful relied on the baptismal confession, which was passed on to and ordinarily memorized by all believers, as a reliable guide to the heart of scripture and a prism through which spiritual interpretations could be assayed.

The Relation of Early Oral Traditions to Canonized Written Texts

Modern criticism has focused on speculative study of the oral tradition that preceded the written text of scripture, attending particularly to supposed differences between the oral and written. Patristic criticism, which was fully aware of the oral tradition, did not speculate so actively on it and did not posit substantive differences between the spoken and written words.

Jesus taught his disciples not by writing, but primarily by his life. The words of Jesus that interpreted his life were only later recalled and in due time written down. In this sense an oral tradition of Christianity may be said to precede the written tradition. Once Jesus' teachings had been written down and been widely received in worshiping communities, however, the oral tradition had, by the second century, diminished in importance.

The apostles received and passed along this same method of oral communication, spreading the good news first by oral preaching, which only later became fixed in writing. In other words, the teaching of the apostles was spoken before it was penned. In early worshiping communities, then, hearing preceded reading. Paul valued highly and commended both the received oral tradition and the received written tradition. He called the Thessalonians to "stand firm" and "hold fast to the traditions *[paradoseis]* which you have learned from us *by word or by letter*"[7]—that is, whether orally or in writing.

Scripture became written in order that the events attested in preaching might be more accurately preserved and remembered. A written text was obviously more stable than an oral tradition, which might always be controverted by another alleged oral tradition. A text, if drafted faithfully, did not distort memory but stabilized it in writing. The written Word of canonized scripture was assumed to be consistent with its anteceding oral expressions, and its transmission stood under the protection of the Holy Spirit, who accompanied the apostolic witness.

The year 51 CE is generally posited as the approximate date of writing of Paul's first letter to the Thessalonians, the earliest of the New Testament canon. We can imagine various possible forms of proclamation that existed in Christianity before that time, but we do not have any of them in written form (except for probable hymn fragments preserved in the written tradition). Hence they do not carry the same weight of reliability and durability as canonized holy writ.

Form criticism has unwisely tended to make normative the alleged oral tradition as a replacement for the written tradition. Only canonical scripture deserves to be given normative value.

Oral preaching preceded the written tradition, which then by liturgical usage and the process of canonization became gradually recognized as received scripture. That scripture in turn served to reawaken the remembering community, which then became the guardian of the deposit of faith lodged in the written Word. Holy writ is the primary source, ground, and criterion of all Jewish and Christian teaching. The faithful of all generations have always known that. Even the heretics appealed to scripture for their arguments. To enter the arena of Christian worship is to enter the arena of scriptural truth.

Why Persecution Heightened the Need for an Unwritten Tradition
Under conditions of persecution, the tormented Christian community had to rely on memory rather than on written texts. The brevity of Mark's gospel, written before 70 CE, may have sprung from a need for a memorizable form of Peter's preaching of the gospel.

It is hard to discern what specific elements of oral tradition may have been left unwritten (or may have failed to survive in written form) because of persecution, and we do well not to speculate wildly. Basil, writing in the fourth century, mentioned holy traditions of triune immersion, common prayer on the first day of the week, bending knees in prayer to rise anew as an analog of death and resurrection, and making the sign of the cross. In all these cases little residue of written apostolic tradition remains, but that absence does not, in Basil's view, diminish their value. These practices, received and conserved consensually as unwritten traditions from the apostles, remain shrouded in silence, noted Basil, "out of the reach of curious meddling and inquisitive investigation. Well had they learned the lesson that the awful dignity of the mysteries is best preserved by silence. What the uninitiated are not even allowed to look at was hardly likely to be publicly paraded about in written documents."[8]

It was remembered by analogy that Moses did not open all parts of the tabernacle to all. Unbelievers did not enter at all, and even the ordinary faithful accessed only its outer precincts. The Levites alone served in worship, offering sacrifices. Only one priest could enter the holy of holies, and that only once each year. In this same tradition of awe, especially under conditions of marginalization and persecution, it was thought that the apostles had passed on certain memories orally, carefully guarding the awful dignity of the mysteries in silence.[9]

Yet oral tradition, however valuable, always falls prey to abuse and uncertainty, as is abundantly demonstrated in the criticism of the oral tradition. Thus the focus of orthodox Christian teaching remains fixed upon the written Word and the early written documents setting forth the meaning of that Word to worshiping communities worldwide.

A Gentle Caveat for Those Who Expect Ancient Writers to Adapt to Modern Assumptions

If one starts with the narrow assumption that modern thought is superior to ancient wisdom, then the classic exegetes will always appear to be dated, quaint, premodern, and hence inadequate. In fact, if judged only in terms set by modern moral criteria, they will seem comic, mean-spirited, or downright oppressive. The deeper critical question, then, is the adequacy of modern moral criteria.

The modern reader has no legitimate right to impose on ancient exegetes lately achieved modern assumptions about the valid reading of scripture. The ancient exegetes worked under their own assumptions: that scripture was revealed truth, and that the full truth of scripture could be discerned only by *living out* that truth. In other words, they believed that no reader could approach even an elementary discernment of the meaning of a text unless he or she took seriously its revelation and sought to live under its terms. They assumed that one must *practice* a passage's truth in order to hear its meaning.

Modern exegesis does not make these rigorous assumptions: it does not allow the orthodox premise of revelation, nor does it submit personally to the radical moral requirement of the revealed text—that it be taken seriously as divine address. Instead, it favors the sort of historical-critical inquiry described earlier, that makes the critic the arbiter of the text.

The rigorous assumptions of the ancient exegetes are often confused with the assumptions of early twentieth-century Protestant fundamentalists. There is no similarity whatsoever between the two groups, however. Modern fundamentalism developed as a reaction against the naturalistic reductionism of recent centuries—that is, against the tendency to see the world and all its creatures in understandable, scientific, "human" terms. The ancient Christian writers, on the other hand—living in a different world—knew nothing of naturalistic reductionism or what we now call fundamentalism. The rabbis and the church fathers objected to a merely literal or plain-sense view of scripture, looking also for spiritual and moral and typological meanings. As we saw earlier, they saw each scriptural text as being clarified and amplified by other texts and by the whole of the history of revelation; they believed that the *whole* of scripture illuminated each *part*.

Whether Misogyny and Anti-Semitism Disqualify Scripture

Some modern critics perceive the ancient Christian writers to be incurably anti-Semitic or misogynous or both. A cautious apology is in order for today's teachers of classic Christianity, but detailed efforts will have to be left to others. I know how hazardous such an apology is, especially when handled only briefly; but it is necessary, because this issue has become such a stumbling block to some modern readers that it prevents them even from listening to the ancient exegetes.

In my view, neither modern anti-Semitism nor modern misogyny entrapped the minds of the ancient Christian writers. The arguments of the ancients were framed not in regard to hatred of a race or gender, but in regard to the place of the elect people of God, the Jews, in the history of the divine-human covenant that is fulfilled in Jesus Christ, and to the role of women in the history of salvation. Patristic arguments may have unintentionally wronged women according to modern standards, but they intended to elevate the dignity and role of women according to apostolic teaching.

To place arguments in a history-of-salvation context does not exhaustively address all of the tangled moral questions regarding the role of Christians in the histories of anti-Semitism and misogyny—questions that require continuing fair-minded study and clarification—but it does help us get at the core of the issue. Whether John Chrysostom or Justin Martyr deserves the label *anti-Semitic* or *misogynist* depends on how the terms *anti-Semitic* and *misogynist* are used, especially whether they have a primarily racial-gender or a religious-typological definition. In my view, most of the patristic texts that appear to modern readers to be misogynist or anti-Semitic fall into the latter category: they have a *typological* reference. In other words, they are based on a specific method of approach to the interpretation of scripture—called the analogy of faith—which assesses each particular text in relation to the whole, the entire trend of the history of revelation. Within this method the differences between Jew and Gentile or man and woman are viewed under messianic assumptions and not merely as a matter of genetics, race, or gender.

Even in their harshest strictures against Judaizing threats to the gospel, the ancient exegetes did not consider Jews to be racially or genetically inferior people, as modern anti-Semites are prone to do. Similarly, in their comments on Paul's strictures against women teaching they showed no animus against the female gender as such, but rather exalted women as "the glory of man."

Compare the writings of Rosemary Radford Ruether and David C. Ford[10] on these perplexing Semitic and sexist issues. Ruether steadily applies modern criteria of justice to judge the sins and inadequacies of the ancient exegetes. Ford seeks to understand the ancient Christian writers empathically from within their own historical assumptions, limitations, scriptural interpretations, and deeper intentions. While both treatments are illuminating, Ford's treatment comes closer to a fair-minded assessment of the writers' *intent*. Early Christian writers would not recognize themselves in modern charges of anti-Semitism and gender preference. If those being scrutinized cannot recognize themselves in the assessment, the discussion turns toward the questions of fairness and empathy: Have modern interpreters respected their assumptions?

Whether Jewish and Christian Orthodoxy Can Respect Each Other in Good Conscience

I have argued repeatedly in earlier chapters that orthodox Jews and orthodox Christians can not only think and talk together, but to some extent believe together in a common history of salvation, according to covenant teaching, and benefit mutually from the strength of each other's faith. As an orthodox Christian, I cherish very warm personal relationships with Conservative Jews without any feeling that I or they have lost integrity or diminished our religious observance.

How do I respond to complaints by those who feel that I have not sufficiently distinguished between the mutual exclusiveness of the two orthodoxies, Jewish and Christian? Would it not be the case, they argue, that if one is true, the other must be false? To affirm Jewish orthodoxy at any level seems to them to deny Christian orthodoxy.

Christian orthodoxy is not invalidated by the awareness that God has elected the people of Israel, nor is Jewish orthodoxy falsified by the premise that God's purpose with Israel has continued and been extended in the events attested in the New Testament.

It is useful to draw a sharp distinction on the crucial question of whether the Messiah has come in Jesus or not. However friendly, Jews and Christians must be utterly candid with each other about how they differ on this pivotal point, and how it affects everything else that they believe and teach. But does granting that difference and its importance foreclose all further discussion of analogies between our lives in covenant with the God of Israel? The early history of discussions between Jews and Christians assumes that this dialogue is important for both parties.

Some Jews and Christians may respectfully object that *orthodoxy* is not the right word to describe what they are seeking (or even what I am trying to argue). They may think, especially out of modern premises, that this project makes conspicuous use of a word that has a tainted history. Why not simply give up the word *orthodoxy* and talk instead about *classic Christianity* or *rabbinic Judaism?* I have no objection to these terms; in fact, I use them frequently. But the term *classic* is not as resolute or definitive as the term *orthodox. Classic* has a much softer nuance and falls prey to nondoctrinal interpretations. Not so with *orthodox.* I have not found compelling reasons why the term *orthodox* cannot be used as a sociological type to describe both Jews and Christians with largely similar views, hopes, texts, and moral teachings (with the exception of messianic fulfillment).

I would like my conservative Christian colleagues to empathize with the intention of my conservative Jewish friends on the question in this dialogue. My Jewish friends would say, I do not cease being an observant and faithful Jew the moment I enter into serious dialogue with Christians who believe that their Christianity is intrinsically grounded in and connected with my Judaism through its history and through our shared history. It is not a mark of orthodoxy to be closed off from dialogue with those who share the history of

Abraham, Isaac, and Jacob. They will say to fellow Jews: Why is my integrity questioned if I talk with Christians about rabbinic exegesis and its parallels with patristic exegesis? Such a discussion holds far more meaning than going together to an ersatz Seder service. Orthodox Jews do not propose to their Christian friends that those friends avoid or dilute their Christian confession, especially when it does not diminish their Jewish faith and identity. Likewise, they do not assume that their own Halakhah is demeaned by a frank and open comparison with classic Christian teaching.

Some may wonder why I have not discussed Christian missions to Jews. To explore this issue in depth would detract from the major agenda of this argument. Yet the question cannot be wholly avoided. This delicate issue especially concerns evangelical Christians committed to the Great Commission. Because of religious liberty concerns, I do not want inordinately to constrain those groups of Christians who believe it is their religious duty to bear chastened and fitting testimony to Jews, provided it does not demean Jewish faith by exhibiting the habits of unseemly proselytism. I concede that the original apostles engaged in a mission to the Jews. But I believe that any missionary effort that fails to honor the election history of those it seeks to serve falls short of charity. I believe that the one covenant with God may be viewed from two different vantage points: one, the elect people of God; the other, the transmutation of the people of God in the light of the ministry of Jesus. Both of these covenant viewpoints are meaningful and honorable and historically true as viewed differentially within the history of covenant. Both need to be affirmed and defended in a constrained way without rancor.[11] The Jews are a special people chosen not by you or me or themselves but God—chosen for special service in human destiny as God's people, a holy nation set apart.[12]

In a wonderful story, my mentor, Will Herberg, tells of his visit with Reinhold Niebuhr, in which Herberg indicated to Niebuhr that he was considering becoming a Christian. Niebuhr urged him strongly to go back and first read his own rabbinic tradition.[13] Niebuhr was bang on in his hunch.

EIGHT

Strengthening the Multicultural Nature of Orthodoxy

The intrinsically cross-cultural nature of orthodoxy provides the third level of evidence of its rebirth. There is a growing awareness within the church at large that orthodox life has a practical capacity to energize greater fairness in social relations and public policy.

Classic Christian orthodoxy has far more potential to work for good as a global and multicultural phenomenon than do strictly secular modern models. It has resources and energies for social transformation that are unavailable to its humanistic and secular counterparts.

There is growing evidence to confirm a recent shift of consciousness in society toward a higher valuation of faith-based charitable networks. The media culture is belatedly recognizing the social value of traditional Jewish and Christian moral reasoning. The sociological evidence is pouring in on what makes for sustainable societies, and that evidence clearly shows that those rooted in classic moral teaching are more effective at designing and implementing behavioral transformation than are supposedly value-free or secular governmental strategies. This evidence rises from scientific social analysis, studies of the relation of religion and culture, cross-cultural studies, and studies of public policy and strategies for social effectiveness.

THE FAIRNESS REVOLUTION MEETS MULTICULTURAL ORTHODOXY

The longest-lasting revolution in human history is under way even today, with fighting on many fronts. The so-called fairness revolution seeks a fair and equitable opportunity for every person in every culture, regardless of gender, race, economic situation, education, and physical capability; and where unfair treatment of people occurs, it seeks legal and attitudinal remedies. There are deep historical connections that lead from religious faith to efforts at fairness as the history of the civil rights movement makes clear. The fairness revolution has two complementary arms, religious and secular, but the former until recently has been less visible.

Although the secular forms of fairness advocacy seek to embrace all human cultures, their typical range of vision is decidedly recent and Western. The mix of voices in classic Christianity embrace many more cultures and generations. Secular models of egalitarianism claim to want to include all cultures in the modern democratic scene, and yet they sustain an intractable prejudice against any culture perceived as premodern and any view that might appear to neglect recent Western expressions of egalitarian democratic idealism. In other words, despite their purported inclusiveness, they are often so narrowly framed (to favor the power of knowledge-elites) that they quickly lose all claim to fairness or even proximate objectivity. This is the *unfair* part of the fairness revolution.

Fairness advocates want to legislate fairness by creating legal penalties for prejudices and by putting restrictions on voluntary associations. Yet in doing so they tend to reduce the vision of human change to mere political manipulation and oppressive legal constraints, missing weightier matters of the heart. They appear to love whales and spotted owls and kangaroo rats, and yet they sometimes show contempt for actual people and organic social processes. They love tearing down any walls that appear to block people out, and yet they detest premodern wisdoms and quickly block out people who conscientiously hold traditional values.

Comparing Orthodoxy's Inclusive Compassion with the Secular World's Efforts at Fairness

The rebirth of orthodoxy interfaces ironically with the miscalculations of the fairness revolution. Orthodoxy views classic Christianity as the historical source of a social compassion that could, if rightly understood, add immense energy to social betterment.

Christian social vision does not stop with governmental efforts but seeks to energize private charities. It does not stop with legal remedies but seeks to redeem the heart. Christian moral sensibilities do not revolve exclusively around the modern ethos but are intergenerational (and hence far more cross-cultural) than those grounded in modern assumptions only. This is in part why faith-based social services show greater imagination and better outcomes than do government-sponsored programs.

Although older secular forms of the fairness revolution still tend to view orthodox moral reasoning with intense suspicion, newer forms recognize classic Christian teaching as a source of motivation, empowerment, energy, prudence, and justice. The anti-religious slant among the older forms of fairness advocacy is based on modern egalitarian assumptions and the premise that bureaucratic planners know what is best for everyone else. This wing of the revolution focuses on governmental executive actions, legislation, and judicial activism, despite the fact that such an approach has resulted in many failed social experiments in the past—experiments often rejected by the very constituencies they were supposed to protect or relieve (as seen in highrise housing, busing, and urban renewal policies). To cite a specific example, aid to dependent children has engendered a fixed dependency class of ensured poverty stretching over generations, with no end in sight.

Though many (if not all) of the secular attempts at fairness are well intended, legislatively enforced efforts at inclusion, such as affirmative action, inadvertently produce policies that tend to ignore merit or pander to politically preferred pressure groups and caucuses. Artificial quotas restrict "democratic" choices to self-serving categories set up by social engineers. They stifle true democracy by turning legislative processes into the artificial manipulation of democratic representation by the selective massaging of preferred minority interests. When leadership is selected on the prejudicial basis of race or gender rather than performance, a process is set in motion that cripples self-esteem, productivity, and fair representation. Because these misfirings of the fairness revolution only reinforce the impotence of the underclass, they highlight the need for a more nuanced understanding of equity and justice and organic social change.

Understanding the Connections Between Classic Christianity and the Fairness Revolution

While it is evident that the fairness revolution itself has grown out of a compassionate multigenerational moral tradition profoundly influenced by classic Christianity, the relationship between orthodoxy and the fairness revolution is not easy to sort out or explain. It is becoming increasingly evident that the religious traditions with millennia of cross-cultural experience have certain forms of wisdom not easily accessible to secular models, and yet secular advocates often promote the fairness revolution as something that only secular agencies are capable of bringing about. This itself is prejudicial and ill informed.

Secular ideologues defend their moral high ground by alleging that classic Christian teaching has been so complicit with corrupt social and economic systems—systems that have, among other things, not only permitted but re-inforced racial and gender inequities—that it has lost all credibility. While these inequities stain the history of Christianity—no argument from me there—they do not express the heart of classic Christianity itself, which brought Western civilization to levels of social justice now being emulated in the Two-Thirds World.

The Enlightenment's record of secular social experimentation is riddled with failures and unexpected secondary consequences. Enlightenment ide-alism transmuted into Communism. The Cambodian revolution was hatched not in Cambodia but in Paris among utopian Marxists. The Nazi experiment, with its superhuman Nietzschean dreams, and the great Cul-tural Revolution in China were disastrous expressions of misguided mod-ern Western planning schemes. None could have been conceived apart from the coercive utopianism of the anti-religious heirs of the eighteenth-century Enlightenment.

Today secular efforts at egalitarianism continue to flounder, largely be-cause secular advocates fail to study secularism's past failures. These advo-cates continue to overleap organic social processes and to ignore standard forms of social wisdom readily available in the classic Western moral tradi-tion—for example, the need for careful checks and balances in government, the dignity of unborn human life, and the protection of noncombatants.

The Practical Value of Orthodoxy for the Fairness Revolution

Because the orthodox tradition has a wealth of historical wisdom inacces-sible to modern prejudices, it offers the fairness revolution profound new insights and energies for social change, moral courage, and persistence. These energies come from gratitude for God's gifts in creation and redemp-tion, not from human imagination alone. And they tend to have staying power, because religiously grounded social motivation is less vulnerable to demoralization than its secular parallel.

Furthermore, the orthodox way is more experienced than secularism at anticipating and avoiding unexpected secondary consequences. The bibli-cal tension between law and gospel, which is refracted in the tension be-tween Jewish orthodoxy and Christian orthodoxy, is a perennial source of profound social realism. Because orthodox biblical teaching gives believ-ers a realistic grasp of the inveterate nature of human self-assertiveness, they are prepared for the possibility of secondary consequences from any policy (and indeed expect even the secondary consequences to carry with them the predisposition to new forms of distortion!). This is the story of human freedom from the beginning of history: it risks fallenness. Thus no good policy can protect itself from distortion or unintended consequences.

And yet we cannot stop trying. The fairness revolution, which has as many failures as achievements, must continue to work toward greater equity and justice. Classic Jewish and Christian moral reasoning offers that revolution a better way toward social fairness—a way that avoids the pitfall of utopian illusion.

Orthodoxy's Call for a More Radical Diversity, Inclusion, Tolerance, and Empathy

The modern idea of diversity is *less diverse* than the ancient ecumenical idea of *oecumenē*. The classic concept of *oecumenē* (universal, the whole world) spans many generations—even millennia—while the modern idea of diversity spans but a single century (or more likely only a slice of that—one generation, or one subset of one generation, such as a particular coterie of youth culture). Because modern diversity has no time to listen to other generations, it risks a massive loss of wisdom.

Likewise, the modern idea of inclusion is *less inclusive* than the classic Christian understanding of inclusion. The classic understanding rises from the more radical inclusiveness of God's mercy toward all, as creator of all, redeemer of all, and consummator of all history. God's work in creation is given to all, even if many refuse the gift. God's action on the cross is offered for all, even if only some accept it. God's promise for the future of history encompasses all, even if some will voluntarily reject grace. The modern version typically focuses on only one particular disenfranchised interest group.

The contrast continues: the modern conceit of tolerance is *less tolerant* than the ancient ecumenical ethic of long-suffering forbearance. Modern tolerance depends on a relativism that gives up on the search for truth before it begins, whereas classic Christian forbearance is based upon the assumption that truth is knowable because God has made it known. Modern tolerance seeks the lowest common denominator, whereas classic Christian forbearance seeks the highest common denominator: our human participation in the divine-human covenant (as represented in repentance, humility, and cross-bearing). Out of this call for participation comes a higher-level energy for social reconstruction unburdened by illusions.

The modern notion of absolute equality embodies *less empathy* than the ancient ecumenical idea of compassion, which puts a neighbor's need above one's own. The modern idea of absolute equality survives on the thinness of passing human sympathies, whereas the classic Christian understanding of compassion radiates the full depth of God's own compassion for all humanity, as shown in God's willingness to become flesh and die for our sins. Classic Christianity is not a substitute for democracy; it is the leading progenitor of it.[1]

The Intellectual Freedom of the Orthodox Way

As noted in Chapter 4, one of the primary reasons that orthodoxy persists is that it possesses an extremely long memory. Orthodoxy offers two millennia of intellectual options, not a single century saturated with experimental failures. It offers vast varieties of intellectual alternatives, acknowledging that these alternatives all come with boundaries.

A veritable feast of learning is offered in the deeply rooted orthodox community. At the table of orthodox learning the believer is offered reliable, ecumenically tested premises to try out: revelation in history, divine providence, the Father's love made known through the Son by the power of the Spirit, the expectation of final judgment. These freeing assumptions manifest themselves in the living communities of worship that embody the orthodox way. There anyone can sit at a large table and enjoy the whole feast.

The steady habit of mind and heart in orthodoxy is attentive listening to history. Thus believers come to the table eager and ready for the feast prepared. Knowing that the ancient way of reasoning cannot be reduced to sociological insights, historical analyses, philosophical arguments, or scientific methods, they eagerly sample options closed by narrowing modern restrictions.

The venerable tradition of ecumenical reflection liberates any community of discourse. It permits the faithful to reason afresh amid their actual unfolding history, but it grounds that reasoning in orthodoxy's distinctive premises of historical revelation and consensuality. Contrary to modern assumptions, orthodoxy grants a high priority to thinking freely out of a wide experiential base of faithful confessors of all times and places.

There is a correspondence of unity and continuity among the leading consensual interpreters of the sacred texts of the worshiping community. This consensus, which cannot be better summarized than in the baptismal confession, must be grasped intuitively through patient historical listening. Subsequent rememberers and guardians of the deposit have respected earlier layers of consensus, because this community of faith over many generations has assumed that the formation of consensual ecumenical teaching was led by the Spirit in the transmitting of Christian truth amid the hazards of history.

It is not the habit of orthodoxy to pit Christianity against critical theory. It is the habit of orthodoxy to incorporate many correlated critical methods and bring them into coordinate accountability within its overarching understanding of the human prospect. Because orthodoxy frees critical reasoning from the templates of narrow modern ideological advocacy, it increases the quality of that reasoning.

CONSENSUS RECOGNITION

We next explore how classic Jews and Christians reached, developed, and maintained cross-cultural consensus over many generations—something that modernity has proven itself unable to do. In the rest of this chapter we will look at how the orthodox experience has engendered forms of consensus that can be practically applied to social maintenance and reconstruction.

The achievement of consensus is an ancient art that was fashioned out of religious communities responding to revelation. Only much later was consensus-formation applied within secularizing environments. Sociological and political processes are surely utilized by the Spirit to enable and activate broad consent on a wide range of issues. While these processes can be fairly examined empirically and sociologically, such an examination does not get at the deeper cause of consensus-formation: the Holy Spirit. The Lord prayed that the Spirit would come to make us one, as he and the Father are one.

The Holy Spirit Speaks All Languages

Much about the work of the Spirit falls entirely beyond our ken. But we do know from experience that the Spirit has found ways to proclaim the same Word of truth to the varied cultures of the world. This continues today.

Almost two millennia ago the life of faith active in love poured forth from Pentecost, a unique language event. Only gradually, as believers through many centuries defended the faith proclaimed at that event, did the full and universal implications of Pentecost become clarified in the believing, consenting community. The conciliar process that followed in later centuries confirmed repeatedly the truth-claims of the early community of faith, until finally a relatively unified consensual understanding of faith gained worldwide consent, reaching out to all cultures.

The language of the apostolic tradition expanded quickly from its original Aramaic to the languages of the fifteen ethnic identities mentioned in Acts 2—Parthians, Medes, Elamites, Mesopotamians, Judeans, Cappadocians, and those from Pontus, Asia, Phrygia, Pamphylia, Egypt, Libya (Cyrene), Rome, Crete, and Arabia. From these peoples, locations, and languages, the gospel soon entered into the wider streams of the two great available international languages of the Greco-Roman world: Greek and Latin. Soon Armenian, Syriac, Coptic, and Georgian would all be claimed by the same Word and the same Spirit. The

Holy Spirit empowered Christian teaching in all these languages; nothing necessary to salvation was forfeited by translation into another tongue.

Note that English, German, and French—indeed, all the languages that we now call European—were very late arrivals in the classic ecumenical tradition. Little Christian teaching exists in these languages prior to the sixteenth century—a fact unknown or forgotten by those who imagine that Christianity is intrinsically a *European* phenomenon. Christianity largely did without Russian and French for about half of its history and without English, German, and Spanish for almost two-thirds of its history.

The general consent of the worldwide laity to Christian truth has never implied that everything worth knowing could be crammed uniformly into one single language pattern or cultural perspective, thereby diminishing the importance of other native and colloquial forms of language and culture. This consent has rejected only those terms and ideas that would mislead the community of believers into false premises or conclusions contrary to the original apostolic deposit of faith. Everything apart from outright heresy has been fair game for debate and due consideration through the centuries.

Protestants have benefited from and contributed to the greater catholicity of the community of faith. These heirs of pietistic revivalism today have the same right as do the Orthodox and Catholics to appeal to the consensual conciliar teachings. They need not remain forever fixated on more recent forms of teaching—forms that have split asunder Christendom.

When differing interpretations of scripture conflict, the simple Deuteronomic question remains: "Ask your father and he will tell you; your elders, and they will explain to you."[2] The command of the orthodox way is simple: "Do not move an ancient boundary stone set up by your forefathers."[3] These boundary stones were firmly established at Sinai, in Jerusalem, and in the early Christian councils (beginning as early as the Council of Jerusalem, about 46 CE). They endure intact in the continuing work of consensual exegetes. Those who "rashly seek for novelties and expositions of another faith" are always eventually going to be found wanting by general lay consent, by "all the people" who respond in faith with one voice within the *consensus fidelium,* saying, "So be it, so be it."[4]

Cross-Cultural Listening for Consensus
The faithful do not assume that absolute unanimity is required for ecumenical consent. If they did, no question could ever be settled. A small cadre of objectors could block ecumenical teaching and unity in Christ. Consent may be perfect among the faithful in the celestial city, but it remains imperfect and debatable among the conditions in transit.

All who sincerely wish to follow the ancient ecumenical consensus must learn to listen for it with discernment, which means "according to the Spirit." Such listening is less a skill than a gift. However, it is a gift not easily received, for its reception requires becoming attuned over a lifetime to the silent heart of the believing community in all times and places. To engage in this kind of consensual reflection demands an absorptive mind and a hunger for exposure to the symphony of voices within classic orthodoxy. Such absorption includes critical reasoning, historical inquiry, and active empathy. Those voices that best sing in ecumenical harmony must be listened to attentively and comparatively, with an ear for the whole range of cross-cultural Christian testimony.

More or less true voices are winnowed in and winnowed out, not by private claimants with individual intuition but by the historically informed faithful who can assess correspondence with the historical consensus. Some voices do not belong in the choir; they quake with uncertain notes in equivocal peripheries of the ecumenical chorus. Others clearly sound in full harmony. When one hears a voice that blends with the saints of all times, its authenticity is easy for the gathered faithful to recognize. They say, "Amen. So be it." On the other hand, when one hears a voice that pretends to sing on key but only imagines itself to be in harmony with biblical faith and historical consent, the faithful easily recognize the dissonance.

Wherever classic consensual Christian teaching differs from one's own local dialect or erratic ethnocentrism, the whole is preferred to the part. But how can one learn a way of listening that distinguishes the dialect from mother tongue? That is a lesson learned by drinking deeply from the spring of worship, praise, and moral reasoning that bubbles up from cross-cultural generations of faithful teaching.

Nothing is more pathetic than a self-centered doctrinal or moral advocate who claims to be centered on God's Word and yet fails to listen to the vast resources of orthodoxy. (I made such pitiful claims myself before meeting the ancient consensual teachers.) Expecting someone to apply ecumenical discernment effectively without sustained exposure to the worshiping community with its ancient texts is like asking a native resident of Tampa to identify the eighty different types of snow known readily to native Inuits.

If one tries to impersonate historical consensus without entering deeply into the worshiping community, without singing the hymns of the church, without being immersed in the written Word, without walking daily in the way, without living life in Christ, his or her voice will quickly betray itself with evidences of dissonance. Such discord can never elicit a broad level of lay trust over an extended period of time. It would be folly to ignore the experiential authority of those who have years of practiced attentiveness to classic consensual teaching. To hear a corrective, one goes back and studies ever more carefully the varieties of expression of the one apostolic mission in its beautiful, two-millennia-spanning multilingual variations—Eastern and Western, African and Asian, Roman and Syrian.

The imperative, in a word, is *Listen!* Heed those most aware of the enormous flexibility and variability of orthodoxy, of its unique ability to transform various cultural traditions, yet who are able to behold within all this variety the unifying work of the Holy Spirit.

Within this huge language universe, orthodoxy makes time and room for many shades of permissible interpretation. Orthodoxy does not seek one exclusive interpretation that would bind up the written Word or make the Spirit strictly subservient to a single transient culture or economic class or political interpretation. It seeks to discover that stratum at which all share equitably in the unity of the one people of God—albeit with varied symbol-systems, constantly changing cultural memories, and even competing economic interests. The orthodox way seeks to make peace between scripture interpreters of different languages, periods, and moral traditions who yet share the same faith in the same Lord and the same baptism by the one God. Only when forced by persistent error does orthodoxy become polemical.

There are those who doubt that unity of the one people of God is possible, that consensus exists in regard to faith. The only way to address that doubt is to go through an exquisitely nuanced listening process. Only then can searchers earn the right to question the existence of established consensual judgment.

Bearing with Misunderstanding

The consensual thought-process of orthodoxy may seem impossibly backward, dated, and reactionary to those who assume without investigation that consensus is impossible. Among evangelicals, for example, orthodox teaching may seem too Catholic. Among Catholics, it may seem inordinately hellenic. Among Greeks, it may seem distressingly un-Greek. Among pietists, followers of the orthodox way may seem like bookish antiquarians who have missed the point (and perhaps even the experience) of being warmly moved by the Spirit. To political liberals the orthodox way may appear hopelessly defensive of economic injustices, while to political conservatives it may seem too multicultural. But to those Christian believers who allow the ancient ecumenical consensus to guide their praying and believing, the orthodox way resonates with the consensus of faith that embraces and guards the dearest treasures of ecumenical, Catholic, evangelical, liberal, and Orthodox traditions.

Ironically, in listening and working for the unity that the Holy Spirit is creating, believers must prepare to bear the burden of being caricatured and pigeonholed into whatever particular niche the puzzled beholder finds convenient. This is a yoke to be borne joyfully, with comic sensibilities where possible and with an awareness of both the incongruity of the divisiveness of human interests and the singularity of the divine intention.

Orthodox believers warily approach any supposed ecumenical voice that has not been thoroughly exposed to the liturgies, songs, prayers, and sacred texts of ancient ecumenical teaching. Not until a person has personally tested such a voice again and again in contemplative scriptural and liturgical meditation can he or she become rationally persuaded of the living fact of its basic consensuality. Just as only after years of bird-watching can a birder accurately identify a whooping crane in flight, so it is with orthodox listening: the argument on discernment cannot become convincing without careful study, earnest prayer, and comparative reading. One cannot expect someone unprepared by this discipline to understand liturgy or make ecumenical judgments or offer reliable moral counsel.

Guarding Consensus Recognition

The *episcopoi* (superintendents, overseers, or bishops) of the New Testament are those to whom the task of defense of the faith has been especially committed (1 Tim. 6:20, 1 Tim. 3:1–7, Tit. 1:7–9), along with elders. They represent the unity, continuity, and integrity of the community of faith. The office of *episcopos* has traditionally borne responsibility for guardianship of the faith, defending it against error and guiding the whole laity toward undiluted apostolic teaching. In the free church traditions, this same role has been found under different names.

In executing their responsibility, holders of the episcopal office remain rigorously subject to scripture and to the historical consent of the whole people of God. This is why, when bishops fail to guard the faith, or when they preach contrary to the faith, the offense is seriously damaging to the whole body.

It is intensely disappointing and ignoble when those in the episcopal office fall into blatantly false teaching. Recent examples are all too numerous: John Shelby Spong, Jacques Gaillot, Raymond Hunthausen, Walter Sullivan, Joseph Sprague, Melvin Talbert, and Walter Righter follow in the wake of historical wayward bishops who have advocated views contrary to classic Christian teaching: Nestorius, Valens of Mursa, Eusebius of Nicomedia, Julian of Halicarnassus. Simply being a duly elected bishop does not guarantee that one has the gift of *episcopos* or that one is orthodox, although there is a strong *presumption* that any bishop will be rigorously accountable to classic Christian teaching.

Those in the office of elder (*presbuteros*) or pastor (shepherd, *poimen*) voluntarily offer themselves to obedience to the teaching of general lay consent, ordinarily under the guardianship of the *episcopos* or its synodal or free church equivalent. Yet regrettably, in recent times the offices of overseer, elder, and pastor have too frequently been used as a weapon for demeaning and rebuking orthodox teaching. Little will change in this regard until the larger body of laity insists that its highest leaders guard ecumenical teaching.

Yet even when counter-consensual voices are recalcitrant or seem temporarily triumphant, the Spirit does not cease to work among them for the peace of the community of faith. The Spirit is not rushed; the Spirit has plenty of time. As history has shown repeatedly, conflicts of doctrine that seem to involve irreconcilable differences often are resolved later, when passions have diminished.

Learning to Trust the Consensus

Once the ancient consensus of the faithful has been defined through due process (meaning that it has been determined to be a cross-cultural, Spirit-led consensus tempered by centuries of experience and time), and once it has entered into liturgy, theological tradition, moral education, and pastoral care, that consensus is taken as reliable unless there are compelling reasons to question it. Debates may continue as to whether particular contested points are to be consensually received, but where lay consent over centuries has firmly defined and confirmed the consensus, it is viewed by believers as cross-culturally durable. The canon of holy writ, the rule of faith, the baptismal formula, and the ecumenical councils, all authenticated many times over by general lay consent, hold time honored and reliable authority. They do not have to be rewritten by every sophomore in Religion 101.

Legitimate ecumenical authority must undergo repeated testing over a period of several centuries, however, in order to retain its legitimacy. Thus we are always free to ask the toughest questions of presumed authorities. As their voices repeatedly radiate the Spirit that guides the worshiping community, gradually the believer begins to trust those authorities on most contested points.

Guarding the Deposit of Faith

Classic Christian teaching, according to Vincent of Lérins, consists in "what you have received, not what you have thought up; a matter not of ingenuity, but of doctrine; not of private acquisition, but of public Tradition; a matter brought to you, not put forth by you, in which you must be not the author but the guardian, not the founder but the sharer, not the leader, but the follower."[5] Thus Paul instructed Timothy to guard the deposit that had been committed to him.[6] The community of believers seeks not to discover a new word but to proclaim the ancient gospel ever anew, so that "by your expounding it, may that now be understood more clearly which formerly was believed even in its obscurity."[7] Clearly, then, interpreters who pretend to improve upon apostolic testimony are tampering with the evidence.

This does not imply that there can be no progress in our ever-inadequate attempts to grasp and articulate ancient ecumenical teaching. On the contrary, Vincent argued that the interpretation of the deposit of faith progressively unfolds. However, progress should not be equated with mere change, since change can be for good or ill. True progress advances in understanding that which has been already once for all given fully and adequately in the deposit of faith.[8] As God does not change in substance over time, so does the Word of God not change, although it may refract differently through cultural change. Being of the very nature of God, the Holy Spirit "works in others a change to grace, but is not changed Himself," says Ambrose. For "how is He capable of change Who is always good?"[9]

It is foolish to think that philosophical imagination or historical inquiry will finally bring the gospel to more perfect clarity than that grasped by the apostles and by the Lord himself. Nothing that modern life offers is able to circumvent or surpass or make dated the apostolic testimony.

The notion that Christian teaching changes substantively from culture to culture is a mistake that orthodoxy perennially disputes. The deposit of faith does not itself significantly shift in content, nor does it alter in meaning from that which was first proclaimed by the apostles. The community of faith remains guardian of the Word made flesh as handed down to each succeeding generation, its sense and meaning unchanged.

Brighter light may be shed by the good news upon present and future generations. Clearer conceptions of the gospel's cross-cultural truth may arise. But the light and truth that may come will not shine unilaterally from the new historical situation; rather, they will shine from the truth of the revealed Word addressing that historical situation.

Myopia in Academic Studies in Religion

As we saw in the previous chapter, the academic study of religion abounds in the prejudices of modernist chauvinism. It is replete with social-location analysis, speculative form criticism, and psychoanalytic ploys. All these methods tend to put the religion critic in charge of the text. The authority of the sacred text as revelation is set aside.

The academic study of religion wants to manage the impression that it is treating classic Christianity objectively and fairly, while actually ignoring or demeaning it and while propagating modern illusions in its stead. With many seminaries desperately trying to "catch up" with the follies of secular academic studies in religion, the chronic neglect of consensuality and continuity persists even in ordination training. The academic religionists have become expert in testing strong faith on the criteria of weak faith, and they are regrettably eager to share their expertise.

Scripture reminds us that the demonic always appears as an angel of light. Echoing from the fourth century, the voice of Hilary of Poitiers is still relevant to this tendency of scholarship: "Since, therefore, they cannot make any change in the [scriptural] facts recorded, they bring novel principles and theories of man's devising to bear upon them."[10] Having found the premodern text itself irritating and unacceptable, modern naturalistic "critics" scramble to imagine some new way of spinning it. The special burden of critical orthodox scholarship is fairly to answer biased assessments of this sort.

Orthodoxy's Humility Requirement

Orthodoxy cries out for modest speech. Orthodoxy's quarrel with modern hubris is precisely the *overconfident* narrowness, prejudice, and limited historical vision of the modernity.

To understand a particular classic text requires hearing it, insofar as possible in its own language and accents, with empathy for its history, nuances, saints, hymnody, liturgy, and history of suffering. This means that orthodox believers must maintain an attitude of meek humility regarding any one person's or culture's capacity to see the whole simultaneously. When we speak of orthodox life rightly, we remember the limits on our own mastery of its language, channeled through particularities, carved out of our own experience of it. Others can more easily perceive our speech as limited than we can.

Orthodox consciousness has produced many different manifestations in history, some culturally akin to those we know well, others greatly distant. The human tendency is to relate empathically to those that are akin but have little patience with those that look radically different. Our familiarity with one of these traditions may lead us to claim that the part we happen to know is the whole of orthodox life, and yet that violates the very premise of orthodoxy. Christians must strive to point not to the part but to the wholeness of the one holy catholic apostolic church. From the orthodox perspective, to point to any one authentic expression of faith is implicitly to point to the church's implied cross-cultural wholeness.

There are two different ways to approach a solution to the problem of trusting the orthodox tradition: first, by critical study; second, by meek obedience. These two approaches (one lifelong and the other here and now) are complementary. By intensive study of the varieties of orthodoxy we learn its subtleties, yet this lifelong task falls short since it is always incomplete. As this incompleteness brings us to our knees, we come to the other simpler approach: an attitude of genuine humility. Our imperfections call us to simple *obedience,* to yield to consensual wisdom even when we do not grasp all its reasons fully.

The orthodox way reminds us of our always limited grasp of time and place. It teaches us to pray: *I acknowledge, Lord, the extreme limitations of the specific forms in which I experience the unity, holiness, catholicity, and apostolicity of the church. Nonetheless, every time that I meet a new form, I give thanks to you that I recognize its correlation with the forms that I and others have known and experienced.*

The Mind of the Believing Community

Can the ancient faith rehabilitate a tradition-deprived culture? Is this asking too much? We can be encouraged by previous historical periods in which such a renewal has in fact happened. But it will happen only if contemporary believers follow the guidance of intergenerational consensual teaching. Only this approach is blessed by the Holy Spirit.

Teaching tested by many generations is stronger than teaching checked out by only one generation. Classic Judaic wisdom insists on the freedom to listen anew to the rabbinic interpreters of law, marriage, the economic order, and human relationships. Classic Christianity insists on the freedom to listen anew to the earliest attesters of Christian faith on these same subjects.

These rememberers aim gradually and fairly to reclaim the institutions and schools and organizations of Judaism and Christianity for their historical communities. Despite the hazardous accommodations of both faiths to modern culture, classic rabbinic and patristic texts are now being reread with respect and integrity. Amid the failure of bureaucratic ecumenism, ancient ecumenical teaching is now being scrutinized carefully. Amid the almost complete disintegration and collapse of the soul of modernizing Judaism and Christianity under captivity to modern thought-forms, believers are finding unexpected wisdom in sacred scripture, in ancient rabbinic and patristic readings of texts, and in the practical application of the orthodox way.

The elect people of God who once appeared so isolated, so vulnerable, are once again gaining confidence in possessing and owning the history of their election and destiny. The bride of Christ herself, who seemed once pro-foundly imperiled, is again rediscovering her secured relation to the groom.

The Spirit continues to work powerfully to restore both communities of faith to their original vision of their essential calling to holiness, their uni-versal significance, and their covenantal mission within history. Evidences of health and new growth abound. Even in the face of congregational divisions, gross cultural accommodations, and leadership apostasies, these worshiping communities are regrounding themselves in their sacred texts.

NINE

Learning to Say No

I now turn to a different level of evidence for the rebirth of orthodoxy: avid new interest in rigorous boundary-definition for Christian teaching. An unexpected body of Catholic-Protestant-Orthodox literature on questions of heresy and apostasy is emerging—literature that indicates we are learning how important it is to say no together on behalf of a larger yes. This trend, called by some *the recovery of ecumenical polemics* (or disputational defense), complements ongoing efforts at *ecumenical irenics* (or peace-making). The new interest in polemics amounts to a retrieval and relearning of once-available critical skills.

Relativism has run its course. Who would have guessed only a few years ago that issues surrounding the definition of heresy would be a major concern of third-millennium religious life?

THE RECOVERY OF CHARITABLE ADMONITION

Serious truth claims require clear denials. Classic Christianity cannot be rightly affirmed without specifying what those affirmations necessarily rule out. To affirm honestly is also to negate; to make claims implies a disclaimer of contrary assertions.

Therefore, orthodox polemics and irenics, with their opposing goals of conflict and peace, stand in an intrinsically complementary relation. Though both are essential to the health of orthodoxy, the latter overwhelmed the former in recent decades. The polemic task was lost for a time in cheap accommodation that made no denials or negations. Now, though, the era of sentimental hypertoleration is fading: the faithful are again willing to speak out in negating terms as circumstances dictate and the Spirit leads.

Even as the church continues to carry out its important irenic task, investigating how diverse expressions of apostolic teaching can be accommodated to the one faith in the one revealed God. Yet it now sees the importance of the polemic task: distinguishing and resisting false teaching. This new interest in thoughtful, targeted ecumenical polemics (in the classic sense, as a sister discipline to irenics) is prompting careful analysis of ancient heretical movements—an analysis that also addresses how such movements recur today, and why and how they must be answered. After many decades of intimidation, Christians are relearning how to draw needed boundaries.

Among articulate writers in this arena, Harold O. J. Brown and Bishop C. Fitzsimmons Allison best exemplify the new orthodox courage. Among Catholic expressions of this habit of mind are Germaine Grisez, Tom Weinandy, Walter Kasper, Joseph Ratzinger, Eleanore Stump, Michael Novak, James Hitchcock, Robert George, Russell Hittinger, Paul Mankowski, Alistair MacIntyre, and George W. Rutler. Among the more astute Protestant practitioners of ecumenical polemics are Robert Jenson, Stanley Hauerwas, Phillip E. Johnson, David Wells, Donald Carson, R. C. Sproul, Os Guinness, Ronald Nash, William L. Craig, Hugh Ross, David Yeago, J. P. Moreland, John Woodbridge, Gary Habermas, and J. P. Moreland. Among Anglicans we find J. I. Packer, Alister McGrath, Vinay Samuel, and Ephraim Radner. Although Orthodox writers tend more natively toward irenics, their most able polemic writers are found today in Patrick Henry Reardon and James Kushiner.

These writers are making a serious effort to reset the boundaries between orthodoxy and heresy. I will argue that this growing critical competence is a constructive dimension of orthodox intellectual vitality, though it is certainly unwelcome in the eyes of hypertolerationists.

In Season and Out of Season

Every battle line against false teaching needs bold and persuasive argument. But this argument itself must be grounded firmly in a charitable irenic spirit that understands where the center lies. In other words, irenics must accompany polemics at every stage. Both feeding and trimming are required to tend the vineyard of the faithful. Pulling out weeds by the roots helps healthy vines take root. Without gentle, critical polemics, irenic efforts are weak and tepid. Without an irenic center, the polemic edge quickly becomes belligerent and prone to hubris.

Irenic argument searches for consensus. Polemic argument points out *dissensus*—the differences that lie beyond the borders of ecumenical consent.

Irenic teaching celebrates what lies peacefully inside the borders of faith. Polemic teaching identifies those assertions that lie regrettably outside the historical consensus.

The modern love affair with relativism and permissiveness has made it easier to blur lines than draw lines, to conciliate than to defend the truth against subtle attack. While peace-making is the normal, native, and continuing task of classic Christian teaching, there are times when defense is required. Unfortunately, the children of toleration are ill prepared for reasoned argument and charitable disagreement with those who have plundered and undermined the classic faith. They are much more inclined to friendly superficial gestures.

Learning to Say a Gentle No on Behalf of a Greater Yes

It is only when the faithful have the courage to say no that yea-saying has plausibility and moral force. Only when Daniel was willing to say no to idolatry in Babylon were the captive people given hope. Not until Athanasius unambiguously challenged Arius did the church's faith become clearly defined. Only when Luther nailed his Ninety-Five Theses to the Wittenberg door did a reformation of medieval abuses begin. Not until the Confessing Church in Nazi Germany boldly rejected the specific idolatries of German Christians did their witness became credible in the Barmen Declaration. The yes to the truth of God does not happen without a tough no to false opposition.

Similarly in modern Judaism, not until Solomon Schechter opposed uncritical Jewish accommodation to modernity did historical Jewish learning find its identity in America. Not until Martin Buber resisted secular individualism was the new personalism of the kibbutz born. Not until Israel Friedlaender said no to Jewish timidity did Israel begin to become a modern nation.

The advice of hypertolerationists to Athanasius and Luther and the Confessing Church and Friedlaender would seem to be: "Back off! Ease up. Be more empathic with the Arians, the indulgence sellers, and the Nazis. Consider them in relation to their social challenges and their psychological histories. Don't forget their good intentions." The faithful answer, "No way. Never again."

Speaking Truth in Love

To those we love who are on the edge of temptation, we owe the duty of admonition. To admonish with meekness is a gift of the Spirit.

Wherever religious leadership has languished in a syndrome of apostatizing, the faithful center must answer clearly and confidently (always in meekness and charity), well instructed by the ancient ecumenical consensus. Where the hearts of duly ordained leaders have turned away to idolatry, permissiveness, absolute relativism, or vague syncretism, they must be met with forbearance and then in due time confronted with patience, civil discourse, and the determination to teach.

We must speak the truth with love amid false hopes. Modern excesses will be corrected only by courageous love, candor, and charitable admonition. Today we continue to hear of many such excesses—for example, rash liturgical experimentation and neo-pagan mockeries of holy communion. These excesses require candor—blatant disavowals of faith can be left ambiguous only at the cost of seared conscience and bad faith—but the candor must be grounded in gentleness and mercy.

The most conspicuous recent prototype of idolatry is Sophia worship, which goes hand in hand with the pagan wiccan (witch) movement. When the goddess Sophia is reified as a feminist deity distinguishable from the triune God, the faithful must be clear in saying no. When wiccan covens pray to goddesses and seek to make witchcraft acceptable within ordained ministry, the faithful laity must speak out in protest. The boundary here rests not on political considerations but on the scriptural command for truth-telling and against idolatry. Such idolatry has no place within the bounds of Christian worship. The worshiping community cannot, under the pretense of toleration, sanction the false implication that the salvation accomplished once for all on the cross is just one among many salvations, or that Christ's tortuous death has no decisive meaning for all humanity. The confession of God Almighty demands a repudiation of those teachings that claim that God cannot be distinguished from creation, that God is ignorant of the future, or that God is finally as limited as we humans are.

Honing a Critical Orthodoxy
Before heresy can be identified, we must be clear about what it is that truth-telling requires.

Christian Truth as Grounding for Christian Unity
Christian unity springs from Christian truth. Unity eludes us when we dodge the truth. Orthodoxy requires the clear rejection of every half-truth. It requires a discerning critical spirit. It can flourish only through constant vigilance precisely at those points where faith is being falsely charged or distorted or intimidated. It listens for points where scripture is being superficially quoted, where false teachers "feigning faith" offer "something like a deadly drug with honeyed wine."[1]

When idolatry sings the same hymns in the same pews, wearing the guise of Christian legitimacy, the sorting task becomes more difficult. Many come to church regularly, kneel at the Lord's table, hear the preached Word, and even receive salaries to provide leadership, yet have not learned the church's most simple and generally received consensual teachings: the triune God, the incarnation, the atonement, the resurrection, and the indwelling of the Spirit. The community of faith cries out for critical discernment wherever heterodoxy has become culturally fused and enmeshed with classic Christian teaching. This requires historical and sociological awareness heightened by careful study of the frequent counterfeits to faith.

Both healthy and polluted fish are caught in the same net of evangelization. But the situation is different in the case of ordained ministers who are specifically set aside to protect the community from toxic teachings, yet they cannot smell the difference. This jeopardizes the center of the integrity of ordination.

The Fantasy of a Center Without a Circumference

It is tempting to fantasize that no boundaries are required in either moral discipline or religious community. This is the defining illusion of hypertoleration. We are mesmerized by the misconception that freedom opposes all limits, when in fact true freedom lives only within lawful limits. A community with no boundaries can neither have a liturgical center nor remain a community of worship.

A center without a circumference is just a dot, nothing more. It is the circumference that marks the boundary of the circle. To eliminate the boundary is to eliminate the circle itself. The circle of faith cannot identify its center without recognizing its perimeter.

The debate over heresy is a struggle to specify the legitimate boundaries of the worshiping community. That it is a necessary struggle is widely acknowledged: even tolerationists who rule the word *heresy* out of bounds (as if it were alien to polite discourse) are themselves asserting a boundary. Absurdly, they are implicitly acknowledging the need for boundary-definition in ruling boundary-making out of bounds!

It is only within the fantasy world of absolute toleration that the very concept of heresy has become unthinkable. Unlimited toleration is one of the controlling myths of the modern world. But there is a catch: we do not live in the modern world anymore. We live in the period following the demise of the modern. This is why we are now talking freely about heresy in a way that would have been unthinkable only a decade ago. In the passing modern world, heresy was hardly ever discussible. The word itself could be spoken only in a sotto voice, and only if it was screened through a thousand qualifiers. But in today's world, after the collapse of controlling modern ideologies, many ideas have been opened for reexamination, including the concept of heresy.

The modern period itself, like all other periods, must now stand under the critical judgment of the norms that historical orthodoxy has applied to heterodox views in other centuries. This discussion is not without its dangers, but to fail to talk about heterodoxy altogether would be far more risky.

MARKING BOUNDARIES

The ancient ecumenical tradition views the study of heresy as logically linked intrinsically with the study of orthodoxy. Heresy is what orthodoxy is *not*. Reflection on heresy is thus a necessary boundary-making function, indispensable to the worshiping community. This community has a confessional core that *without boundaries could have no definable center*—hence no existence whatsoever. How can the faithful converse about the center of faith at all without some implicit discussion of the boundaries that demarcate life around the center?

Some would prefer that the Christian tradition be endlessly plastic, flexible, malleable, with no boundaries at all. But such plasticity can be accomplished only by constantly twisting the sacred texts of the tradition, forcing interpretations, and resorting to bizarre speculations.

Meanwhile, the apostolic testimony itself remains eternally pertinent to variable human cultures. In its firmness, it retains an inwardly centered flexibility capable of correcting human folly in all times and places.

Transcending Allergic Reactions to Boundaries

Some think that to specify any boundaries at all will carry the taint (and prompt a recurrence) of abuse of state police power, smearing the church with blood and strife. Not so. The community of faith, under the guidance of the Spirit, has learned that strife and hubris are tamed and purified, not increased, by stating clearly and accurately where the boundaries lie.

Yet some cannot entertain the thought of boundary-definition without immediately rehearsing the most flagrant examples of the loss of civil liberties. The Spanish Inquisition remains the defining example of the dangerous extremes conjured by the very word *heresy*. Modern upwardly mobile people, with all their guarantees of civil liberties, wildly imagine that they will be again subjected to some new potential "inquisition" if the H-word is even mentioned. But the Spanish inquisitors had state power behind them, while classic Christians worshiping within democracy exercise no unilateral coercive power—and desire none. Wherever misguided church leaders confuse coercive political power with faith, they cease being grounded in the meekness of the orthodox way.

Rather than fixate on the civil abuses of the *last* five centuries, with that period's tortured witch-hunts, the community of believers today is returning to the *first* five centuries of flourishing ecumenical consensus. That consensus, much of it cast and molded amid conflict and even persecution, marks clear boundaries between belief and unbelief. Those boundaries still function to distinguish between what Christianity is and what it is not. We disdain them at our peril.

Guardians of the deposit of faith are legitimately concerned when boundaries of faith become so permeable and diffused that they all but disappear. Never are we completely exempt from the temptation once again to embrace the ancient heresies, especially when they reappear under the guise of newness and creativity.

REGAINING EQUILIBRIUM

The need to mark clear boundaries is easily recognizable in childcare, education, and sexuality, but these limits are harder to mark in religion. Now, though, as more and more people are searching for boundary-definition in Christian teaching, the historical meaning and dynamics of heresy are being reexamined.

Heresy Classically Defined

The root meaning of *heresy* is "arbitrary self-willing." The Greek root *hairesis* derives from the metaphor of arbitrary choice. The self-chooser wills to stand against authenticated, settled truth, opting for independent, arbitrary self-willing "other than" *(heteran)* or contrary to the settled historical reasoning confirmed by the intergenerational community of believers.

Hairesis presumes that it is improving upon the apostolic testimony. It defiantly chooses a path thought to be better than that of the apostles. Marcion, Montanus, Praxeus, Arius, and the Donatists all sincerely believed that they had discovered a better way.

Hilary of Poitiers distinguished heresy from consensual teaching in this way: "For there have risen many who have given to the plain words of holy Writ some arbitrary interpretation of their own. This they prefer to its true and particular sense"—namely, that sense celebrated consensually by the mind of the believing community under the guidance of the Spirit. "Heresy lies in the sense assigned [by *hairesis*, by arbitrary interpretations], not in the word written. The guilt is that of the expositor, not of the text."[2]

The Disequilibrium of Mistaking the Part for the Whole

If heresy is a persistent disequilibrium or loss of balance in walking according to the wholeness of faith, sound Christian teaching seeks a good balance in walking that path. Believers are gradually regaining the equilibrium of the ancients, temporarily lost amid the excesses of recent decades.

Heresy chooses willfully to depart from the internal cohesion and fine dialectical balance of classic Christian teaching. Because heresy asserts severed, segmented fragments of religious truth in disconnection or imbalance, it lacks the wholeness, composure, and equanimity of the New Testament faith. It carves and slices the wholeness of faith into parts and then chooses or discards elements based on its own private preferences. These fragments are often so disconnected that they lose all affinity with the wholeness of ancient Christian teaching. In isolation they become unrecognizable.

Heresy can thrive only where some legitimate dimension of faith is elevated out of proportion. Asserted asymmetrically, that dimension loses equilibrium and proposes itself as a new principle of interpretation for "correcting" the whole pattern of Christian teaching. This results in the denial of the unity and proportionality found in classic ecumenical Christianity.

Orthodox proportionality has been tested by generations. Its balance emerges in scripture study through detailed comparison of prophetic and apostolic testimonies and through scrupulous comparison of scripture with scripture.

Think of a delicately designed brocade tablecloth, its design spanning the whole cloth. Clearly, cutting the fabric into pieces would distort the wholeness of the design. So it is with Christian thought. In heresy the innovator fixates on one piece of the whole pattern of Christian truth and cuts it out of the whole. This distorts the larger subtle design of the ancient catholic faith.

Think of the power, beauty, subtlety, and exquisite proportionality of a painting by Tintoretto. Suppose some self-assured critic focused on one square inch and said, "This is the decisive aspect of this portrait—the hair in the left ear." That assessment misses precisely the wholeness of the painting that makes it memorable. In the same way heresy, in making its private selection of preferred glimpses of Christianity, misses the wholeness, internal cohesion, and reasonableness of the historical consensus of faith.

The Inadvertent Providential Contribution of Heterodoxy

In every unbalanced heterodoxy, however, the Holy Spirit gives the community of faith a new opportunity to clarify once again the finer, subtler equilibrium of faith. Providence permits heresy to strengthen the community's grasp of the wholeness of faith.

Heresy has never been regarded as entirely beyond the bounds of providence. *Nothing* is. Thus classic Christian teaching looks for the providential design lying hidden within the divine permission that allows the faithful to struggle with heresy. The inadvertent contribution of heretics to the formation of orthodox consensual exegesis has caused the faithful of two millennia to marvel at God's providential working. The faithful celebrate with the fourth ecumenical council—the Council of Chalcedon (451 CE)—that the true faith is "defended with the best results, when a false opinion is condemned even by those who have followed it."[3]

As Cyprian noted, some fragment of truth always lingers even in those ideas that are falsely asserted.[4] Heresy begins with truth, after all: it is the exaggeration of some aspect of the truth into false proportion in a way that neglects the wholeness of catholic faith.

There is good reason today, as in past centuries, to reexamine the ancient heresies carefully in order to grasp anew the fragmented elements of truth that they sought awkwardly or insufficiently to bring forth, keeping in perspective their exaggerations and distortions. Within orthodoxy, heresy has been as rigorously studied over the years as orthodoxy itself. The two inquiries belong together, everywhere interfacing. When new heresies appear, usually they turn out to be the old ones reinvented. Fortunately, we have the great advantage of being able to appeal to orthodoxy's historical memory. Without this historical awareness, the contemporary community of believers would be left defenseless.

Schism, Apostasy, and Heresy

Wherever heresy has led to a breach of unity in the community of believers, that breach is called *schism*. This word may signify either strife within the community or, more particularly, separation from it.

The rebirth of orthodoxy is *not* schismatic. The orthodoxy of today ceaselessly works for the reunion of the divided body of Christ on the basis of ancient ecumenical teaching. Though the dissenting tradition of Protestantism often resorted to asserting its orthodoxy by schism, such an approach appears more out of place in the current environment of a new ecumenism. The rebirth of orthodoxy must not add to further divisions within the whole body.

Apostasy is different from schism. Historically, it refers to a (generally massive) falling away from the apostolic truth consensually received. Apostasy is most disturbing when asserted by ordained ministers who have been voluntarily commissioned and have solemnly covenanted to defend the faith, yet openly oppose classic Christian teaching.

The lay membership of mainstream Protestantism is far from apostate, as you will see if you join the average congregation in singing the hymns of the church, celebrating the eucharist, engaging in a life of prayer, and doing charitable acts. These faithful believers are not apostate, though they sometimes wonder if their leaders are. As the laity watch much of the leadership of mainline Protestantism succumbing to wild experimentation and counter-ecumenical (and even schismatic) impulses, they are puzzled. They know that views are being asserted at the leadership level that run counter to ancient ecumenical Christianity, and they do not understand why. This is the irony: the clergy betray their promises to the laity—the people most vulnerable to being hurt—when they fail to guard the integrity of Christian teaching.

The Letter to the Hebrews anticipated both this falling away and its remedy, asserting that we need "someone to teach [us] the elementary truths of God's word all over again."[5] The more erased the boundaries of faith, the greater the need for gentle admonition and doctrinal precision.

The Culture's Revulsion Against Permissiveness

There is a quiet revulsion against permissiveness. There is a whiff of commonsense recognition of the comic vulnerability of absolute relativism.

The rediscovery of legitimate boundaries to faith is becoming a central feature of the rebirth of Jewish and Christian moral life, which has so long been deprived of having legitimized space for boundary questions. Classic Christianity and Judaism are increasingly gaining the courage to ask what the church or synagogue looks like when it becomes accountable to its sacred texts. Religion cannot befriend absolute relativism. Exaggerated egalitarianism imperils the Jewish and Christian search for truth.

Rebounding from the Default of Ordained Leadership

During the last four decades many men and women ordained and remunerated to guard the Christian faith have failed to do so, either because they have not known how or because they have not understood why. Imagining themselves to be "creative" or "prophetic," they have followed a new path and lost the ability to articulate the orthodox consensus.

How far should those who mock the creed be left uncontested—or even applauded or further remunerated? Should church bureaucracies and boards of ministry and seminaries continue with impunity to employ and promote those who ignore the most elementary Christian teachings on the authority of scripture, the divinity of Christ, and the sanctity of marriage? It is painful even to have to ask these questions, but ask we must.

That certain leaders of the church have been unable to discipline themselves is due to the overindulgence and permissiveness of modernity's religion. In recent years sacred ministry has often been reduced, with higher ecclesial blessing, to political strategy to wanton desturction of tradition (or worse), whether in a diocese or a parish. The church is learning only belatedly how to admonish and discipline and speak the truth in love, calling to account clergy who are seeking liberation *from*, rather than *within*, classic Christianity.

It is the laity who are learning this lesson best. Ordained ministers commissioned to teach faithfully out of the apostolic tradition who publicly declare themselves to be agnostics, pantheists, pagans, or pedophiles are no longer being left unchallenged by their congregations. When unfaithful clergy in high positions of religious leadership are protected by colleagues and by due processes that they themselves finessed, the faithful laity are seeking alternative solutions. When other remedies have been exhausted, they often resort to withholding funds.

The problem of unfaithful clergy extends to our seminaries as well. Candidates for ordination often come to their education strongly motivated to study the self-disclosure of God according to scripture. (I have seen them come and go through the years. This is my world.) These ordinands are often surprised to find themselves steered away from scripture toward tendentious gender studies, nihilistic deconstruction, uninhibited liturgical experimentation, the ubiquitous (and speculative) historical criticism, and counterproductive psychotherapies. The fair-minded know that this must and will end. But by what means? By now the end is clear—reform of ministry—but the means are uncertain.

The ordination process itself has been corrupted—sexually, politically, and spiritually. The more it resists correction, the more it begs either disrespect or comic ridicule. Who surveils the surveillors, after all? This is the dilemma that the faithful are now gaining the determination to address. We see abundant signs of the rebirth of orthodoxy, but not enough has yet happened to override tenure administration, trustee negligence, and sexual abuse in our religious institutions.

When faithful laity become powerless to effect the reform of education for ministry, a profound crisis arises. When historical doctrinal standards are debunked, when tenure rules prevent redress, new remedies are required. The absence of such remedies explains why confessing and renewing movements have arisen throughout mainline Protestantism.

The Renewed Engagement of the Laity in Guarding Christian Education

It is supremely ironic that today's laity are becoming the mentors of today's clergy. It is the clergy into whose hands lay believers have solemnly entrusted themselves and their faith. And yet, when the clergy have fallen further away from faith than the laity, the laity are now taking the lead.

Those who fund ordination education have a legitimate interest in ensuring the clergy's apostolic guardianship role—something that the clergy itself rightly ought to have ensured, of course (and that the clergy have *promised* to ensure). The laity have discovered that they cannot allow the clergy to be seduced by fad after fad. Those to whom ordination has been entrusted have voluntarily given up their right to teach conjectures that defy settled Christian doctrine, and they must be held to that.

Lay trustees at religious institutions are now demanding an accounting. With their help, the support structure is being eroded out from under "cloned" faculties that persistently exclude evangelicals, the orthodox, and liturgical traditionalists. Clergy education can no longer remain aloof from engagement with believing, supporting lay constituencies. Its professors can no longer be presumed to have unlimited license to teach anything they please under the sullied banner of academic freedom. When all boundary issues are indiscriminately wrapped in the incontestable flag of academic freedom, academic freedom loses its moral high ground. The faithful laity recognize this; they understand that they have a decisive interest in the quality of the ordained ministries that they are asked to trust as apostolic, holy, and catholic.

TEN

Recentering the Mainline

A much more visible arena of evidence of the rebirth of orthodoxy is found where it might be least expected: in the liberal Protestant mainline churches. Just at a time when evangelicals and Eastern Orthodox Christians seem to have given up on the mainline, the mainline churches themselves are crying out for recovery of their orthodox and evangelical roots. Scratch the surface of any mainline church congregation and you will find believers who hunger for a return to classic Christianity.

This is far from a reversion to introverted denominationalism, although it is occurring within the old denominational territories. Rather, it is a startling rediscovery of the ancient ecumenical center, once prized, then almost lost, but now being actively reclaimed by Presbyterians, Methodists, Episcopalians, Lutherans, and others. These denominations who for a half-century have championed modern bureaucratic ecumenism are now turning to ancient ecumenism.

RECLAIMING LAPSED INSTITUTIONS
Typically in North America, the label "mainline" refers to member churches of the World and National Councils of Churches. Among the clergy of these mainline churches, classic Christian teaching has been too often overshadowed by theological experimentation and egalitarian idealism. A careful look at the journals of these mainline denominations makes this all too clear. The evidence in these in-house publications of boards and agencies is that these church bureaucracies have offered the mainline churches an unsupervised

playground for experimentation in political messianism, utopianism, sexual liberation, and anti-market economics.

I speak particularly and penitently of my own tradition, the United Methodist Church, whose lobbies, agencies, and activists, despite their pious Wesleyan history, have been leading supporters of zany causes. Similar experimentation is found among the liberal bureaucracies of the Presbyterian Church USA, the United Church of Canada, the United Church of Christ, the Disciples of Christ, the Evangelical Lutheran Church in America, and the Episcopal Church USA.

Each of these mainline communions has suffered a four-decade slide in vitality, membership, and social witness. But recently, promisingly, within each there has emerged an active movement aimed at the renewal of classic Christian teaching. These reform groups include the Confessing Movement Within the United Methodist Church, the Confessing Churches Movement of the Presbyterian Church USA, the Presbyterian Lay Committee, Disciples for Renewal, the Center for Catholic and Evangelical Theology, Good News Heritage Fellowship, and three reform movements within the United Church of Canada.

These scripture-centered accountability movements are gaining rapid momentum. Their journals thrive as their voices grow more confident of being heard. They have registered unexpected legislative victories in the national assemblies of their parent bodies. The expectation is increasing that they will *reform* the decaying mainline. Together they are often called *the confessing movement,* focused on rightly confessing the ancient faith, or *renewing movements,* focused on reclaiming the institutions of the faith confessed. These are distinguishable but complementary movements.

The Moral Crisis Facing the Mainline

Can the loyal remnant within the mainline churches cope with ongoing temptations to walk away and abandon the struggle? Can those who hold steadfastly to classic Christian teaching find strength to challenge the long dominance of doctrinal latitudinarians who want the church to be all things to all people? These questions are being contested at a thousand different levels in every mainline local church, regional office, and legislative assembly.

A massive moral crisis now faces the defensive mainline leadership, its lobbyists, its academic institutions, its public relations offices, and its bureaucracies. A common vision shared by evangelicals, orthodox (both uppercase and lowercase), moderates, and traditionalists is gradually taking shape: the repossession of those church institutions that have fallen into forgetfulness. Orthodox voices are exercising increasing influence within denominations previously written off as incurably permissive.

Many evangelicals and Catholics who do not view themselves as being in any way connected, even sentimentally, to the North American mainline, are nonetheless involved in analogous battles being fought in varied worshiping communities on all continents. I only wish to signal, in an effort to hearten the faithful wherever they serve, what a great work God the Spirit is doing within these churches.

Can classic Christians and confessors of apostolic faith in the mainline churches cooperatively form a plausible accord that effectively resists the apostatizing temptations endemic within the unregenerate mainline? Can they unite with a trustworthy and viable agenda for reclaiming the community of faith to doctrinal integrity? Can they set a trajectory that will neither slide toward heterodoxy and imprudence, nor turn inwardly toward resentment and reactionary defensiveness? The battle line lies just here.

Information Sources on Renewing and Confessing Movements Within the Mainline

The evidence for the growing influence of orthodox and evangelical voices within the mainline is seen in the breadth and variety of renewing and confessing movements within churches ordinarily regarded as liberal or doctrinally latitudinarian. Such movements have a broad and snowballing presence among the member churches of the National Council of Churches. They are increasing because of needs unmet by the elite central organizations. Only a few year ago they were almost invisible. Now they are ubiquitous and expanding.

Every one of these denominations (Lutheran, Episcopal, Methodist, etc.) has actively working within it at least two or three, and in some cases more than a dozen, movements dedicated to renewing theological and moral integrity and biblical regrounding. This distribution and vitality can easily be grasped by simply reviewing the following roster of confessing movements, renewing organizations, and publications within the mainline churches. (Additional information about publications and websites is given in the endnotes.)

Episcopalian Confessing Movements. Among Episcopalians the influence of the American Anglican Council is growing. This council publishes the journal *encompass* "to fulfill the Great Commission through mission, proclaim the Biblical and Orthodox faith, [and] transform the Episcopal Church from within."[1] Episcopalians United produces an online report called *Anglican Voice.*[2] Scholarly Engagement with Anglican Doctrine (SEAD)[3] brings together leading orthodox theologians of the Anglican (and other) traditions for major conferences on classic Christian teaching. The signers and supporters of the Baltimore Declaration[4] and the contributors to Mission and Ministry[5] are to be numbered among renewing influences in the Episcopal Church USA, along with the South American Mission Society (SAMS) and the National Organization of Episcopalians for Life (NOEL), which publishes *NOELNews.*[6]

The largest grassroots movements are found among Presbyterians and Methodists. These movements were considered pariah organizations only a few years ago, but by now they have gained substantial influence in their recovering denominations, winning major yet still inconclusive legislative, judicial, and constitutional victories.

Presbyterian Confessing Movements. Among the Presbyterians, the Presbyterian Lay Committee sends *The Presbyterian Layman* to almost a half-million people, urging that "official church bodies refrain from issuing pronouncements or taking actions unless the authority to speak and act is Biblical, the competence of the church body has been established, and all viewpoints have been considered."[7] In less than a year over twelve hundred Presbyterian churches have joined the fledgling Confessing Church Movement to affirm that "Jesus Christ alone is Lord of all and the way of salvation; Holy Scripture is the triune God's revealed Word, the Church's only infallible rule of faith and practice; God's people are called to holiness in all aspects of life. This includes honoring the sanctity of marriage between a man and a woman, the only relationship within which sexual activity is appropriate."[8] Presbyterians for Faith, Family, and Ministry seeks "to restore the strength and integrity of the PC(USA)'s witness to Jesus Christ as the only Lord and Savior," publishing splendid articles in *Theology Matters.*[9] The group Presbyterians for Renewal publishes *reNEWS.*[10] Presbyterians Pro-Life publishes *Presbyterians Pro-Life News.*[11] Presbyterian Action for Faith and Freedom publishes *Presbyterian Action Briefing.*[12] All these in only one denominational tradition, but largely cohesive in their measured critique of the Louisville bureaucracy!

United Methodist Confessing Movements. The Confessing Movement Within the United Methodist Church began with one hundred and three church leaders in 1994 and now has a constituency of over six hundred thousand, including over three thousand Confessing Churches, publishing *We Confess.* "Confessing Jesus Christ as Son, Savior, and Lord, the Confessing Movement exists to enable the United Methodist Church to retrieve its classical doctrinal identity, and to live it out as disciples of Jesus Christ."[13]

The senior renewing movement within United Methodism for over a quarter-century is Good News, A Forum for Scriptural Christianity Within the United Methodist Church, publishing *Good News: The Magazine for United Methodist Renewal,* with over thirty-five thousand subscribers.[14] That group's work is complemented by the Renew Network, for the renewal of United Methodist Women, publishing the *Renew Newsletter;*[15] the Taskforce of United Methodists on Abortion and Sexuality, the pro-life witness in the UMC, publishing *Lifewatch;*[16] Bristol House, publishing *We Believe* and other biblical curriculum materials for the renewing and confessing churches;[17] and the Mission Society for United Methodists,[18] which sends witness and service missionaries to areas neglected by the General Board of Global Ministry. Several of these organizations joined together to form a coalition called Decision 2000 at the Cleveland General Conference at the turn of the century. (The outcomes of that conference, reflecting the influence of the Decision 2000 coalition, are reported later in this chapter.) Other participating organizations included United Methodist Action, publishing *UMAction Briefing;*[19] and Transforming Congregations, a ministry "to all persons affected by relational brokenness, resulting in sexual sin."[20]

The scholarly society of the John Wesley Fellows seeks to support and bring together young evangelical scholars in the United Methodist Church for integrity in theological education, publishing *Catalyst.*[21] The United Methodist Renewal Generation publishes *Josiah Journal.*[22] The Coalition for United Methodist Accountability (CUMA) focuses on judicial challenges and questions of the administration of discipline and church law within the United Methodist Church.[23] Aldersgate Renewal Ministries holds large annual meetings of Methodists.[24] The group Concerned Methodists publishes *The Christian Methodist.*[25] The Methodist Laity Reform Movement publishes a newsletter.[26]

Among the most beleaguered denominations, burdened with faltering and diluted theological leadership and the fastest rates of membership decline, are the United Church of Christ, the Disciples of Christ (Christian Churches), and the American Baptists. To counter this decline, all these have active renewing movements:

United Church of Christ Confessing Movements. In the United Church of Christ (UCC), arguably the most liberal of the mainline denominations, there are the proactive orthodox advocacy efforts of the Biblical Witness Fellowship, "a confessing church movement in the United Church of Christ," publishing *The Witness.*[27] There is also Focus Renewal Ministries;[28] the Mission Renewal Network, "mobilizing missions among Churches serving Christ in the Evangelical, Reformed and Congregational Christian Heritage";[29] and Confessing Christ,[30] composed chiefly of UCC theologians and pastors. The Renewal Fellowship of the UCC is "a transdenominational association of evangelicals building on the biblical roots of the Reformed, Congregational, Evangelical and Christian heritages," publishing *Renewal Life*.[31] Advancing Churches in Mission is "a movement committed to awakening and equipping the local church for accomplishing God's global purpose."[32] All of these groups are working proactively to regenerate and renew the United Church of Christ.

Disciples of Christ Confessing Movements. Disciples Renewal and its partner organization, Disciples Heritage Fellowship, form "a fellowship of believers from Christian Churches, from the Campbell-Stone Heritage working for change and reform in the Christian Church (Disciples of Christ)," providing resources for a growing network of Disciple Renewal Covenant Churches; they publish *Disciple Renewal*.[33]

American Baptist Confessing Movements. Among American Baptists are the American Baptist Evangelicals, committed "to serve the renewal of American Baptist churches by building partnerships to serve, connect, nurture, and grow healthy congregations,"[34] and American Baptist Friends of Life.[35]

United Church of Canada Confessing Movements. The United Church of Canada is viewed by its own renewing groups as a basket case of dysfunction, arrogance, and coercion against evangelicals. Seeking correctives are the Community of Concern of the United Church of Canada;[36] National Alliance of Covenanting Congregations of the United Church of Canada, "upholding historic Christian faith and traditional Christian morality";[37] Church Alive, of the United Church of Canada;[38] the Evangelical Fellowship of Canada, "committed to bringing Christians together for greater impact in mission, ministry and witness," publishing *Faith Today*.[39] *Fellowship Magazine*[40] is co-sponsored by the Community of Concern of the United Church of Canada, Church Alive, and National Alliance of Covenanting Congregations of the United Church of Canada. Despite their minority status, the nationwide meetings of these groups garner large numbers of energetic lay and clergy participants at huge rallies.

Lutheran Confessing Movements. Among Lutherans[41] there is a significant variety of movements, not all of which share the same views on questions of polity and church order, but which are basically committed to a deepening of classic Christian teaching within the liberalizing Lutheran tradition. They include the American Lutheran Publicity Bureau, publishing *Lutheran Forum;*[42] the Great Commission Network of the Evangelical Lutheran Church in America, publishing *Networking Together,* calling for "a renewed commitment to Biblical and confessional authority";[43] the Fellowship of Confessional Lutherans;[44] Lutheran Renewal;[45] the Center for Catholic and

Evangelical Theology, publishing *Pro Ecclesia;*[46] Lutherans for Life; the Word Alone Network;[47] and a new online service called Kairos News.[48]

Coordinating the Confessing Movements. The Association for Church Renewal (ACR) brings together and coordinates the work of executive directors of renewing and confessing movements in North America[49] committed to "classic, orthodox Christianity." Composed of more than forty executive officers and leaders from more than thirty renewing and confessing movements within mainline Protestantism, it is the sponsor of the first-ever gathering of evangelical, confessing, and renewing Christians in the mainline churches of North America, which in 2002 joined many of the grassroots participants in organizations listed above for the first time. It has formed the Confessing Theologians Commission of the Association for Church Renewal, "to advise the renewing and confessing movements in mainline churches on biblical, theological and moral issues and concerns."[50] The mainline evangelicals are very loosely linked with the National Association of Evangelicals (NAE) through the Association for Church Renewal, which is a member of NAE.[51]

The Institute of Religion and Democracy, publishing *Faith and Freedom,* coordinates in cooperation with ACR several renewing ministries within mainline churches[52] and sponsors the Ecumenical Coalition on Women and Society. The wonderful Fellowship of St. James publishes *Touchstone,* a magazine of "mere Christianity."[53] In addition to these there are a number of special ministries serving the mainline, such as Alpha North America;[54] Prayer Summit;[55] *The Just Cause,* an online newsletter;[56] and *Regeneration,* a model for youth ministries in renewing congregations.[57] The Center for Theological Inquiry at Princeton has sponsored major consultations of ecumenical theologians from mainline and other church traditions. The Alliance of Confessing Evangelicals serves confessing movements partly within but largely apart from (even over against) the mainline churches, but concerned with the renewal of Reformed teaching. It is the publisher of *Modern Reformation* and sponsor of Reformed Theology Conferences and the fascinating radio program, *The White Horse Inn.* These outlets provide "a forum for confessional theologians to discuss the possibilities, strategies, and proposals for a vigorous initiative in relating orthodoxy to contemporary challenges and opportunities."[58]

What do we learn from this remarkable roster?

- Every mainline denomination has not one but many renewal organizations seeking to strengthen classic Christian teaching.

- Most renewal groups publish newsletters or journals as well as occasional white papers and studies of subjects often neglected in publications of the denominational bureaucracy.

- Investigative and free advocacy journalism is alive and well within the mainline churches. Because most of these movements do not get funds from their own denominational headquarters, they are free to critique denominational policies in ways that in-house, centrally controlled publications ordinarily cannot.

- The websites listed in the endnotes continually post current data, activities, and articles pertaining to renewing and confessing movements. The response of the NCC and mainline bureaucracies has been largely to ignore and dismiss this vast and growing network of confessional initiatives.

MARKING THE CENTER

How is the recovery of classic Christianity within mainline Protestant denominations an evidence of the rebirth of orthodoxy? In this section I will take one denomination, the United Methodists, as a case in point.

How the Traditional Coalition Is Reshaping the Mainline: A Case Study

A stone's throw from the Cleveland football stadium, the United Methodist Church General Conference convened in May of 2000. Church representatives met to engage in their quadrennial showdown of legislative and media battles. Near the Rock and Roll Hall of Fame, the Civic Center rocked with inflamed rhetoric outside the assembly, but within the legislative process a new spirit of doctrinal and moral conservatism rolled in.

Legislating within the huge mainline churches encompasses a vast, complex, and messy democratic process, with many voices at the table. The record of this particular conference offers a brief glimpse into the struggle within *all* branches of the mainline. The evangelicals, orthodox, and traditionalists can take heart from what happened in Cleveland, as these fifteen actions illustrate:

- The conference acted to require evangelism in the curriculum for ministerial ordination. Furthermore, it obliged curriculum planners, lay speakers, and candidates for ministry to follow Wesleyan evangelical doctrinal standards.

- It defeated radical feminist attempts to impose nontrinitarian language on the liturgy.

- It affirmed Jesus as only Lord and Savior of the world against efforts to legitimize the doctrine of universal salvation as if it were a standard Christian teaching.

- It resisted an attempt to dilute confessional membership vows for professing members.

- To prevent regional legislative bodies from defying the church's long-established sexuality standards, it affirmed that regional annual conferences cannot nullify the Book of Discipline.

- The conference received a declaratory decision from the Judicial Council upholding the Book of Discipline as the law of the church, so that regional "covenant" experiments cannot take precedence over churchwide law (as liberal bishop Melvin Talbert had maintained in a disciplinary case where charges were dismissed against sixty-seven clergy who participated in a blessing of a "same-sex union").

- The conference defeated an attempt to create a new layer of world Methodist bureaucracies. It mandated a policy to limit bureaucratic stockpiling of unrestricted reserves—stockpiling intended to make the denomination less accountable to the will of the laity in stewardship.

- It permitted annual conferences to distinguish relief giving from conference benevolences, so as to acknowledge greater respect for the conscience of the laity in stewardship decisions (in the context of bureaucracies that have had a history of spending general church gifts for ideologically unacceptable purposes).

- Talk of a church split was decisively avoided by the reaffirmation (by increasing majorities) of the church's traditional teaching on sexual "fidelity in marriage and celibacy in singleness." The conference resisted persistent challenges to allow the blessing of homosexual unions. It firmly retained language declaring that "homosexuality is incompatible with Christian teaching," defined "practices incompatible with Christian teaching" as "chargeable" offenses, and added the prohibition of performing same-sex unions to the "duties of the pastor." While affirming evangelical reparative therapy and transforming ministries to homosexuals, it defeated proposals to require the hiring of homosexuals in church positions and to require church-sponsored Scout troops to accept homosexual leaders. Homosexual advocates experienced the conference as a major setback, with charge after charge being decisively defeated.

• For the first time, the United Methodist Church voted to seek observer status in the National Association of Evangelicals and the World Evangelical Fellowship.

• For the first time, it opposed partial-birth abortion by a vote of 622 to 275, in contrast to its adamant pro-choice stance of previous years. For the first time, the conference officially supported voluntary prayer in public schools and an International Day of Prayer for the persecuted church.

• For the first time, 40 percent of the delegates voted for redefining the formula for distributing the twenty-million-dollar seminary funding scheme, showing a large measure of dissatisfaction with current seminary curricula and faculties. (Seminary accountability will become a growing issue for future general conferences.)

• The conference showed surprisingly strong support, though insufficient for a majority, for an Evangelical Missionary Conference in the West as a haven for evangelical churches marginalized by liberal leadership.

• The conference revised delegate representation to reflect growth in traditionalist areas in the South and South-Central Jurisdictions and in the Central (overseas) Conferences, ensuring a stronger evangelical vote in future general conferences and fewer delegates for the predominantly liberal western states.

• The Conference elected three evangelicals to the increasingly important nine-member Judicial Council.

These fifteen actions illustrate an important point: after years of attempts, Cleveland 2000 marked a year of unexpected victories by orthodox voices within the United Methodist Church. These gains came largely as a result of a preceding and continuing network of prayer, a coalition of numerous renewing and confessing movements working closely together, and widespread demoralization among the old-guard liberals. These may seem like modest gains, but they are among the first evidences of the growing ability of the orthodox center to effect basic change in mainline churches.

A similar story could be told of the turnaround in the Presbyterian Church (USA), led especially by the Confessing Church Movement and *The Presbyterian Lay Committee*. While Episcopalian, American Baptist, and other communions' successes are less sweeping, each denomination shows signs of growing orthodox legislative effectiveness. The contests will continue.

Emerging Evangelical Leadership in the Mainline

It is a profound embarrassment to liberal leadership that during its hegemony, the seminaries, and the bureaucracies, the churches have lost ground in a massive membership hemorrhage. Liberals go into a cold sweat trying to explain how, while they owned the infrastructure, the money, the publications, and the leadership, they failed even to hold membership steady. They still nurture the fantasy that they have the high moral ground on sexuality issues, politically correct policing, and standard liberal theological issues such as universal salvation. The liberal leadership is now faced with the desperate dilemma of trying to secure trust and support from its ever-diminishing numbers of constituents.

Evangelicals view scripture as the norm of faith and life, with a stress upon the believer's experience of a personal relationship with Jesus as Lord and Savior, the only Son of God, and the Holy Spirit as enabler of a world-wide mission of proclamation. They maintain a biblical doctrine of the incarnation, atonement, and the Lord's return. They focus on personal conversion and the witness of the Spirit, and they place a high priority on evangelism. An evangelical Christian is one who reads the Bible as God's Word, who lives out of a personal relationship with Jesus Christ as the only Lord and Savior, who is saved by grace through faith active in love, and who has a lively commitment to the Great Commission.

Evangelicals are now in a determined struggle to recover endowments, libraries, and institutions that have been virtually lost for four decades. (Almost half a century of opportunities for advancement of the gospel wasted!) Ironically, evangelicals have been cast as pariahs within the mainline. The exclusion and marginalization of this sizable constituency—the faithful evangelical minority—has been attempted by those who often imagine themselves as inclusive, tolerant, generous, and liberal.

Why Remain Faithful to an Apostatizing Church?

Many free church evangelicals rank liberal mainline struggles very low on their list of matters of importance. They say: So what? Why don't orthodox believers just walk away from a church long locked in secularizing ideologies?

The renewing and confessing movements are growing firmer in their answer: The mainline is a sleeping giant still capable of recovering its earlier history of evangelical witness and leadership. Its institutions are worth recovering and cannot easily be replicated. Much will be lost by their almost total collapse, as we have seen in the United Church of Canada.

Those involved in confessing and renewing movements within the mainline see the church's present dilemmas in a very long historical perspective, not merely in relation to the next petty legislative battle. They look not simply to a quadrennium or decade, but to twenty centuries of *consensus fidelium*. They hold as a model the courageous evangelical Anglicans of the nineteenth and twentieth centuries, who remained faithful over many decades until they at long last gained significant voice within worldwide Anglican counsels, as seen in Lambeth 1998.[59] Mainline evangelicals have reason to think that they can reclaim their captive institutions, as have Anglican evangelicals in significant ways. They have good reason to ask other orthodox believers to pray for their efforts to reground the mainline in the gospel, to transcend the secularizing and liberalizing temptations of the last half-century.

Confessing movements within the Protestant mainline have potentially major repercussions for the future of both Catholic and Orthodox traditions, as well as for the future ecumenical vision. A deepened, chastened, penitent conversation is taking shape between those mainline evangelicals and those Catholic and Orthodox believers who are learning from our mistakes and excesses. Alongside this there is an emerging dialogue between Reformed evangelicals and Anglican-Wesleyan-Holiness tradition evangelicals, who are learning how much they have missed by not listening to each other for 250 years.

Countering Schism

Underlying these rather general responses to the question of why faithful believers in mainline churches are called to remain within their conflicted communions to renew and reground them lie specific, well-reasoned arguments:

We are sternly warned by scripture against schism. We dare not further divide the church, which has suffered enough already under the divisiveness of false teachers and ideological advocates who presume to speak for the future of Christianity.

None of us heard the gospel apart from the community of believers who transmitted it to us. To quit contending for the faith is to hold cheap our baptismal vow, which ties us to the larger body of faith. To leave our communion tempts us toward a despairing act of voluntary abandonment of communities and institutions to which our forefathers and foremothers gave blood, sweat, prayers, and tears, and through which the apostolic teaching has been transmitted.

We in the confessing movements do not deny that a sincere believer may leave a faltering church or denomination for good cause, but to leave one structure is to embrace another—and that second structure may have similar limitations or worse. Furthermore, to quit is to leave behind mounting problems that will *never* be solved unless the faithful are willing to roll up their sleeves and help. The churches need loyal and steady critics more than purists or loners or deserters.

The faithful in our communions have remained voiceless long enough. They stand in need of articulate argument and wise, coordinated strategic action to counter waywardness.

Though I respect and empathize with those who have found the reform of mainline communions virtually impossible, I believe that a turning point has been reached. It seems to me that the apostatizing voices in church leadership, with their weak arguments, are already aware of their approaching collapse. The Holy Spirit is working to renew the church, and we are invited to participate in the renewal. To abdicate our own historical mainline communion now would be wasteful and negligent. It would be like leaving a family in distress just at a time when a fresh start is possible.

Some worshipers, conceding the above arguments, agree to remain within the mainline communion but choose to stay out of the fray. Although it is possible to remain a faithful worshiping member of a local parish and pay no attention to the contested judicatories, people who walk away from the legislative bodies and seminaries of the church may only make things more difficult for the next generation. It is possible to ignore perverse agencies and harebrained publications, but if we do, we deepen the quagmire. The longer we wait to clean house, the harder the recovery of classic Christianity will be.

Although it is sometimes argued that the mainline churches have so fundamentally deteriorated that they are intractable and practically unreformable, the confessing movements disagree, arguing that the Holy Spirit has not given up on our local churches with their families, their roots, their histories, and their promise. Proponents of church reform believe that the Holy Spirit has called us to pray for the various communions that brought us to faith and to remain as agents of witness and reconciliation within them.

It is for all these reasons that we in the renewing and confessing movements are committed to remaining within our communions, however far they may have fallen into confusion and disobedience.

RECOVERING MISLAID ASSETS

Another evidence of the rebirth of orthodoxy in the mainline lies in an emerging determination to recover lost institutions, reclaim meandering establishments, and recoup lost assets.

Tracking the Money Trail

For over 160 years Protestant women have given monthly sums to world mission programs focused on preaching the gospel on all continents and serving others in Christ's name. My grandmother proudly wore her fifty-year pin as a longtime participant in the Methodist Women's Society of Christian Service, as did my mother. Every month these societies would meet and hear of preaching missions and relief efforts, giving generously in response. For over sixteen decades these monies have collected in the General Board of Global Ministries and its predecessor organizations.

This board, despite its anti-capitalist rhetoric, has by now garnered vast capitalist endowments. And how is it using those resources? Despite the board's anti-colonial language, it has spawned little colonies of regulatory political advocacy all over the world; despite its anti-oppression rhetoric, it has colluded with Cuban and North Korean regimes on foreign policy issues. Ironically, the only contacts the Methodist Board actively encourages with the Chinese churches are those approved by the Communist government. The same holds for Cuba, where the Castro government line has been repeatedly echoed in the literature of the mission board.

We are not talking about peanuts in these endowments: there are hundreds of millions of dollars held in reserve! The United Methodist Board of Global Ministries alone had $481,440,325 in 1998, according to the official *Daily Christian Advocate.*[60] Why do the various boards of the various denominations need these vast reserves? Self-protection, pure and simple. The religious hierarchy needs a hefty financial reserve in order to survive the years of drought that would follow, should they face a strong conservative challenge that would dismantle their patronage system. These boards want to keep enough dollars under their control to sustain several years of scarcity if necessary, so that they do not have to bother listening to those circles of local church women. They oppose designated giving (by which local churches specify where their apportionments go) for the same reason.

In the late 1960s the General Board of Global Ministries was overtaken by political activists dedicated to regulatory economics, dependency politics, and government expansionism. The official literature of this board makes clear that this now wealthy bureaucracy casts a cold eye on preaching aimed at conversion. Judging by their publications and their actions, they do not believe in conversion. They believe in treating all faiths equally, as if all paths to the truth are equally valid. This board, after years of collecting money for the preaching that it was created to do, has virtually ended its support for ministries of proclamation! Today it defines "mission" efforts largely as grant-making to social action projects.

It is easy to detect this new definition of mission in the rhetoric, programming, and publications of the board (now caught, for example, in the grip of proactivist lesbian advocacy). Local church women, however, are still asked to provide financial support, often as if preaching and conversion were still involved. Mystified by the isolation and silence of the leadership, these reluctant supporters look for explanations.

The Donor's Complaint

Orthodox believers are making this complaint about self-preserving liberal bureaucracies:

You own our seminaries, you own our boards, you have rewritten our histories, and you are now using our money for purposes we think unconscionable. Given all that, we would like to discuss the ethics of being responsible about gifts and donations received over generations.

The charge of misuse of funds is a serious one indeed, but it is a hard one to deny: millions of dollars now sit in banks, the interest reserved for projects that have nothing whatever to do with the purpose for which they were given. Critics believe that there is at least the potential of actual fraud in the administration of some of these funds, meaning that administrators, if challenged, could be found culpable under law. Orthodox believers see this financial and moral dilemma as evidence of the continuing untimely sway of a bureaucracy that has outlived its usefulness.

The orthodox faithful have seldom felt a vocation to enter into the nittygritty of legislative activism, or to organize a populist counter-movement, or to plan to elect delegates or a fair judiciary. Evangelicals have preferred to get busy with the Great Commission to make disciples all over the world, abandoning political machinations to those who are perhaps wise as serpents but considerably more harmful than doves. Recently, though, the curve of evangelical political and strategic intelligence is sharply up. This is evidence of the rebirth of orthodoxy.

Redressing Institutional Theft

When property is ripped off, its owners usually inventory precisely what has been lost and then follow a legal due process for making an accurate claim for recovery. The faithful laity are now registering such a claim. This is their

social justice issue: they are respectfully asking that specific properties be returned—gifts and endowments designated specifically for evangelical purposes, such as libraries, educational institutions, and income from invested
funds.

Religious institutions and publishing houses and mission boards and
seminaries have been seized in an unfriendly takeover by liberal church leadership—a takeover that the denominations, filled with permissive apologists
for secularization, have permitted to happen. Ironically, even when outvoted
in legislative processes, such apologists have retained their tenure and pen-
sions in church agencies and educational institutions. The longsuffering
laity know this, having watched their finest church and academic institutions erode and disappear at the hands of leaders bitterly intolerant of traditionalists. They know that nothing can be done until the faithful, both lay
and professional, first gain a new will and courage to speak the truth in love
and then work cooperatively and proactively to recover what has been lost.

There is little hint of recognition among those who have stolen the institutions that they are the least bit culpable. They shamelessly imagine themselves to be heroes—even heroes of *faith*. Among the most insidious
offenders are the liturgical experimenters, the sexual liberators, and the doctrinal revisionists who occupy lecterns and pulpits yet remain functional agnostics and deliberate agents of secular liberation. It will not be easy to tell
these unfaithful ones the truth or to break through their self-deceptions. But
this is precisely the task that faces the faithful today. Little will change until
charges are stated clearly and evidence is presented in fair hearings. Insofar
as courage is lacking to do this, the precipitous decline will worsen.

Consciousness-raising is needed among those who have benefited from
institutional theft and intellectual duplicity. These wrongdoers need to
understand precisely what damages they have inflicted on the faithful. They
need to recognize their own collusion, understand exactly what has been
stolen, and help determine how it can be justly returned to its rightful
owners: those who understand and guard the ancient ecumenical consensus of the faithful of all times.

The mainline is striving to extract itself from the desperate desire of its
erstwhile leaders to be *totally liberated from classic ecumenical Christianity*.
As a former full-time card-carrying freedom-seeker, I know from experience
how mesmerizing this fantasy can be. *Liberation* is a term these activists
apply to themselves; not a metaphor imposed upon them by others, it is
their own intentional naming of themselves.

They must now cope with a wholly unexpected situation: the decline of
modern consciousness, the collapse of modernity. They have attached

themselves to ultramodern values just at a time when those values are expiring.

The orthodox laity pray for the return of these wanderers. Having virtually no immune system against heresy, no criteria for weighing or even testing out the legitimacy of counterfeit religious currency, the faithful laity (who have too long delayed gentle admonition) must now enter the conflicted arena of rebuilding, healing, and regrounding religious governance and discipline. This rousing is slow, but it is already firmly under way. The articulate laity have come to understand that they have a decisive interest in the renewal of the institutions and ministries that they have been asked to trust.

Widowed Institutions After the Death of Modernity

The religious community that fastens itself parasitically on the latest movement in modern thought does not easily survive the collapse of that movement. When its host is dead, the parasite loses its nourishment. As modernity collapses before our eyes, those who think of themselves as most up to date are being abruptly outdated. They are the last to recognize the rebirth of orthodoxy.

What is happening amid this hazardous historical situation is a joyous return to the sacred texts of scripture and the consensual guides of the formative period of its canonization and early interpretation. These times call not merely for generating moral outrage. Rather, we are rediscovering how the Spirit is descending upon the faithful, reclaiming them to ancient faith and calling them to repossess captive institutions.

ELEVEN

Rediscovering the Classic Ecumenical Method

Having presented evidence from biography, the history of exegesis, the fairness revolution, ecumenical boundary-definition, and the recentering of the mainline, I now turn to the description of the crowning act of reconstruction. This is the most heartening evidence of the rebirth of orthodoxy: Christians are quietly relearning how to think ecumenically in classic terms.

AN AID TO REMEMBERING

The presentation of this new evidence is best begun with the telling of a story. Let me tell you about Vincent of Lérins, introduced in earlier chapters, who with his simple faith shaped the course of Christianity.

The Classic Method of Reliable Remembering

Shortly after the Council of Ephesus in 431 CE (the third ecumenical council), and sometime before 450, an obscure but well-informed Christian monk withdrew from his very active life of traveling (doing what, we do not know). He retreated to a monastery off the southern coast of France. We know him only as Vincent. He used his time in the monastery to summarize what he had learned during his travels about the classic ecumenical method for discerning the truth.

He chose, for his place of study, a quiet monastery located on the beautiful island of Lérins, off the coast of Cannes, now the playground of film stars. The monastery had been founded in 410 CE by the saintly Honorat, later bishop of Arles (d. 430, a contemporary of Augustine). Lérins soon became the liveliest center of monastic spirituality and inquiry in the West. It was as important to the future of the West as were the monasteries of Scetis in Egypt and Saba in Palestine.

Soon the tiny island of Lérins developed into a major center for ecumenical classic Christianity, for spiritual counsel, for ascetic exercise, and for East/West dialogue. There more than anywhere else the vital energies of Eastern monasticism were transmitted to the West. Its influence spread to Ireland. Key monastic leaders such as John Cassian, Honorat, Hilary of Arles, and Vincent were among those who came to this little island for spiritual rejuvenation.

It is likely that Vincent himself had some form of firsthand information regarding the process that had led up to the decisions made at the Council at Ephesus, where the complex biblical and liturgical issues of Theotokos and Nestorianism (issues focused on Mary as mother of the Incarnate God, and the relation of Christ's divine and human natures) had been debated and decided. It is not difficult to imagine that he himself had attended the council. It is entirely plausible that he knew key figures who had attended. His "act of remembrance" (or *Commonitorium,* as his major writing is known) shows every evidence of being a report on the ecumenical method that had preceded Ephesus and that had once again been tested (and had prevailed) at Ephesus.

Vincent of Lérins's Way of Consensual Recollection

While modern bureaucratic ecumenism is languishing, ancient ecumenism and its methods are being intensively studied and rediscovered. This new interest in the texts, methods, and decisions of ancient ecumenism provides the final touch of the argument for the rebirth of orthodoxy. We are witnessing a profound reexamination of how the ancient consensus was formed in the early Christian centuries, along with a growing conviction that the same method of consensuality remains viable for us today. In this final chapter I will set forth the argument of the defining primary text of ancient ecumenical method and show how it is being rediscovered and reappropriated.

The decisive classic text for orthodox ancient ecumenical method is Vincent's great *Commonitorium* (generally referred to as *Commonitory* among English speakers)—an "act of remembrance" that is still pertinent to our remembering today.[1] Vincent's brilliant analysis, conceived in the fifth century, remains the most significant text on ecumenical method of the first millennium. In that analysis he shows how scripture repeatedly reawakens the tradition-bearing community and how tradition guards scripture.

The contemporary revival of the Vincentian rule is closely interwoven with the rebirth of orthodoxy. In the pages that follow I will cautiously unpack his argument, setting forth a straightforward description of the process of consensus-recognition and orthodox tradition-transmission as understood by the ancient church.[2] The Vincentian method is being actively reappropriated and redeployed, because the *new* ecumenism is grounded in *ancient* ecumenism; the *new* irenics is based upon *classic* irenics.

When, Where, and Why Commonitory *Was Written*

The Latin title of Vincent's ecumenical exercise implies that it is a "recollection of a wanderer." Vincent himself is the wanderer, the peregrine, the soaring bird that circles high above the vast land and surveys it. Vincent identifies himself only as a traveler, a pilgrim, an outsider, a foreigner. Aside from this enigmatic signature, we know little of him except what can be inferred from his text.[3]

Vincent reveals straightaway why he is writing this study of how to discern classic Christian teaching: as an *aid to recollection*. This seasoned ecumenical itinerant sets out an aid for the proper recollection of the worldwide community of prayer. It is intended to serve both as an aid to his own memory and as a means for helping others to recollect rightly what all informed believers at that time already knew. It is addressed to anyone who wants to think intergenerationally with the whole community of believers under the authority of scripture about the apostolic testimony, resisting odd and idiosyncratic views of scripture.

Vincent appears to have in his possession a torrent of information that issued from the Council of Ephesus. He seeks to condense it into a compact, systematic statement of classic ecumenical method. He shows every evidence of having been steadily engaged in a profound dialogue with both Eastern and Western church voices during this tumultuous crisis, whose subtle decisions would reverberate for centuries through the whole Christian world.

Picture Vincent in his monastic library, with manuscripts strewn around: he seeks to discern the central intent of the mind of the believing church; he listens carefully to the varieties of cultural voices within worldwide Christianity; he attends to the broad database of evidence leading to and following from the Council of Ephesus.

All his attention now focuses on this simple question: If believers quote scripture with different meanings, who is to decide which interpretation is correct? Or more precisely: How do believers who quote and understand scripture in differing ways come to the truth of Christianity in a manner that can be ecumenically validated so as to transcend mere cultural and linguistic variables and private opinions? Let us look over the shoulder of this pilgrim as he explores this question we still face.

Vincent describes himself as having been "long involved in various unstable and saddening whirlpools of secular strife."[4] What was this secular context? The Hun tribes were threatening the peace of the church and the empire all across the northern perimeter of the Mediterranean, steadily encroaching over the Alps. The worldwide Christian community, stretching from India to Spain, struggled for some semblance of unity amid enormous historical diversity. Vincent evidently knew, all too familiarly, the secular strife of a divided world.

But now, in the sanctuary of Lérins, Vincent is standing at a distance from these whirlpools, taking ample time in a quiet place to recall accurately the complex process of ecumenical consent. Having been out there on the seas of historical struggle, he is grateful to be safely in this quiet harbor to reflect on his journeys. Amid the swirl of historical changes going on around him, Vincent seeks to account meticulously for the deliberative process by which the heart of what has been generally received as unchanging apostolic faith was defined. He feels a distinct vocation for this task of remembering accurately. By recalling the ecumenical process of weighing and defining received teaching, he hopes to prevent time from snatching away the specific contours of his memory immediately following the Council of Ephesus.

At Lérins nothing distracts Vincent. He can daily practice what is sung in the liturgy. He can be still and know that God is God. In the solitude of monastic life he can draw together the tumultuous recollections that form his vast experiential database. But as he takes pen in hand, his mind focuses not only on the integrity of his task as a historian; it focuses also—indeed, more so—on accurate remembering *in the presence of God*. It is as if his remembering process is taking place in a divine theater, with God as the audience. He sees his accuracy as having eternal consequences. He is aware not only of the dangers of shipwreck on the stormy sea, but even more so of the final judgment to come.

Behind this remembering attempt lies a crucial premise: the Holy Spirit has promised to help believers remember accurately. The Advocate (or Helper), the Holy Spirit, "whom the Father will send in my name, will teach you everything, and will call to mind all that I have told you."[5] Vincent does not view himself as a value-free, autonomous observer at work on his own, without accountability before God in the midst of a remembering community. Rather, he sees himself as actively living in a community of worship to whom his memory is strictly accountable. Therefore, he does not think of his writing as an exercise of private opinion or ecstatic vision. On the contrary, he believes that he is following a reliable spiritual process that can be objectively and dispassionately—even scientifically—observed, reported, and described. He expresses gratitude for the active help of the Holy Spirit in remembering the truth which is being reappropriated consensually in each new generation.

The Contemporary Revival of the Vincentian Method

A growing body of scholarly literature seeks in our time to explicate this ancient method and explore its undertones and consequences.[6] Fifteen hundred years after Vincent first stated his argument, it still remains the definitive expression of the orthodox ecumenical method. This methodological rediscovery is a key evidence of the rebirth of orthodoxy.

My purpose here is to set forth a concise exposition of Vincent's calm description of that process of conciliar deliberation, definition, and decision. I present this exposition not as a history that means nothing to me but as an inquiry that touches the heart of what I too believe. It describes what I have come to regard as most eminently trustworthy in scriptural testimony, for I too live within this worshiping community, as one baptized within it and willing to die for its truth.

Picture Vincent again in the monastic library, hard at work. Although writing for his own self-clarification, he is aware that this memorandum might, even inadvertently, fall into someone else's hands. So he takes special care to describe the remembered consenting process precisely. Suppose, he imagines, that his description of the ecumenical process might come into the hands of a godly person who would have an intimate primary knowledge of the councils, the apostolic tradition, and its consensual exegetes who best know the mind of the believing church—would he not want such a person to vindicate his report readily? In this task, then, he cannot be a partisan; he must accurately remember the remembering process.

Vincent is not attempting to address the general intellectual culture or the civil order in his *Commonitory,* but those who already best know the faith. Hence this is less an apologetic exercise intended to convince unbelievers than a recollection of and for believers already convinced. Vincent has no thought or pretense of teaching the faithful what they already know. Rather, he is simply trying to state accurately just how they came to know what they know, so as to warrant and obtain their wholehearted confirmation.

His account is intentionally stripped of all autobiographical references, because the rememberer is not the subject of the remembering exercise. Rather, the fixed center of his attention is what is remembered. His own opinions, inclinations, and impulses do not appear within this frame. He does not set forth his own subjective feelings about the process or his personal "reader response" to the conciliar method. Instead, he sets forth the historical church's recollection of how it gained consensus on the apostolic testimony to God's incomparable revelation.

Hence we know almost nothing of Vincent's biography. We barely know his name! Yet we walk away from his recollection with a very clear picture of the process he is describing.

How Vincent Discovered the Rule

In preparation for his quiet reflection, Vincent reveals that he has long been engaged in what we today would call an *empirical inquiry,* a careful sampling process, something like a poll-taking exercise. He has been deliberately inquiring of many believers, especially those well-grounded in sanctity, asking this simple question: How does the whole church come to distinguish the truth of Christian faith from falsehood amid conflicted opinions? He has been traveling widely and cross-culturally among dioceses, meeting with confessors, bishops, theologians, monastics, and articulate laypeople. Everywhere he has been, he has asked the faithful: Is there a reliable way to sort out wheat from chaff amid serious doctrinal disputes? Suppose I wanted to look for a reliable rule that would distinguish fraudulent expressions of faith from true faith. How would I find it?

He was astonished: virtually every believer had the same core answer! Its short form had two parts: (a) scripture and (b) the central tradition that guards scripture. But to say only that would oversimplify.

This short answer led Vincent to inquire further with believers: If we have scripture, why do we even need a continuing authoritative tradition? Is the scriptural canon itself not complete? Is it not sufficient? What more needs to be said? In other words, why do we need councils and contemporary Christian teachers if we have scripture?

Answer: All agree on which scriptural texts apply. That has been well established in the scriptural canon,[7] the list of writings recognized East and West as fit for reading in worship. But not everyone fully concurs on what canonical scripture as a whole conclusively *teaches.* Key areas of disagreement remain on the particular interpretations of many sacred texts, and on plausible ambiguities within and among those texts. If Valerius reads a particular text one way, Arius another, and Eunomius, Sabellius, and Pelagius in other ways, how can we know who comes closest to the truth of that text?

Vincent concludes that the trend of the interpretation of the prophetic and apostolic texts must be understood in accordance with some general rule—a rule plausible cross-culturally to the church universal as to what constitutes the mind of the believing church.

But what is that rule? Again the answer rings clear from all whom he asks—an answer that has become known as the Vincentian rule: *In the world-wide community of believers every care should be taken to hold fast to what has been believed everywhere, always, and by all.* Its Latin form reads: *Quod ubique, quod semper, quod ab omnibus creditum est.*[8] This short answer comes from the hearts of virtually everyone Vincent interviews. It is not a rule that Vincent *invents*, then, but one that he acknowledges was widely understood long before his inquiry. He seeks only to articulate the rule accurately.

Everywhere, Always, and By All

Classic Christian teaching holds fast to what has been believed and consented to around the world by Christians of all times and places. Individuals who likewise hold fast to that consensual belief can rest assured that they are following orthodox faith. Three Latin words—*ubique, semper, omnibus* (everywhere, always, by all)—sum up the ancient ecumenical method of scriptural discernment. Thus the direction and momentum of orthodox interpretation are guided by a process of fair-minded historical inquiry, aided by the Holy Spirit, into what has been believed in all cultures where faith has been lived out, and believed from the beginning of the apostolic witness, and believed by general lay consent in the whole church over the whole world in all generations.

We may summarize these three criteria as *universality, apostolic antiquity,* and *conciliar consent.* To be trustworthy in accordance with these criteria, any assertion of faith must

Be the same faith that the church confesses the world over

Be the same faith confessed by the apostles

Survive testing by cross-cultural generations of general lay consent through a trustworthy process of conciliar agreement

If an assertion passes these three tests, it may be said to express the mind of the believing church, and thus can be accepted as trustworthy. If an assertion fails any of these tests, it cannot be confidently termed classic Christianity (though it may still be open to ecumenical debate).

As we weigh the many conflicting assertions that claim to be Christian in today's world, we can examine their reliability by asking the same three questions:

1. *Universality.* Does this opinion echo out of a particular locale, or is it shared generally by the whole community of believers around the world?

2. *Apostolic antiquity.* Is this claim something new, or is it grounded in ancient intergenerationally received faith?

3. *Conciliar consent.* Has this teaching been confirmed by an ecumenical council or by the broad consensus of the ancient Christian writers? Do we have a documentary tradition of the consenting laity generally affirming it? Has it been duly expressed through the liturgy and prayers of the church?

Hence truth-telling within Christianity takes place within three arenas: a *spaceframe,* a *timeframe,* and a *fairly ordered consenting process.* It has a cross-cultural sociology and geography—*everywhere!* It moves through all times following the ancient apostolic witnesses—*always!* It is constantly being tested out by a fair-minded, comparative, deliberative process under contrary challenge—by *all the faithful* (not clergy alone, but laity as well)!

The Vincentian rule is presented graphically in Table 3. Anyone who discovers agreement at all three levels depicted there—spatial consent, temporal consent, and fair deliberative consent in the face of challenge—can be assured of reliable ecumenical truth.

TABLE 3:
THE THREE ARENAS OF CHRISTIAN TRUTH-TELLING

Everywhere	*Always*	*By All*
Cross-cultural space	Intergenerational time	Fair deliberative process
Universality	Apostolic antiquity	Conciliar consent

Does the consent needed at the three levels shown in Table 3 require absolute unanimity? No. The respondents to Vincent's inquiry did not absurdly insist that all consent must be plenary or perfect; they did agree, however, that it must be reasonably firm. It is seldom (if ever!) possible within any historical process to obtain an absolute, hundred-percent vote, nor is it required. Every important question has been contested. But here only those scriptural interpretations that have most influentially adjudicated are here under examination. Vincent is looking practically for the center of an orthodox method of reflection, especially in the case of issues whose veracity has been decisively debated. He seeks not an absolute or unanimous perfectionism, then, but a reliable reverberation of the symphony of faith.

Can we, using these three criteria, summarize briefly and surely what Christians believe? The answer to this must emerge clearly from general lay consent, having been confirmed intergenerationally. This we already have in what we today call the Apostles' Creed (the ancient baptismal rule of faith learned upon entry into the believing community). That creed sufficiently expresses the same ancient ecumenical faith into which all Christians have been baptized. Its triune structure substantively corresponds to the same *credo* as the Nicene-Constantinopolitan Creed and the Quiqunque Vult (sometimes called the Athanasian Creed). These are the three creeds that have enjoyed the widest ecumenical consent over the longest period of time across the broadest span of geography.

To answer in greater detail why Christians believe what they believe requires a larger database of historical information, beyond this baptismal summary, as to how the Holy Spirit has led the community of believers into general consent. Vincent is poised to describe that larger pool of information.

While all Christians have access to this summary of baptismal faith (and closely analogous forms of it), not every lay believer has the time or interest to investigate its history and related texts systematically as a historian. Each believer is assured of the trustworthiness of the core memory of the meaning of baptism, but not everyone has the opportunity or inclination to analyze why the general lay consent has become so enduring and firm.

Vincent renders a service to ordinary believers in the worshiping community by attempting to account for the continuity and authenticity of their common worship of God revealed in scripture. He does this by examining case studies of historical crises, showing how issues have actually been resolved using the clear criteria of the ecumenical rule.

FOUR DECISIVE CRISES OF CONFIDENCE IN GENERAL CONSENT

The consenting community has undergone a series of major crises of confidence in the process of testing the authenticity of tradition-transmission. Vincent explores four of these as decisive model cases—each beginning with "What if?" Each reveals the providential path by which the faithful have gained confidence in the consenting process. These four specific challenges, each of which threatened breakdown in the consenting process, have brought the truth of Christianity into greater clarity and general consent. The conclusion reached by consensus in each case can now be commended as reliable teaching to the worshiping community (now and in the future).

Vincent's four crises of confidence are logically related questions that together exhaust most challenges: What if a part rejects the whole? (The faithful applied *ubique*.) What if a "new gospel" is preferred to the apostolic faith?

(The faithful applied *semper.*) What if the ancient witnesses themselves might be wrong? (The faithful applied *ad omnibus* and conciliar consent.) What if no conciliar precedent is defined? (The faithful again applied a refined form of conciliar consent.)

1. What If a Part Rejects the Whole?

The first crisis of confidence is a disruptive scenario: What if some few members break away from the communion of the previously received faith? This crisis emerges when an idiosyncratic, particular regional minority voice rejects the cross-cultural, worldwide orthodox consensus that has emerged under the guidance of the Spirit.

If scattered, isolated contemporary members abandon the historical faith, the ecumenical remedy is clear and straightforward: the faithful appeal to the coherence and "rationality of the body universal instead of the blighted idiosyncrasies of the corrupt member[s]."[9] In other words, the soundness of the body universal ought rightly to hold against the variability and fragility of a few.

Christian teaching under that first challenge prefers the universal to the particular, the classic to the eccentric, the whole to the part. Orthodox faith looks to the cross-cultural, intergenerational community of believers for validation rather than to a few individual voices, to alleged private revelations, or to bizarre egocentric reasoning. Built into classic Christian thinking is a consensual principle that anticipates later democratic forms that would point toward approximate political consensuality.

There can be no true consent if the consent achieved is not *global.* Regional consent is not *ecumenical* consent. Insofar as possible, orthodox teaching must be shown to be received and owned worldwide by the worshiping community. Having once been so shown, the consensus does not need to be forever retested, however.

Suppose, while claiming to stand in the apostolic tradition, I put together a small caucus or regional group that claims to represent better "apostolic teaching" than that previously held in cross-cultural Christian communities everywhere. Suppose I further claim that I have a particular interpretation of key scriptural teaching which supersedes even that which has been universally accepted. How would the orthodox way respond to that challenge? It would fairly compare the proposed view with what general Christian consensual teaching has most broadly concluded. Universality is an objective, testable criterion. It requires comparison of the proposed local view against judgments shared by the whole historical community of experience.

In countering such a claim to "improved" faith, it is appropriate first to refer to scripture itself. But if the interpretation of scripture is then contested, or if one canonical text is pitted against another, these "regional" views may be tested against the whole body of classic Christian consent that addresses the pertinent text. Orthodoxy thus provides a counter-individualistic criterion: the universal, historical, community memory stands more reliably than the partial, regional, ecstatic, or individualistic memory.

Does this imply that no local or regional or individualistic scholarship can ever be orthodox? No. It means that local views that inveigh against the consensual memory must be tested against that memory.

This is the first criterion that has to do with cross-cultural consent. It applies a geographical, *spatial* metaphor to the question of truth: Is the assertion in question believed *everywhere*?

The second criterion is different. It has to do with *time*: Has the assertion *always* been believed?

2. What If a "New Gospel" Is Preferred to the Apostolic Faith?

The second scenario is all too familiar to the faithful: What if a new and contrary teaching pretends to supersede the received gospel, the canon of apostolic testimony? What if some contemporary members, perhaps even in huge numbers, have abandoned the historically received recollection and are asserting contemporary opinion as if it were historical faith? Or consider the scenario's worst-case expression: What if even the *majority* of the worldwide Christian community in a given period has temporarily broken away from the historical apostolic faith?

Orthodoxy confidently answers all these queries in Vincent's voice: "Then, one will endeavor to adhere to the voice of antiquity, which is evidently beyond the danger of being seduced by the deceit of some novelty."[10]

This second level of crisis emerges when a new branch of the vine falls temporarily into degeneration. In that event, the believing community does not have merely the first level of appeal: to believers everywhere *(ubique)*. It also has the second level of appeal: to antiquity *(semper)*, the ancient apostolic faith which obviously precedes and regulates the newer proposal. Orthodoxy argues not only from cross-cultural experience (universality), but also from intergenerational experience (faith shared over time from antiquity). Thus this is a very different criterion from the first.

This criterion applies even when the vast number of believers wrongly consent to temporary error. Against any emergent voices, even those claiming to be a majority, orthodoxy still can appeal to antiquity, because antiquity is beyond contamination from contemporary distortion.

Athanasius used the appeal to antiquity, drawing on pre-Nicene formulations in response to the Arians. Augustine made a similar appeal to Paul against the Pelagians and Donatists. Luther (like Augustine) appealed to Paul against late-medieval scholastic misreadings of the relation of grace and freedom. They believed, as the orthodox faithful have always believed, that even if bandwagon theologians are enamored for a time with some alleged "death of god" or some cult of the "new age" or some such thing, that does not change one iota the continuity of classic Christian teaching.

We might say that apostolicity trumps contemporaneity. Only a dozen apostolic votes of duly elected original eyewitnesses to revelation easily override a gazillion opinions of those who were not eyewitnesses to revelation, no matter how well intended their thinking.

Does this imply that no new scholarship can be orthodox? No. It means only that any new scholarship claiming fidelity to the apostolic tradition must be tested by the texts of the written Word and by the historical memory of the meaning of the written Word.

The distinction between Vincent's first and second criteria was fleshed out centuries later in the political arena. In subsequent democratic theory a great debate emerged between those who focus democratic representation on *constituency* and those who focus it on *conscience*. In preparing for a vote on the floor, ought the legislator weigh constituency numbers or listen to his or her own conscience? The first criterion of classic Christian teaching is more akin to constituency than conscience, while the second is more akin to conscience than constituency (assuming that apostolic teaching guides conscience). The genius of ecumenical method is the tension and equilibrium between these criteria.

In Christian teaching the "constituency" is never merely a *contemporary* group. The pertinent community is the whole historical community of believers who have given voluntary consent to living in Christ according to apostolic teaching. Hence when a novel idea of Christianity arises, it must accord with ancient apostolic teaching. If consistent, it can fit in under the larger orthodox umbrella. If not, it is subject to assessment under the criterion of apostolic antiquity.[11]

3. What If Ancient Witnesses Themselves Might Be Wrong?

Now we come to a harder case, the third scenario, which is very pertinent to our present secular situation: What if the ancient intergenerational faith itself, and even the criterion of antiquity, comes into question? Suppose its claims are argued as unreliable or outmoded: How can apostolic antiquity remain a reliable criterion if apostolic antiquity itself is charged with being unjust or stupid or wrong? What if a new teaching claims to supersede entirely the alleged truthfulness of the old faith?

If antiquity itself is challenged, or if an error is detected in an otherwise trusted ancient consensual writer, then we must refer the issue to a conciliar process—typically that of an ecumenical council—to settle the matter fairly in accordance with the unity of the faithful in all times and places. The conciliar process must look diligently for what is consistent with apostolic teaching as generally received cross-culturally and intergenerationally. If searchers can find this third level, they have identified classic Christian teaching. If an Arian Christology should arise today, it is an easy matter to compare its assertions with conciliar consent: Arianism has been once for all ecumenically rejected.

Suppose someone comes along and says with a straight face, "The sacred text itself errs. Look how unjustly it colludes with slavery and the oppression of women!" Suppose the prophets and apostles themselves not only disagreed among themselves, but also erred substantially on crucial points, whether morally or reasonably or with faulty memory. What if it is claimed that the transmitted text itself is spurious or untrustworthy? In that case orthodoxy appeals to an entirely different principle that completes and amplifies both universality and apostolic antiquity. This third criterion is a textually tested combination of the first two criteria applied in history by means of *conciliar consent*. But remember that the concept of conciliar consent makes no sense at all without the premise that the Holy Spirit is guiding that consent.

Take an argument such as the premise of Elisabeth Schüssler Fiorenza's *In Memory of Her: A Feminist Theological Reconstruction of Christian Origins* (NY: Crossroad, 1983), (which is that scripture confirms modern feminist arguments). She argues from supposed deep antiquity—in fact, from what she conceives to be the earliest layer of *oral, prewritten* tradition. Yet her argument arises from speculations about the oral tradition informed heavily by contemporary ideological premises prone to tendentious, instrumental use. Result: her interpretations of the early oral tradition turn out to sound exactly like modern feminists. Sounds like a very recent question: Is it legitimate to appeal, as form criticism often does, to an unwritten oral tradition as more apostolic than the written tradition? The answer, of course, is no.

How would an orthodox perspective evaluate proposals of this sort? It would compare each assertion with written apostolic testimony, in the light of intergenerational consensual exegesis of the apostolic testimony.

To recapitulate these first three crises in light of Vincent's criteria of universality, apostolic antiquity, and general intergenerational lay consent documented by conciliar action:

1. If some isolated contemporary members abandon the historical, universally received worldwide faith, you prefer the universal to the particular.

2. Even if the whole community of believers for a certain period of time seems to go astray in a new culture with a new idea unfamiliar to the apostles, you appeal to antiquity above innovation.

3. If the reliability of apostolic testimony itself is questioned, you appeal to ecumenical conciliar precedent by looking at conciliar decisions and canons, where almost everything important has been already debated.

Any believer may freely question the authenticity of a supposed inauthentic Christian tradition. That is done by submitting the historical evidence and awaiting the confirmation of general ecumenical consent. If that consent is not forthcoming or is unclear, however, then Vincent's first three criteria need to be supplemented by a fourth, which we now consider. (The fourth, actually a subcategory of the third, might better be viewed as "3b.")

4. What If No Conciliar Precedent Is Defined?

Now we come to a fourth scenario, a variation of the third. What if a contested case arises in which arguably no council has ever acted upon the particular question at issue? If there is no cross-cultural, intergenerationally received conciliar act or document to which to appeal, how could we settle such a case (short of seeking to call an ecumenical council)? What if an alleged truth claims to be apostolic but has never been adjudicated as such by fair conciliar process?

This brings us to the more complicated fourth scenario described by Vincent. In most cases, as he pointed out, an issue can be settled on the basis of the first three criteria. The fourth criterion offers a more discriminating level of appeal: if after you have pursued the three previous criteria uncertainty remains, then you interrogate the prevailing opinions of *the most reliable consensual teachers of the ancient Christian tradition*, who have lived in various periods and at different places but have nevertheless remained in communion with the broadest consensus of the one worldwide, transgenerational community of faith. This criterion of the ecumenical exegetes, which amounts to an extension of the third criterion of general consent, focuses on commentary on key scriptural texts under dispute.

In appealing to the ecumenical exegetes, we are still seeking what we have sought all along: consensuality—the Spirit-led voice of the one holy catholic and apostolic community of believers. Thus we should interrogate not just contemporaries, as would Schleiermacher, but also (and especially) those classic teachers who best span the bridge between the apostles and all later generations, over a long chronological plane, and the widest possible geographical frame—in short, those most generally received, East and West, in the furthest range of time and space by the *communio sanctorum.*

But how do we identify those interpreters most frequently and persistently received ecumenically, who have held and taught what has generally been received as the mind of the believing church? Should we treat the question numerically, counting the number of quotations that have been most widely distributed geographically in the whole transgenerational Christian community? However intriguing that might seem to those accustomed to quantification, it is not the way of orthodoxy. That would be less reliable than the way the Holy Spirit has in fact led the consenting community of faith to unity and consensus through an actually lived history.

The Consensual Exegetes

As a matter of fact, the conciliar process has already identified its most consensual interpreters. They are frequently specified in the documents of the ecumenical councils and in subsequent decretals (authorized collections of papal decrees). They are at least eight fathers most often referenced: four great "doctors" of the East (Athanasius, Basil, Gregory of Nazianzus, and John Chrysostom) and four great "doctors" of the West (Ambrose, Augustine, Jerome, and Gregory the Great). Virtually all who have thought seriously about any ecumenical question would include these "doctors of the church" in the effort to identify classic consensus on questions not decided by official conciliar actions.

Classic Christian teaching listens most often and most intently to these eight voices. Because it perceives them as most generally received by the whole church for the longest period of time, it sees them as trustworthy interpreters of the apostles.[12] These are teachers of scripture whose names have been widely respected not for a few decades but throughout almost three-fourths of the history of Christianity. They are widely attested as best representing the broadest consent of the believers of all cultures and periods in rightly discerning Christian truth.

This is not merely *my* opinion, mind you. It is a documentable fact that these eight great doctors have been more widely received (through both space and time) than any others as perennially reliable consensus-bearers.[13] That does not imply that they possessed infallible judgment and never made a misstep. In fact, they themselves warned against making that assumption. Still, they have been on virtually everyone's list of ecumenical teachers through the ages.

The tradition of identifying key ecumenical teachers established itself early. By 495 CE the Gelasian decretal commended to all as consensual teaching not only the canons of Nicea, Ephesus, and Chalcedon "to be received *after* those of the Old or New Testament, which we regularly accept. Likewise the works of blessed Caecilius Cyprian . . . *and in the same way* the works of Gregory Nazianzen, Basil, Athanasius, John Chrysostom, Theophilus, Cyril of Alexandria, Hilary, Ambrose, Augustine, Jerome and Prosper."[14] The fifth ecumenical council—the Council of Constantinople II, in 553—urged believers to "hold fast to the decrees of the four councils, and in every way follow the holy Fathers, Athanasius, Hilary, Basil, Gregory the Theologian, Gregory of Nyssa, Ambrose, Theophilus, John Chrysostom of Constantinople, Cyril, Augustine, Proclus, Leo and their writings on the true faith."[15] Earlier the Council of Ephesus had also cited four leading bishops of Alexandria as generally recognized reliable witnesses.[16]

There are many others who speak in the same voice as these reliable consensual teachers, but none that is more generally acknowledged to have rarely led the laity astray. Minimally these eight are consensually reliable voices, expressing the mind of the believing church. Excepting Gregory the Great, who came later, all these were writing just after the earliest ecumenical councils had winnowed away much chaff, when the early vitality of the church of martyrdom had not waned, and when the disciplined spirit was still vital. We listen to them because the more we know scripture, the more we realize that they understood well and early just how the consenting community should read and compare the texts of scripture.

If the faithful discover again and again certain exegetes who displayed the best habits of mind, the highest competencies, and the greatest faithfulness, would it not be self-evident that those exegetes should be especially trusted? This is what the laity in fact has discovered about Athanasius, Basil, Gregory of Nazianzus, John Chrysostom, Ambrose, Augustine, Jerome, and Gregory the Great. Orthodoxy has learned not to be afraid of any of these voices. It has learned to listen trustingly to all, hearing them in a complementary pattern so that each might benefit from the critique of the others.

In summary, then, there are four filters through which to sift Christian truth-claims—four strata of referees, if you will:

1. The universal prevails over the particular (the whole is preferred to the part).

2. The older apostolic witness prevails over the newer alleged general consent.

3. Conciliar actions and decisions prevail over faith-claims as yet untested by conciliar acts.

4. Where no conciliar rule avails, the most reliable consensual ancient authorities prevail over those less consensual over the generations.

Covering the Nakedness of Noah

Vincent presents another case study revealing the deepening complexity of assessing consensuality:[17]

Suppose that in promoting theological innovation we discover that some well-respected ancient Christian author inadvertently advocated a wild or unconscionable nonconsensual view. Suppose we then argue in favor of that ancient innovation on the basis of its being held by that esteemed early author, even if not by the larger community of believers.

This supposition ostensibly appeals to antiquity, but functionally it is a disingenuous appeal to individuality and novelty. This academic game is all the rage these days. Some people take ignoble delight in using secular legalism to first expose an "embarrassment" in Christian history and then propound their proposed remedy for the misstep as a kind of "reform"—as if it were an "achievement" of revolutionary proportions. They might quote an obscure passage from an established figure—a passage that by the standards of modernist chauvinism would be seen as excessive or embarrassing to the author.

Vincent, in his case study, asked how orthodox rememberers might prudently deal with such a maneuver. He then used a striking metaphor to show the orthodox way. Those who practice this evasion are like those who desecrate the remains of holy venerated persons, he said. They defame in public what ought to remain wrapped in silence. Vincent then examined the biblical prototype of this deception. These people are like Ham, he said—Ham, who *failed to cover the nakedness of Noah*, who held Noah (his father) up to ridicule: "And Ham, the father of Canaan, saw the nakedness of his father, and told his two brothers outside. Then Shem and Japheth took a garment, laid it upon both their shoulders, and walked backward and covered the nakedness of their father."[18] Ham typifies a tendency of heretical self-assertion: it dearly loves to expose the nakedness of the father, while faith would cover that nakedness.

Vincent countered what later would become a psychoanalytic preoccupation: exposing the nakedness of the saint. Embedded in his fifth-century analysis we find a penetrating critique of what we today call *criticism*. The critical approach often cynically demeans and dismisses religious texts or persons by showing their partiality, vested social interests, or unseemly motivations. The critic then becomes the master of the text, presuming to know more about it than the author ever did or could.

Vincent regarded this attitude as a violation of filial piety: he likened it to usurping authority and scattering the ashes of the fathers. He believed that when someone fails to cover the nakedness of a good man, or the unintended vulnerability of the ancient trusted writer, the orthodox way calls us to respond with the opposite affection: it seeks to cover the nakedness, foreswearing the voyeurism of seeing saints trip or martyrs stumble.

Suppose the object of criticism is a respected teacher such as Clement of Alexandria or Eusebius, both godly men in their time. Yet each had certain special obstacles and challenges that the fault-finding critic would never understand or want to empathize with. In responding to these challenges, they displayed character flaws that led to subsequent misinterpretation. This nakedness we can either gaze upon, as did Ham, or cover up, as did the brothers of Ham. When the saints and fathers are accused of unintentional or sporadic misdemeanors (which may in fact have emerged out of laudable actions or intents), how will we choose to respond?

The orthodox disposition is to not hold up to ridicule the apostle Paul for not overtly opposing the view of slavery that prevailed universally in his time, since he was thoroughly engaged in something far greater that was redeeming slavery from the heart: proclaiming the gospel. If James does not expressly state justification by faith, but does so only implicitly, the tendency of Ham would be to gaze upon that nakedness. Orthodox sympathies, on the other hand, would give the apostles the benefit of the doubt, reading James in the light of Paul, and vice versa.

THE APOSTOLIC MODEL OF ORTHODOX REMEMBERING

After addressing the four crises of confidence in consensuality detailed above, Vincent asks whether there is a biblical prototype for right remembering of the truth of Christianity. He shows, in the *Commonitory*, that right remembering has been a concern of the apostolic tradition from the outset. He points especially to the key model of the orthodox way of interpreting scripture: the apostle Paul himself.[19] He demonstrates that the apostolic way of remembering is not a method that emerged incrementally generations after Paul. Rather, it was clearly and repeatedly articulated in the Pauline letters themselves.

The Apostle Paul as the Prototype Rememberer

As Vincent points out, Paul showed, in his many writings, that the gospel moves from culture to culture without changing. The gospel addresses all audiences (via various languages) with the same truth. It flows within a huge, continuous wave of historical flux but does not itself change. It enters freely into new language structures, but in doing so it remains faithful to the same word as that received through revelation. John Henry Newman translated as follows Vincent's metaphor of development, that Vincent saw prototypically in Paul: "Let the soul's religion imitate the law of the body, which, as years go on, develops indeed and opens out its due proportions, and yet remains identically what it was. Small are a baby's limbs, a youth's are larger, yet they are the same."[20]

The gospel as Paul told it was not bound to a single or particular cultural context. On the contrary, his mission was to show the gospel's universal relevance. And he was successful: his letters have circulated among all the churches in the known world, wherever the gospel has been preached, in each subsequent generation. Paul was right: the apostolic teaching is not reducible to a particular, culturally relativistic premise; it is offered to *all* cultures and remains intrinsically transgenerational.

Paul's remarks were clearly not addressed merely to a single, particular congregation. In Colossians, for example, Paul gives greetings to the "brothers and sisters in Laodicea, and to Nympha and the church in her house. *And when this letter has been read among you, have it read also in the church of the Laodiceans, and see that you read also the letter from Laodicea.*"[21] Because Paul clearly assumes that his letters will be passed from church to church, we cannot reduce his arguments to instructions intended only for one setting regarding one particular crisis.

Thus when Paul, in Galatians 1:6–7, attacks those who have deserted to another gospel, following their own desires, he is speaking to the whole worshiping community; when he warns against turning away from the truth that the Galatians originally received, and against forgetting their loyalty to the tradition they had heard preached from the outset, he is aiming for a broader audience.

Paul speaks of the gospel *we* first preached, meaning the shared confession, the common faith of the worshiping community, the first faith received from apostolic testimony, including his own, received through revelation. If someone should preach an idea contrary to that which *we* have received, he says—even if it seems to come from an angel—if it goes against the gospel you first heard, do not trust it.[22] Against the frogs, gnats, and dayflies who imagine that they have a new and improved interpretation better than the received tradition, Paul exhorts his readers to hold fast to the gospel "we preached to you," and not "a gospel contrary to that which you received."[23] Vincent thought of his ecumenical method as merely another way of stating Paul's intent in Galatians 1:8–9.

The purity of the gospel is obviously of central concern to Paul. He writes to Timothy and Titus, warning them not to make void their first faith[24] and cautioning them against defiant dissenters who preach "contrary to the doctrine which you learned."[25] Innovators will cause the shipwreck of faith[26] (he tells them), subverting whole houses for filthy lucre's sake,[27] confusing gain with godliness,[28] infecting the body with diseases that spread like cancer.[29] These innovators are busybodies who go from house to house blabbering about what would be better left unsaid,[30] causing dissension and offense, always chasing after the latest fad, while never attaining knowledge of the truth.[31]

The Spirit Guides Remembering

Those individualistic Christians who steer intuitively by the seat of their pants, without classic standards, cannot avoid eventual review under due process by those who remember accurately the classic standards. Every generation is subject to being reminded when necessary where the center is.[32]

Only right remembering can remedy our persistent tendency toward self-righteousness. Since believers as well as unbelievers remain tempted to sin, we all may tend toward what Vincent calls an "insatiable lust for error."[33] Our sinful nature is "possessed by a permanent desire to change religion, to add something and to take something away."[34]

But through the guidance of the Holy Spirit, the apostles remembered events accurately and transmitted them reliably in the written Word. The faithful can entirely trust the received apostolic teaching that emerges out of that memory. The Christian community is not merely a human institution that needs constantly to be protected by human guarantees of justice. It stands under the protection of God the Spirit, who helps the faithful to remember rightly. The one who pushes through a hedge— that is, deviates from the cleared path—is more likely to get bitten by a snake, as we are told in Ecclesiastes.[35]

In 1 Timothy 6:20, Paul urges Timothy to avoid an excessive interest in "the profane novelties of words."[36] Paul's words strike like a hammer: Keep away from empty discussions. Avoid futile phrases. Shun novelty (which is fleeting) in favor of apostolic truth (which is enduring). Avoid the contradictions of supposed knowledge elites (gnostics) who, though professing faith, have fallen into error. These innovators, as Paul's warning reminds us today, promise a great deal but deliver little of durable value.

Paul warns against novelty peddlers who claim to know the truth but are ignorant. These tempters, Proverbs tells us, are like a harlot who, though seductive, wreaks havoc. She "sits at the door of her house, on a seat at the high places of the town, calling to those who pass by, who are going straight on their way, 'You who are simple, turn in here!' And to those without sense she says, 'Stolen water is sweet, and bread eaten in secret is pleasant.' But they do not know that the dead are there, that her guests are in the depths of Sheol."[37]

Why Promptness Is Required in Admonition

In another case study Vincent focuses on the need for promptness in response to unbalanced heterodox challenges. The Arian persecution taught the community of believers this correlation: that "the more devout a person is, the more prompt he is to oppose innovations."[38]

The case that Vincent recalls for us is that of Stephen of Rome, in which Bishop Agrippinus of Carthage had wrongly asserted, contrary to orthodox memory and earlier received ecumenical practice, that rebaptism was permitted. Before Agrippinus the clear rule had been that anyone baptized in the name of the Father, Son, and Spirit need not be baptized again. Agrippinus decided that baptism by heretics was invalid, even if carried out in the triune name, and decreed that people whose baptizers were shown to be unfaithful needed to be rebaptized.

The superior to whom Agrippinus reported was Stephen of Rome, head of the apostolic see. Stephen could have opted to do nothing about Agrippinus's novel practice. Instead, against the advice of colleagues, Stephen promptly contested the innovation, viewing it as a challenge to the apostolic tradition he was pledged to uphold. To protect the intergenerational cohesion of the people of God, Stephen countered, "Everything [should] be transferred to the sons in the same spirit of faith in which it was accepted by the fathers; . . . religion should not lead us whither we want to go, . . . (rather) we must follow whither it leads; . . . it is proper to Christian modesty and earnestness not to transfer to posterity one's own ideas, but to preserve those received from one's ancestors."[39]

Two insights are confirmed in this incident. First, Stephen was transferring to Agrippinus the precise tradition he and all before him had received from the apostles, and that tradition was understood in the same spirit in which it had been received; it had not been tampered with or violated. Second, recollection does not require our embroidery, for we do not transfer our own ideas, but the ideas and the language preserved by the blood of the apostles, martyrs, and confessors.

When an unprecedented claim on such an important subject as baptism stands in direct contrast to the previous consensual memory, it has to be rejected promptly and firmly.[40] Stephen of Rome is commended by Vincent especially for his promptness. Why? Because fewer distortions of faith will occur if novel practices are promptly met by those with teaching authority in the community of believers. Delay compounds any such problem. Promptness is thus an important aspect of the virtue of vigilance within orthodox witness. And it paid off in the example Vincent gives us: after Stephen's prompt response to the practice of rebaptism, the historical precedent was reconfirmed so conclusively that the issue was seldom reviewed again until much later.

CASE STUDIES TESTING UBIQUITY, ANTIQUITY, AND CONSENT

In the cases that follow, Vincent holds close to his central theme: offering an aid to remembering the faith that has been believed everywhere, always, and by the general consent of all who believe. Vincent proceeds to unfold and elaborate the three-part rule by showing how it has been applied in contentious historical circumstances. The following series of case studies illustrates major challenges to universality, apostolic antiquity, and general lay consent through conciliar definition and consensual exegesis.[41]

The Case of the Donatists and the Arians

Vincent tests the ecumenical rule by comparing the cases of the Donatists and the Arians. First the Donatists, who argued (against apostolic tradition) that the validity of any sacrament depended on the holiness of the celebrant, and who—like Agrippinus—believed that rebaptism was necessary for those baptized by heretics. The Donatists constituted for Vincent the clearest test of the challenge to the rule's spatial-geographical criterion (everywhere, *ubique*), because they garnered a large portion of the young regional church to their point of view. The question that the Donatists raised for Vincent was: Suppose a view, even if wrong or unwise, becomes normative in a particular area—even a vast area, such as Africa (as Donatism did). Does it not deserve to be respected as highly as the fuller consent of the worldwide worshiping community? The answer reached by the faithful was no.

Donatism had its day, a long day, but it eventually dwindled and disappeared. Even though for almost a century it held sway over an immense section of North Africa, it was rejected because it was not *catholic*, but *regional*. The larger church held that any doctrine had to show concurrence with prevailing worldwide, intergenerational Christian lay consent. Thus the rule: The universal was preferred to the particular (regional Donatism).

Both Donatists and Arians at their peak controlled vast territories and gained the consent of large numbers of laity and clergy. While the Donatists were largely concentrated in one continent only, the Arians (who denied that the Son is of the essence of God) had influence in virtually all the territories of the Roman world, and their views were espoused for decades in the fourth century by emperors and civil authorities. With Arianism enjoying extensive official civic sanction, orthodox leadership everywhere was being pressed to accept a revisionist view on a matter so crucial as the personal identity of Jesus Christ as true God.

At one time a large number of *bishops* were Arian—the doctrine had for a time been that pervasive. Would not that tend to legitimize Arianism as a broadly consensual teaching? No, says Vincent—and no, said the early church—because its dominance was limited to only a few generations. Arianism could not be found either in the apostolic teaching or in other generations before Arius.

Nonetheless, the controversy confused believers, who heard voices of ecclesial authority arguing for both sides of the issue. Arianism is a tragic example of how great the calamity can grow when novelty parades as orthodoxy and deception wears the garb of apostolic faith. The movement was doubly poisonous because it appealed to both antiquity and universality on the thoroughly unbiblical point that the Son of God is not quite God. The controversy is pertinent to our time because we too are experiencing vast distortions of Christian authority, memory, and doctrinal definition masquerading as Christian teaching.

Vincent attributed the power of Arianism to four causes, each of which has a current analogy:

1. *The lust for novelty.* Arianism thought of itself as a new corrective to older, distorted views of the sacred text. Its modern equivalent is a chauvinism that assumes that anything recent is superior to anything older. The premise of superiority has its counterpart in the intrinsic inferiority of antiquity.

2. *The neglect of the balanced consensus that was Spirit-led in the original apostolic eyewitnesses.* Arianism treated the apostolic testimony selectively. It did not sufficiently compare text with text by the analogy of faith under the guidance of the Spirit.

3. *The widespread default of the teaching office.* In Arian teaching, the history of apostolic interpretation was judged less important than contemporary interpreters. Where the teaching of the elders is taken

captive to novelty, how can the laity trust the faithful transmission of
the tradition?

4. *The violation of the authority and legitimacy of established institutions
of tradition-transmission.* Well-grounded apostolic communities were
undermined and ruined by the facile novelties of Arius, ending in the
temporary overthrow of clear apostolic testimony in favor of political
powerbrokers.

As a result of these four influences of Arianism, says Vincent, the "jails
and mines were overcrowded with saintly persons. Most of them, forbidden
to enter the cities, hunted and exiled, exposed to life in deserts, caves, among
wild beasts and amid rocks, exhausted by exposure and hunger and thirst,
perished."[42] What finally mattered most in the struggle against Arianism was
the willingness of ordinary faithful laity to give their lives in defense of classic Christian teaching.

It took a century and a half of that willingness for Arianism to be generally exposed as a distorted innovation. While its voices still echo today, it
is now nothing more than a nonconsensual relic—only a vestige, a shadow
of its former self. The faithful eventually defeated Arianism by showing
that it was in fact new—it had no significant exponents before Arius—
and that it therefore lacked the continuous consent of earlier generations
of apostolic memory.

Having laid a foundation with his general discussion of Donatism and
Arianism, Vincent then leads the orthodox rememberer through several particular test cases—those of Nestorius,[43] Photinus,[44] and Apollinaris.[45] He repeatedly observes that what the false teachers meant for ill, God turned to
good. In each heretical challenge, orthodoxy grew closer to the truth by responding with the wholeness of scripture's teaching.

The Case of Nestorius: Whether Mary Is Rightly Called God-Bearer

Vincent rehearses the infamous case of the former patriarch of Constantinople, Nestorius, who changed from sheep into wolf. Once a revered teacher
of orthodoxy, he misled the flock of Christ with a different teaching than
that received in scripture and liturgy.

Nestorius had been elected to his high office after a careful, judicious examination. He was endowed with exceptionally good pastoral qualities and
was a zealous and articulate teacher of doctrine. Honored with the episco-
pacy and with his people's great affection, he assumed vast responsibilities
as patriarch of the great see of Constantinople. How could he, of all people,

possibly fall into a fundamental error on such a crucial teaching as the identity of Jesus Christ? How implausible! It might seem odd that God permitted, rather than prevented, his disaffection. But, says Vincent, the saints teach that God permits such distortions to test and further refine biblical teaching of the divine and human natures of Christ.

Nestorius developed an innovative theory of the person of Christ: that it is better to speak of him as having *two* persons than *one*. One person, he contended, is the man who was born, suffered, and died; the other person is the divine Logos, eternal and unbegotten. One person is begotten of the mother; the other of the Father. Nestorius advocated changing the prayers of the eucharist to reflect that belief. Change the liturgy, he proposed, to speak of Mary not as *Theotokos* (mother of God), but only as *Christotokos* (mother of Christ), because she gave birth not to Christ as God but only to Christ as man.

Yet every baptized Christian knew by heart, both from scripture and from liturgy, that Mary had given birth through the Spirit to the eternal Son of God. The worshiping community had long been accustomed to remember Mary in prayer as the one who bore God the Son, the mother of God. It was clear from the liturgical tradition that she, the mother of the God-man, was thus the mother of God incarnate, who from the beginning was born as *one* person— truly human, truly divine. It was this one person to whom Paul referred when he said that the civil authorities had "crucified the Lord of glory."[46]

It is crucial to the proper idea of the incarnation that the eternal Word of God is born of Mary as one person, not two. All the baptized already knew this. Nestorius the patriarch had missed the mark drastically. The unity of the person of Christ was not formed after the birth but was knitted in the womb. Yet even with all of his good qualities of eloquence and brilliance, Nestorius had misplaced the apostolic teaching of Christ as the truly human son of a human mother and the truly divine Son of the eternal Father, in one person.

Why did God in his providence allow this challenge to faith from its highest official leader? If the teaching of Mary as mother of the incarnate Lord had never been challenged, says Vincent, the incarnational teaching might lack the careful refining and strength it came to have. Through the wrenching agony of the Nestorian controversy, the ecumenical body of Christ came to a clearer understanding of the incarnate Lord. So what others meant for evil, God meant for good.

The Case of Photinus: How Good Qualities Can Become Distorted

Next Vincent presents the case of Photinus, bishop of Sirmium. Although he, like Nestorius, was admitted to leadership with general consent, he eventually put the community of faith on trial—not only in Sirmium but everywhere.

Photinus had extraordinary qualities. A person of genius and an excellent educator (working competently in both Greek and Latin), he was trusted, wrote books against false teaching, and was taken seriously by the faithful on a wide scale. Ironically, it was precisely those special gifts that created a problem for those who worked under his spiritual guidance: because of his credentials, people listened trustingly when (against Philippians 2 and Colossians 1) Photinus questioned the preexistence of Christ.

Vincent argues that it was providential that the laity and clergy entrusted to Photinus cared less about their leader's eloquence or genius or inventiveness than about the faith of their baptism. The people held firm, and his novel teaching (that Jesus became the Christ only at his baptism) was rejected by the Council of Constantinople in 381. God permitted this challenge to strengthen the right remembering of Christ as truly human, truly God, according to apostolic testimony.

The Case of Apollinaris: An Excess of Creative Imagination

Vincent then offers the even stranger case of Apollinaris, who (like Photinus and Nestorius) displayed admirable qualities of intelligence, versatility, and erudition. He gained the trust of those committed to his care and developed the reputation of being an opponent of false teaching. "How many heresies did he crush," Vincent quips, "in as many volumes!"[47] He wrote no fewer than thirty books in defense of orthodoxy. Could not he, above all, be trusted?

It was the creative imagination of Apollinaris that led to his downfall. He had an overweening desire to invent something, a curiosity so abundant that it became character flaw. His imagination eventually undermined the rest of his teaching. It was like leprosy, Vincent observed: one infected with a runaway imagination tends to infect everyone he touches. So a fallen champion of orthodoxy may become an even greater temptation to the community of faith than others in less conspicuous positions of leadership.[48]

Apollinaris introduced this curious speculation: that there was no human soul that dwelt in the body of Jesus, and that Jesus' flesh was not joined with a human mind. Along with this he proposed another odd notion: that the flesh of Jesus did not come from the flesh of Mary but descended from heaven into the virgin. According to Apollinaris, after the virgin had brought forth Jesus, the two persons then were united in Christ. In other words, there was a time when there were *two* Christs, one born as an ordinary man, the other descended from heaven. After the birth of the human child Jesus, the person of the Word descended upon him.

These distortions, which became known as Apollinarianism, were in favor for a time. After much consideration, however, the faithful realized that they ran counter to apostolic teaching and rejected them definitively.

The Case of Origen: How a Teacher's Speculation Can Become the Church's Trial

Of all the heresies, scarcely one compares in importance to the temptations created by one of the community of faith's greatest teachers, Origen. He presents the greater challenge to the faith not because of his ignorance but because of his genius.

Origen's family had become famous and revered through martyrdom. Living the life of holy poverty, he himself had suffered bravely for confessing the faith. Eusebius reports that Origen had endured imprisonment, the rack, and threats of torture by fire. He became a teacher of extraordinary influence. His renown was such that the mother of the emperor sent for him to listen to his opinions. He was also sought out by the great Porphyry, a leading pagan thinker, who traveled to Alexandria as a young boy to hear Origen (who was said to possess knowledge as comprehensive as any of his day).

Origen did not fail to speak out against heretical distortions as they arose. Few of his contemporaries were as vigilant. It was precisely his genius, as one who knew intimately the vast literary sources in Greek and Hebrew, that caused so many to follow him. His intellectual authority intensified the church's temptation to trust him even when he went astray. It prompted some to say, "It is better to err with Origen than to be right with others."[49]

If Origen did so much right, what went wrong? He speculated too much, according to Vincent, skewing the integrity of the apostolic faith and "neglecting the old simplicity of the Christian religion; because he presumed to know more than all the others; because he despised ecclesiastical traditions and the teaching of the fathers and interpreted some passages of Holy Scripture in a novel manner."[50] Vincent is less interested in detailing *specifics* of Origen's speculations than in showing their persistent form as an idiosyncratic turning away from the reliable consensual tradition toward novel, experimental opinion. Still, the specifics indicate how far from the center Origen eventually shifted: he propounded the transmigration of souls, the eternality of souls, the souls as stars, and other novelties.

Vincent is aware that certain of Origen's writings might have been falsified by copyists. That presents an intriguing complication, and Vincent wishes it were so. But he concludes that he cannot enter into conjecture on that point with any confidence. The fact remains, he says, that books published under Origen's name—whether authored by him or not—are read and loved not as books by someone else but as books by the venerated Origen. On Origen's authority (whether with his agreement or not), they have tempted readers to err. The point: when the writings of a widely respected teacher expound error, the worldwide community of faith undergoes a great trial.

The Case of Tertullian: Do Ill-Advised Decisions Disqualify an Otherwise Good Teacher?

As Origen was the leading exegete in early Greek Christianity, so was Tertullian in African Christianity. Who among the Latin Christians of his time was better equipped, had a better command of philosophy, demonstrated more keenness of mind, exhibited more eloquence, and understood careful argument better than Tertullian? All of his opponents—Praxeus, Marcion, Hermonoges—experienced the power of Tertullian's mind as if struck by lightning. Tertullian spent most of his life as a thoroughly trustworthy orthodox theologian, with his energies blessed under the rule of the orthodox consensus.

But Tertullian proved to be not steadfast enough in the universally received faith to resist following after the eccentricities of Montanus, who taught as true prophesies the imaginings of seers who claimed special revelation.[51] In his commentary on Matthew, Hilary wrote of Tertullian: "By his subsequent error he deprived even his commendable writings of their full authority."[52] No matter how reliably Tertullian expounded other points of orthodox faith, insofar as he erred significantly in his teaching of revelation and inspiration, he diminished his full credibility.

TREASURES OLD AND NEW

The power to transform societies and to redeem the human condition finds roots in the stored wisdom of the human past. Classic Christianity and Judaism conserve key aspects of this long memory. The new depends upon the old, and the old forms itself once again in the new. Jesus said to his disciples after telling them in parables about the kingdom of heaven: "Every scribe who has been trained for the kingdom of heaven is like the master of a household who brings out of his treasure *what is new and what is old.*"[53] Commented Augustine: "If he should bring forth new things only or old things only, he is not a learned scribe in the kingdom of God presenting from his storeroom things new and old."[54]

Accumulated Experience in Countering Errors

Confronting the dilemmas presented in the above cases helped the community of faith grasp afresh the central New Testament teaching that God became human in person. In his personal coming, God truly *assumed* humanity (rather than just *appearing* to assume it). His manner of life was not artificial or synthetic. This personal coming was not an *impersonation*. Unlike an actor on a stage, says Vincent, the triune God does not change roles, at one time playing a king, at another time a priest, at another time a prophet, so that at the end of the play the persons being impersonated cease to exist.[55]

In Jesus Christ we have true God become true human in one person. The faith of our baptism centers on one God made man, who assumed our human nature, not artificially, but in reality. He *became* that which he embodied. He was just like us—who are precisely who we are, not players on a stage. Each of us exists as a person of flesh and spirit, soul and body. We do not *imitate* ourselves; we *are* ourselves, says Vincent.[56] God the Word did not *pretend* to suffer in the flesh; he indeed *did* suffer in the flesh. He truly assumed humanity without ceasing to be God the Son.

The one theandric (divine-human) person is God and man, created and uncreated, unchangeable and suffering, at once coequal and voluntarily submissive to the Father, begotten of the Father before time and born of a human mother in time. Fully human, his flesh (like our flesh) comes from his mother, and it has a soul endowed with intelligence, mind, and reason. It is only "by a wonderful and ineffable mystery [that] divine action can be ascribed to man and human action to God," and "that on earth God was made, suffered, and was crucified as man."[57]

These nuances would not have been refined so precisely had not the Nestorian and Apollinarian and other challenges required faith to become explicitly accountable by comparing scripture with scripture. The reality of one person—truly human and truly divine—had to be tested out in every possible way to prove that the incarnation was not an imitation or a fiction. The consenting community had to say no, one by one, to these heresies of Nestorius, Photinus, Apollinaris, and a host of others who had departed from the baptism into which the faithful were all baptized.[58]

The error of even the best teacher can be a temptation to believers. The greater the error, the greater the temptation. Whenever distortions of faith arise, and whenever the authority of scripture is abused by departing from the allegiance of sound faith as consensually defined, the faithful need reminding of who they are and where the center lies. Vincent's *Commonitory* is intended as that reminder. He exhorts all believers to "accept the teachers with the church, and not desert the faith of the church" by following teachers who provide substandard alternatives.[59]

Vincent's Proximity: Only Ten Generations Away from the Originating Event

Vincent was the first to bring to clear statement the long-established procedure for how one discerns Christian truth precisely when that truth is disputed by conflicting voices that appeal to the apostolic tradition. We can trust his distillation of that procedure, because he lived only ten generations from the first generation of apostles (if we assume a quarter-century as the span of a generation).

Consider this succession of witnesses: Paul knew Polycarp, who knew Irenaeus, who knew Callistus (d. 222), who knew Dionysius of Alexandria (fl. ca. 200–265), who knew Anthony of the Desert (d. 355), who knew Athanasius (d. 373), who knew Damasus (d. 384), who knew John Cassian (d. 432), who knew Honorat, who was the abbot of Lérins, who knew Vincent. In these ten generations separating Paul and Vincent, the guardianship of the apostolic witness was taken with absolute seriousness and defended to the death. Only ten generations. But it took these generations to test out false alternatives.

Vincent wrote shortly after the deaths of Augustine and Jerome, during the time of Cyril of Alexandria (412–444), less than eighty years after the death of Anthony of the Desert, less than three hundred years following the *Didache*, Polycarp (d. ca. 155), and Justin Martyr (d. ca. 167). Thus even by Vincent's time a vast accumulation of valuable consensual experience had developed out of which to assess the method of deciding contested Christian truth.

A century before Vincent wrote, the Council of Nicea had met in 325 to engage in a major debate and make a crucial decision about the weak Christology of the Arians. The kernel of the method of classic consensual thinking thus already existed rudimentarily by that time. The unpretentious method that Vincent explicitly described around 432 was fully operational at the time of Nicea (and embryonically operational in Paul, according to Vincent), even though it had not yet been explicitly articulated and systematically explained.

The council fathers of Nicea repeatedly said of their own decision-making process that it was not new, that they were only confirming what had been believed by the community of faith since the apostles. They insisted that their way of settling the Arian dispute was the same method by which the worshiping Christian community had always decided cases of contested doctrine. This process became further refined at the Council of Constantinople in 381 and (especially) at the Council of Ephesus in 431—the very process that Vincent would describe around 432. Augustine, before Vincent, utilized much the same method for discerning the truth, but it remained to Vincent to state the method in a detailed, systematic form and defend it as a historical hypothesis.[60]

By the time Vincent provided its classic expression, this method had already had more than three centuries of testing. By then, through many contested issues, it had proved its durability. Though the Vincentian rule bears his name, Vincent was not the *inventor,* as we have seen; he only gave expression, according to his own testimony, to a process that had been rigorously tested for ten generations.

Faith's Regenerating Power

This stubborn fact remains: a single cohesive deposit of faith, formed and shaped by the Spirit, and confirmed by free mutual consent to revelation, has persisted for two millennia. Translated into many tongues, this consensus has formed (and been affected by) many cultures without losing its core identity. The Spirit has enabled mutual general consent on key points of interpretation of canonically received holy writ in ways that are sufficient not only for eternal salvation but also for better life in this world. In this cohesive teaching lies special power to transform societies.

This Spirit-led process has defined, remembered, and safeguarded consent to apostolic testimony over many centuries. The laity, quite capable of understanding and assessing the fairness of this process, should be given every opportunity to study how the great consensual teachers have fairly gained uncoerced consent from generation to generation over two millennia. Orthodox, Catholics, and Protestants can, despite diverse liturgical and cultural memories, find unexpected common ground ecumenically by returning to classic interpreters of scripture texts that still stand as authoritative for teaching today.

Concluding Imperatives

In Part 1 we saw how orthodoxy persists despite all contrary predictions, and how worshiping communities are now moving confidently beyond the constricted future of modern failures. Amid the modern impasse, the classic religious traditions are being rediscovered by both Jews and Christians, who together have received and continue to guard the memory of God's revelation in history. Orthodoxy has all the advantages of long-term memory unavailable to modern consciousness. The faithful who are willing to suffer for truth are more ecumenical than so-called modern bureaucratic ecumenists. They are opening doors for wider intellectual freedom than is available within modern assumptions.

In Part 2 I set forth a wide constellation of evidence for the rebirth of orthodoxy:

- Personal narratives of regeneration

- Academic studies in the history of exegesis

- A more inclusive multicultural celebration of catholic consensus

- Boundary-definition that draws clear lines between orthodoxy and heresy

- Renewing and confessing movements within drifting religious institutions

- The redefinition of ecumenical thinking in our time

These signs of new birth all point to the gift of regeneration. To rightly lay hold of the power of this gift requires more than description or argument, however. It requires an act of willing and the risk of obedience—the risk of making behavioral changes. Six imperatives follow:

- Tell others the true story of your own rediscovery of ancient religious teaching.

- Study the classic religious writers.

- Enjoy and respect the cross-cultural, intergenerational nature of the religious community.

- Live within doctrinal and moral boundaries fixed for millennia.

- Reclaim faltering religious and educational institutions.

- Apply the ancient ecumenical method of discernment to contested questions.

The purpose of this book is not simply to make the case that an orthodox movement has emerged in contemporary culture, as if that had no moral consequences. This is not just a descriptive exercise to point to a populist movement. On the contrary, the description bears an invitation to take an active part in it. It asks you not whether you are convinced that orthodoxy has been reborn, but whether it is being reborn in *you*.

LIST OF BIBLIOGRAPHICAL ABBREVIATIONS

ACCS   Thomas C. Oden, ed. *Ancient Christian Commentary on Scripture.* 10 vols. to date. Downers Grove, IL: InterVarsity Press, 1998–.

AF   Jack N. Sparks, ed. *The Apostolic Fathers.* New York: Nelson, 1978.

ANF   Alexander Roberts and James Donaldson, eds. *Ante-Nicene Fathers.* 10 vols. 1885–1896.

CC   John H. Leith, ed. *Creeds of the Churches.* 3rd ed. Atlanta: John Knox Press, 1982.

CFBJ   Jacob Neusner. *Christian Faith and the Bible of Judaism.* Grand Rapids, MI: Eerdmans, 1987.

CH   Eusebius of Caesarea. *Church History.* NPNF, series 2, vol. 1.

COC   Philip Schaff, ed. *Creeds of Christendom.* 3 vols. New York: Harper & Bros., 1919.

CTJ   Clemens Thoma. *A Christian Theology of Judaism.* New York: Paulist Press, 1980.

FC   Roy J. Deferrari, ed. *Fathers of the Church: A New Translation.* 100+ vols. to date. Washington, D.C.: Catholic University of America Press, 1947–.

FEF   William A. Jurgens, ed. *The Faith of the Early Fathers.* 3 vols. Collegeville, MN.: Liturgical Press, 1970–1979.

FEH   Will Herberg. *Faith Enacted as History.* Edited by Bernhard W. Anderson. Philadelphia: Westminster Press, 1976.

Inst.   John Calvin. *Institutes of the Christian Religion.* LCC, vols. 20, 21.

JCD   David Novak. *Jewish-Christian Dialogue.* New York: Oxford University Press, 1989.

JJW   John Wesley. *The Journal of the Reverend John Wesley.* 8 vols. Edited by Nehemiah Curnock. London: Epworth, 1909–1916.

JPC   Fritz Rothschild, ed. *Jewish Perspectives on Christianity.* New York: Crossroad, 1990.

KJV   King James Version (1611).

LCC   John Baillie et al., eds. *The Library of Christian Classics.* 26 vols. Philadelphia: Westminster, 1953–1966.

NEB   New English Bible (1970).

NIV   New International Version (1984).

NKJV   New King James Version (1982).

NPNF   Philip Schaff et al., eds. *A Select Library of the Nicene and Post-Nicene Fathers of the Christian Church,* series 1 and 2. 14 vols. each series. 1887–1894.

NRSV   New Revised Standard Version (1989).

RSV   Revised Standard Version (1946).

OF   John of Damascus. *On the Orthodox Faith.* NPNF, series 2, vol. 9; FC, vol. 37.

SCD   H. Denzinger, ed. *Sources of Catholic Dogma (Enchiridion Symbolo rum).* Translated by Roy J. Deferrari. St. Louis: Herder, 1957.

SCF   Henry F. Jacobs, ed. *A Summary of Christian Faith.* Philadelphia: General Council Publication House, 1905.

SCG   Thomas Aquinas. *On the Truth of the Catholic Faith (Summa Contra Gentiles).* 4 vols. New York: Doubleday, 1955–1957.

WJW   Thomas Jackson, ed. *Works of John Wesley.* 14 vols. London: Wesleyan Conference Office, 1872.

NOTES

Works frequently cited are abbreviated here, with full publication information given in the List of Bibliographical Abbreviations. (For example, in the first note, CTJ indicates *A Christian Theology of Judaism*.)

CHAPTER 2

1. Samuel Freedman, *Jew vs. Jew*, New York: Simon & Schuster, 217, 218, cf. 23–29, 338–359.

2. Clemens Thoma, CTJ 30.

3. Will Herberg, FEH 32.

4. Abraham J. Heschel, "No Religion Is an Island," JPC 314.

5. Ibid., 310.

6. Ibid., 311.

7. Martin Buber, "Der Preis," *Der Jude*, Oct. 1917; cited in Will Herberg, FEH 41.

8. Tikva Frymer-Kensky, David Novak, Peter Ochs, and Michael Signer.

9. Pro Ecclesia Vol. X, No. 1, p. 5.

10. Dabru Emet, pp. 5, 6.

11. Dabru Emet, p. 7.

12. Eph. 2:12–19, KJV amended.

13. Gal. 3:29, NKJV.

14. Abraham J. Heschel, "No Religion Is an Island," JPC 322.

15. Ibid., 316.

16. Ibid., 311.

17. David Novak, JCD 113.

18. Franz Rosenzweig, "The Star of Redemption," JPC 197.

19. Jacob B. Agus, "Franz Rosenzweig," in *Modern Philosophies of Judaism* (New York: Behrman's, 1941), 193, cited in Will Herberg, FEH 58.

20. Jacob B. Agus, "Franz Rosenzweig," in *Modern Philosophies of Judaism* (New York: Behrman's, 1941), 193f. For further discussion of this issue, see Nahum N. Glatzer, *Franz Rosenzweig: His Life and Thought* (New York: Schocken Books, 1953), 343–344; cf. Fritz Rothschild, ed., JPC.

21. David Novak, JCD 108.

22. Will Herberg, FEH 49.

23. Gal. 3:14, KJV.

24. Will Herberg, FEH 92.

25. Richard Neuhaus and Leon Klenicki, *Believing Today: Jew and Christian in Conversation* (Grand Rapids: Eerdmans, 1989).

26. For further inquiry: Marcel Simon, *Versus Israel* (Oxford: Oxford Univ. Press, 1948); Miriam Taylor, *Anti-Judaism and Early Christian Identity: A Critique of the Scholarly Consensus* (Leiden: Brill, 1995); Daniel Boyarin, *Dying for God: Martyrdom and the Making of Christianity and Judaism* (Palo Alto: Stanford Univ. Press, 1999); see also works by James Parkes, Gregory Baum, Rosemary R. Ruether, James Dunn.

27. Bernhard Casper, "Introduction, Rosenzweig," JPC 167.

28. John C. Merkle, "Introduction, Heschel," JPC 267.

29. Abraham Heschel, "From Mission to Dialogue," *Conservative Judaism* 21 (Spring 1967): 11.

30. Franz Rosenzweig, letter to Rudolf Ehrenberg, Oct. 31, 1913, JPC 170.

31. Franz Rosenzweig, "The Star of Redemption," JPC 225.

32. Fritz Rothschild, "General Introduction," JPC 7.

33. Jakob J. Petuchowski, "A Jewish Response to 'Israel as a Theological Problem for the Christian Church,'" *Journal of Ecumenical Studies* 6, no. 3 (Summer 1969): 349.

34. Fritz Rothschild, "General Introduction," JPC 15.

35. Clemens Thoma, CTJ 27, 29.

36. Declaration *Nostra Aetate,* n. 4, in Clemens Thoma, CTJ 174.

CHAPTER 3

1. Or, more accurately, the Septuagint translation of the Hebrew Bible.

2. In the Greek Septuagint or Old Latin or later Vulgate versions, for first-millennium Christians.

3. Gal. 1:8, 9, NIV amended. Anathema = eternally condemned.

4. Matt. 28:19.

5. Irish Articles, 75, COC 3:539.

6. Second Helvetic Conference, CC 135.

7. Within the restricted view of modern assumptions, "paleo" carries many negative nuances: passé, antiquated, obsolete. Indeed, at the heart of the disappearing era of Western modernity lies the dubious premise of the absolute superiority of newer to older ideas. That premise is being reversed. Paleo-orthodoxy is a term that promises to be more plausible as this reversal matures.

   The rebirth of orthodoxy is a theme that I first sketched out with rough colors in my *Systematic Theology* (1987–1992). Now I am expanding it in some ways, digesting it in others, and presenting the heart of it to a general secular audience of nonprofessionals.

8. Vincent of Lérins, *Commonitory,* ch. 6, FC 7; 273.

9. Heb. 11:35b–38, NRSV.

10. Vincent of Lérins, *Commonitory,* FC 7:273.

11. Athanasius, *Defence of the Nicene Definition,* NPNF 2 IV:149ff; Calvin, Inst. 1.6.12–13.

CHAPTER 4

1. 1 Cor. 9:19–22.

2. Rom. 11:4 NIV.

3. Second Helvetic Confession, CC 148; cf. 1 Kings 19:18; Rev. 7:4, 9.

4. 2 Tim. 2:19.

5. John 16:6, 13.

6. Acts 14:17.

7. Augsburg Confession, Art. VII, CC 70.

8. Methodist Church, *Book of Worship* (Nashville: Methodist Publishing House, 1965), 12.

9. 1 Cor. 11:26b, NIV.

10. Matt. 16:18, KJV.

11. John 14:16; Matt. 23:20.

12. Matt. 7:25.

13. 1 Pet. 1:23–25, NIV.

14. Matt. 28:20.

15. Jude 1:3 KJV.

16. CC 143.

17. John 14:26, NIV.

18. Isa. 55:11, NIV.

19. Zacharius Ursinus, *Commentary on the Heidelberg Catechism*, 3ʳᵈ U.S. ed. (Cincinnati: Bucher, 1851), 291.

20. John 15:1–5; Col. 1:18.

21. Pascal, *Pensées*, cited Henry Jacob, SCF 378.

22. Council of Nicea I, SCD 54, p. 26; Basil, Letter 114, FC 13:241–242; Gregory of Nazianzus, *On the Great Athanasius*, Orat. XXI, NPNF 2 VII:269–280; Cyril, Letter 39, FC 76:147–152.

23. Phil. 3:10; Cyprian, *On the Lapsed*, ANF 5:437–447; Kierkegaard, *Kierkegaard's Attack Upon "Christendom"* (Princeton: Princeton University Press, 1944).

24. 1 Pet. 4:13–5:9; *The Martyrdom of Polycarp*, ANF 1:37–44.

25. Matt. 24:9 NEB; Irenaeus, *Against Heresies*, IV.33.9, ANF 1:508.

26. 2 Tim. 2:9 NEB. The naturalistic explanation of this resilience falls pitifully short. The willingness to suffer for the truth is explained away as if it came from unconscious sexual passions, the desire for religious ecstasy, or some hidden desire to harm oneself (i.e., a masochistic motive). Reasons grounded in salvation history are ruled out; hence the phenomena are misunderstood.

27. Vincent of Lérins, *Commonitory*, chs. 4–5, FC 7:272–275.

28. Acts 5:40–42; 9:15–16. The Greek *martus* simply means "witness." The martyrs were willing to suffer gladly "for the name" (Acts 5:41b, RSV). While a witness bears testimony by his preaching, a martyr bears testimony by his death (*Martyrdom of Polycarp*, ANF 1:42, 14:2; 16:2). Stephen was the first martyr (Acts 22:20), but other Christians who suffered death for their witness also came to be called martyrs (Rev. 2:13, 17:6). Disciples were warned by their Lord that God's messengers are often persecuted (Matt. 23:34–35). They were called to take up their cross and follow him (Mark 8:34–38). Scripture tells us that discipleship requires readiness to suffer for the truth for Christ's sake (Phil. 1:29–30; 1 Thess. 2:14–15; 1 Pet. 3:14).

29. Vincent of Lérins, *Commonitory*, ch. 5, FC 7:275.

30. Ibid.

31. Ibid.

32. Ibid.

33. Cf. Ambrose, *On the Duties of the Clergy*, I.35–42, NPNF 2 X:30–35.

34. Heb. 11:37–38, NIV.

35. 1 Cor. 1:23 NEB; 1 Peter 2:8, KJV.

CHAPTER 5

1. The Lambeth Conference of 1998 brought Anglican prelates together from all over the world, where chic bishops such as John Shelby Spong painted themselves into an untenable corner, outwitted by the bishops of the two-thirds world. The National Council of Churches (NCC) is struggling mightily with deficit spending and financial crisis, deteriorating mainline denominations, and the threat of complete collapse.

2. Here is another, related analogy. Think of the new ecumenism as somewhat analogous to home-schooling as distinguished from public-schooling in this sense: home-schooling arose as a common alternative only when the failure of many public schools became evident. Professional administrators and teachers (along with their unions) had been assumed capable of managing public education until it became obvious that they were not. Home-schooling is now proving its effectiveness. Similarly, the new ecumenism arose only upon recognition of the incompetence (indeed, utter failure) of the old, nonrepresentative forms of political ecumenism. The laity are saying that they can embody ecumenism better than the pros.

3. A favorite nickname for the National Council of Churches headquarters at 475 Riverside Drive, New York.

4. Paul Ramsey, *Who Speaks for the Church?* (Philadelphia: Westminster Press, 1967).

5. It took only two decades (1948–1966) for the old ecumenism to be taken captive to utopianism of the left, statism fantasies, planned economies, and moral relativism.

6. In describing two ecumenisms, I am speaking of two competing alleged *universals,* two contrary claims to the idea of the whole body of Christ.

7. The crisis of ecumenism is the crisis of two contrary and largely incompatible views of Christian unity. It is the crisis of conflict between apostolic testimony ecumenically received versus the presumed legitimacy of modern truth-claims relativistically conceived. One is grounded in revelation; the other, in modern assumptions (always bent toward reductive naturalistic arguments).

8. The new ecumenism is still reaching out for wisdom and well-grounded apologetic strategies in the arenas of parenting, schooling, the complementary relation of men and women, international relief, world debt, microeconomics, the environment, trade policy, taxation, terrorism, nuclear energy, technological change, economic development, biomedical dilemmas, life-and-death questions, popular culture, and social welfare.

9. Take, for example, the doctrine of justification by grace through faith active in love. Under the rules of the old ecumenism, an effort was made to bring bureaucracies together to talk about justification and see if there could be any agreement on it among modern theologians, historians, and exegetes. The Joint Declaration of Lutherans and Catholics is a laudable expression of that sort of quest for unity. (In fact, it is among the better expressions of the old ecumenism.) Yet it proceeded with almost no recognition of the ancient Christian consensus of exegesis on passages of scripture on justification by grace through faith active in love. Patristic exegesis is virtually identical with Reformation exegesis on key texts on justification (Eph. 2, Galatians, Rom. 3–11), as I show in my book *The Justification Reader* (Grand Rapids: Eerdmans, 2002). The rediscovered unity of the body of Christ is being regrounded in patristic exegesis of passages that became divisive in the sixteenth century. We must now go back to the first millennium of consensus to recover from the division of the second millennium.

10. The living body of Christ is growing precisely under conditions of persecution, unjust accusation, imprisonment, and state terrorism. This courage amid peril can only be a work of God the Holy Spirit. No one could have predicted that the Chinese church would grow so fast under such limiting conditions, but the Spirit has enabled this. What has happened to Chinese Christians is subject to objective historical reportage and analysis. It is all too obvious to any worshiping Christian who reads the Bible what the Holy Spirit is doing in China and the Sudan and Cuba and Indonesia.

11. The non-Chalcedonian communions are coming into a greater recognition of what they can and do honestly share with the Chalcedonian tradition.

PART 2 INTRODUCTION

1. Contrast the authors listed in the table with writers generally unsympathetic to orthodoxy: John Hick, Donald Cupitt, Rosemary Radford Ruether, Rudolf Bultmann, Maurice Wiles, John S. Spong, John Cobb, Jacques Derrida, Geoffrey Lampe, Robert Funk, Joseph Sprague, Morton Borg.

2. Why 1989? In my view 1968 and 1989 bracket key turns in recent cultural history. The year 1968 saw the moment of collapse of the old pre-hippy, pre-Woodstock, pre-drug-culture consensus. The year 1989 heralded the collapse of the Marxist dream. Nietzsche, Freud, and Darwin all lost legitimacy in 1989 amid the collapse of Marxism. It was the year of the Lausanne Congress on World Evangelization in Manila in which the weight of world evangelical voices shifted decisively toward Asia and Africa. It was the year that Hugh Ross wrote *The Fingerprint of God,* Peter Gilquist wrote *Becoming Orthodox,* and Francis Fukayama wrote *The End of History.*

3. "Back Toward Orthodoxy: A Conservative Resurgence Sweeps American Religion," *The American Enterprise* 13, no. 3 (2002), www.TAEmag.com.

CHAPTER 6

1. It is epitomized by Gregory of Nazianzus's *Flight to Pontus* and Augustine's *Confessions*. Among extensive biographies are Athanasius's *Life of Anthony*, Jerome's *Lives*, Chrysostom's feast-day homilies, Theodoret's *A History of the Monks of Syria*, and Gregory the Great's *Dialogues*.

2. The personal narratives of Peter Toon, Dallas Willard, Paul Vitz, Philip Yancey, Charles Colson, and Tom Howard fill in moving details.

3. Biographical narratives of orthodox conversions have been powerfully honed by Will Willimon, Peter Gilquist, Andrew Walker, Keith Fournier, and George Weigel.

4. Indeed, the social, fleshly, objective, and consensual aspects of orthodox teaching usually are thought to stand as a critique of highly subjective pietism, which so often focuses too sentimentally upon highly personal storytelling.

5. This evolutionary socialism, in the tradition of Norman Thomas and Henry Wallace, gave him a deep distrust of concentrations of wealth.

6. For me Marxism became radicalized early in the 1950s, and personalized in the figure of Ho Chi Minh, whom I unreservedly idolized as an agrarian Communist patriot ten years before America's entry into the Vietnam war. My major mentors were almost all socialist or quasi-Marxist. Long before Vietnam I was a pacifist. Before Vietnam my ideology was formed around the group that wrote the Port Huron Statement; that same group later shaped the founding of the Students for Democratic Action.

7. First at Southern Methodist University (1958–1960) and then at Phillips Seminary, Enid, Oklahoma (1960–1970), before coming to Drew University in January of 1971.

8. Although I was paid to be a Christian theologian, my social vision was basically Marxist, my psychology was Freudian, my understanding of the change process was Rogerian, and my ethic was situationist.

9. After Yale, while something deep in my heart remained intuitively Barthian, my head was spinning with Heidegger. My scriptural knowledge came from Bultmann, my social vision from Tillich, and when I confessed my sins it was in a Niebuhrian voice. I was neo-orthodox to the core.

10. Tillich's cultural analysis, Bultmann's demythology, early feminism, and secularization theology.

11. As a former convinced proponent of the radical demythologizing biblical criticism of Rudolf Bultmann (on whose research I wrote my dissertation and my first scholarly book), I am now deconstructing Bultmann.

12. Though I resisted telling the story of my own personal regeneration within classic Christian teaching as if it were a nameless temptation—worse yet, a plague—I never objected when others called my story a *conversion*, because the

experience was as close to a radical spiritual reversal as anything that has ever happened to me.

13. As an infant I received my Christian name (*Thomas* for the apostle and *Clark* for my mother's family name) and the pledge of faithful parents and church to teach me the faith through the scriptures. There was, of course, a silent assumption underlying this identity: my baptism needed my free confirmation. I did belatedly confirm my baptism, but only after a very long detour. The detour occurred during my preparation for ordained ministry, when I lost confidence in the central affirmation that God has come in the flesh and risen from the dead.

14. My parents were right to date my being a Christian to my baptism. But I was a slow learner. There was nothing deficient in my baptism; it was I who was tardy in becoming doctrinally centered and accountable. Now I see the irony in the fact that it was my liberal-activist heritage that gave me triune baptismal faith and my earliest Christian vocabulary. However far I may now have departed from liberal activism (in its pacifist, existentialist, psychoanalytic, and socially idealistic expressions), I remain its grateful son. I regret neither having learned it nor having had to unlearn most of it. It remains highly valued, even when transcended and reconfigured.

15. These I defined in *Agenda for Theology* (1979) as hedonic self-actualization, autonomous individualism, reductive naturalism, and absolute moral relativism.

16. Vincent of Lérins, *Commonitory,* ch. 1, FC 7:270.

17. Written in the early seventies but published in 1976 by HarperSanFrancisco.

18. 1 Sam. 15:29, NIV.

19. Mal. 3:6, NIV.

20. James 1:17, NIV.

21. "Frost at Midnight," *Coleridge: Poetry and Prose,* ed. Carlos Baker (New York: Bantam Books, 1965), 75

22. William Butler Yeats, "O do not Love Too Long." In : "The Collected Poems of W.B. Yeats." Edited by Richard J. Finneran. Rev. 2nd ed. (NY: Simon & Schuster, 1996), 84.

23. Job 1:21b, NEB.

CHAPTER 7

1. Scholars fluent in the original Greek and Latin and other languages have long enjoyed and benefited from the high quality of textual work in *Sources Chrétiennes, Corpus Christianorum* (series *Graeca* and *Latina*), *Corpus Scriptorum Christianorum Orientalium, Corpus Scriptorum ecclesiasticorum Latinorum, Texte und Untersuchungen zur Geschichte der altchristlichen Literatur, Die Griechischen Christlichen Schriftsteller, Patrologia Orientalis,* and *Patrologia*

Syriaca. In digital form many of these texts are available in *Thesaurus Linguae Latinae, Thesaurus Linguae Graecae,* and the *Cetedoc* series.

2. John Wesley, "Address to the Clergy," i.2, WJW X.484.

3. A Roman Catechism, with a Reply, "Preface," *WJW,* X:87, italics added; cf. JJW 1:367.

4. Mark 9:24b, NKJV.

5. Luke 18:13b, NIV.

6. Irenaeus, *Against Heresies,* III, ANF I; Origen, *De Principiis,* IV, ANF III; *Against Celsus,* V.60, VI.7, ANF III; Tertullian, *Against Praxeas,* 18–21, ANF III.

7. 2 Thess. 2:15, NEB, italics added.

8. Basil, *On the Spirit,* XXVII.66, NPNF 2 8:42.

9. Basil applied this analogy: "If, as in a court of law, we were at a loss of documentary (written) evidence, but were able to bring before you a large number of (oral) witnesses, would you not give your vote for our acquittal?" On this basis Basil cherished the phrase "with the Spirit" in the doxology "as a legacy left me by my fathers"—and here he specifically cited Irenaeus, Clement, Origen, Dionysius of Rome, Gregory Thaumaturgus, Firmilian, Eusebius, and Africanus. Basil did not want to be falsely perceived as "an innovator or creator of such new terms." These precious oral traditions, he argued, go back to those who were "pillars of the church and conspicuous for all knowledge and spiritual power." Thus he argued that memories and practices evidently familiar to those generations immediately following the apostles and "continued by long usage" should remain highly valued in Christian teaching. These words were passed down by champions of the Word to "whole nations, cities, customs going back beyond the memory of man." (Basil, *On the Spirit,* III.29, NPNF 2 8:45–47; cf. Augustine, *Letters,* FC 12:252–253).

10. Rosemary Radford Ruether, *Gregory of Nazianzus: Rhetor and Philosopher* (Oxford: Clarendon Press, 1969); Rosemary Radford Ruether, ed., *Religion and Sexism: Images of Woman in the Jewish and Christian Traditions* (New York: Simon & Schuster, 1974); David C. Ford, *Men and Women in the Early Church: The Full Views of St. John Chrysostom* (South Canaan, PA: St. Tikhon's Orthodox Theological Seminary, 1995). Cf. related works by John Meyendorff, Stephen B. Clark, and Paul K. Jewett.

11. Have I thus become a judaizing Christian? Have I given up on the Great Commission? No. I do not promote, for Christians, circumcision, kosher food, or the observance of Jewish festive seasons. My writings show a clear record of defense of the classic Christian teaching of justification by grace through faith active in love. The critical issue hinges on the teaching of the covenant: Did God covenant with our elder brother, the Jews, in such a way that we are engrafted on the original olive tree, not as if superseding Israel, but rather dependent upon Israel? With Paul, I say we are engrafted.

12. It may give me a kind of pleasure when one of my Jewish friends recognizes in Christian orthodox teaching something in which they too believe, or some way in which they can confess with me faith in Christ without ceasing to be Jews. But it does not give me pleasure to think of them disavowing their own election as people of God or their distinctive Jewish destiny.

13. Bernhard Anderson wrote: "Herberg has related to me that he used to discuss with Niebuhr the possibility of his moving into the Christian community; but Niebuhr counseled against it on the ground that he should not become a Christian until first he was a good Jew," FEH 14. According to Harry Ausmus, *Will Herberg: From Right to Right* (Chapel Hill: Univ. of North Carolina Press, 1987), Herberg "told numerous people that when he was moving toward a formal religious position in the early 1940s and he considered becoming a Roman Catholic, Niebuhr convinced him to remain true to his Jewish heritage," 231.

CHAPTER 8

1. Contemporary democratic theory would benefit by being regrounded in a longer-term view of history, and in the premise of long-term general consent over millennia. Our ancestors cannot vote but in our vote we can respect our ancestors.

2. Deut. 32:7, NIV.

3. Prov. 22:28, NIV.

4. Lateran Council, 649, SCD 274, 105.

5. Vincent of Lérins, *Commonitory,* XXII.27.

6. 1 Tim. 6:20.

7. Vincent of Lérins, *Commonitory,* XXII.27, FEF 3:264–265 (2173).

8. Vincent of Lérins, *Commonitory,* XXIII.28, FEF 3:265 (2174).

9. Ambrose, *Of the Holy Spirit,* V.65, NPNF 2 X:102; cf. John of Damascus, OF I.9, NPNF 2 IX:12; Thomas Aquinas, SCG I.13, 86–89.

10. Hilary of Poitiers, *Trinity,* II:2, NPNF 2 IX:53, translation amended.

CHAPTER 9

1. Ignatius, *To the Trallians,* 6, AF 94.

2. Hilary of Poitiers, *Trinity,* II.2, NPNF 2 IX:53.

3. Ecumenical Councils, Chalcedon, Tome of Leo, NPNF 2 XIV:258.

4. Cyprian, *Letters,* FC 51:176–192, 237ff., 259–312.

5. Heb. 5:12, NIV.

CHAPTER 10

1. 1110 Vermont Ave. NW, Suite 1180, Washington, DC 20005; 800–914–2000; info@americananglican.org; www.americananglican.org.

2. PO Box 797425, Dallas, TX 75379; 800–553–3645; eunited@worldnet.att.net; www.episcopalian.org/eu.

3. 126 Coming St., Charleston, SC 29403; 843–224–9161.

4. St. John's Church, 3738 Butler Road, Glyndon, MD 21071.

5. Trinity Episcopal School for Ministry, 311 Eleventh St., Ambridge, PA 15003.

6. 405 Frederick Ave., Sewickley, PA 15143; 800–707-NOEL; NOELife@aol.com; www.episcopalian.org/NOEL.

7. PO Box 2210, Lenoir, NC 28645; 828–758–8716; ptw@layman.org; www.layman.org.

8. *The Presbyterian Layman* (April 2001): p. 1.

9. PO Box 10249, Blacksburg, VA 24062; 703–552–5325; scyre@swva.net.

10. 8134 New La Grange Road, Suite 227, PO Box 22069, Louisville, KY 40222–0069; Joe@pfrenewal.org.

11. PO Box 11130, Burke, VA 22009; 703-569–9474; PresProLife@compuserve.com.

12. 1110 Vermont Ave. NW, Suite 1189, Washington, DC 20005; 202–696-8430; www.ird-renew.org.

13. 7995 E. Twenty-First St., Indianapolis, IN 46219; 317–256–9729; www.confessingumc.org; confessingumc@iquest.net.

14. 308 E. Main St., Wilmore, KY 40390; 606–858–4661; jim@goodnewsmag.org; www.goodnewsmag.org.

15. PO Box 889, Cornelia, GA 30531; 706–778–4812; renewl@hemc.net.

16. 512 Florence St., Dothan, AL 36391; 334–794–8543; tumaslw@sprynet.com; www.lifewatch.org.

17. Bristol303@aol.com; www.bristolhouseltd.com; 800–451–7323.

18. Info@msum.org; www.themissionsociety.org; 800–478–8963.

19. 1110 Vermont Ave. NW, Suite 1189, Washington, DC 20005; 202–696–8430; mtooley@ird-renew.org; davejeanie@muscanet.com.

20. PO Box 7146, Penndel, PA 19047; 215–752–9655; www.transformingcong.org; TransCong@aol.com.

21. Ed Robb Evangelistic Association, 2904 Victory Drive, PO Box 1945, Marshall, TX 75671, publishers of *Challenge to Evangelism Today;* www.edrobb.com; 903–938–8305.

22. PO Box 186, Marshallville, GA 31057; JosJournal@Prodigy.com.

23. 1217 Northern Sky Ave. NE, Albuquerque, NM 87111; Gallaway@swcp.com.

24. PO Box 1205, Goodlettsville, TN 37070; 615–0851–9192; www.aldersgaterenewal.org; gmoore@aldersgaterenewal.org.

25. PO Box 2864, Fayetteville, NC 28302.

26. PO Box 209, Muscatine, IA 52761; 800–334–8920; mreform@yahoo.com; www.mreform.org.

27. PO Box 102, Candia, NH 03034; 800–494–9172; areformer@aol.com.

28. PO Box 330, Sassamansville, PA, 19472; 610–754–6446; frmucc@aol.com.

29. *The Mission Herald,* PO Box 102, Candia, NH 03034; 800–494–9172.

30. PO Box 495, De Forest, WI 53532–0495.

31. 422 Sante Fe Circle, Chanhassen, MN 55317–9722; 763–546–5122; 612–645–5122; Busware@aol.com.

32. PO Box ACMC, Wheaton, IL 60189–8000.

33. PO Box 109, Lovington, IL 61937; 217–873–5126; dhf109@aol.com; www.disciple-heritage.org.

34. 10855 Irma Dr., Suite B, Northglenn, CO 80233; 303–252–7902; 877–223–8264; www.abeonline.org.

35. A pro-life ministry.

36. 800–465–7186; publishing *Concern,* Box 79013, Garth Postal Outlet, Hamilton, Ontario L9C 7N6, Canada; 905–318–9244; 800–465–7186; www.unityofconcern.org.

37. 489 East Osborn Rd., North Vancouver, British Columbia V7N 1M4, Canada; 604–987–9876; blckbrn24@hotmail.com; Geoff_Wilkins@telus.net; www.unitedrenewal.org.

38. Lakeshore Road W, RR 2, Port Colbourne, Ontario L3K 5V4, Canada; 905–835–2884.

39. MIP Box 3745, Markham, Ontario L3R 0YR, Canada; 905–479–4742; ft@efc-canada.com.

40. Box 237, Barrie, Ontario L4M 3T2, Canada; 800–678–2607; 416–767–0300; felmag@on.aibn.com; www.fellowshipmagazine.org.

41. Of the Evangelical Lutheran Church of America (ELCA), as distinguished from other Lutheran bodies such as the Missouri Synod.

42. PO Box 327, Delhi, NY 13753–0327; 607–746–7511; dkralpb@aol.com; Fjschum@attglobal.net.

43. 11633 Wren St. NW, Minneapolis, MN 55433; 763–754–4860; gcnusa@aol.com; www.gcnusa.com.

44. 333 El Molino Way, San Jose, CA 95119; 530–241–8801; SchaeferHG@aol.com.

45. 2701 N Rice St., Roseville MN 55113; 651–490–1517; www.lutheranrenewal.org.

46. PO Box 327, Delhi, NY 13753.

47. 2299 Palmer Dr., Suite 220, New Brighton, MN 55112–2462; 651–663–6004; www.wordalone.org.

48. Kairos news@yahoogroups.com.

49. 308 E Main St., Wilmore, KY 40390; 606–858–4661; jim@goodnewsmag.org; www.acrchurches.org.

50. 6024 Queens Gate Road, Oklahoma City, OK 73132; 405–721–3515; to-moden@aol.com.

   The Association for Church Renewal has sought out leading theologians, those already well informed on church renewal issues in their own mainline churches, who have shown the courage to speak out even when there are contravening pressures to keep silent. Each Commission theologian has a demonstrated record of engagement in the issues that actively occupy the renewing movements. Each has already provided useful counsel for confessing and renewing initiatives within their own communions. They have agreed to provide ongoing counsel for analogous movements and initiatives in the mainline Protestant denominations viewed conjointly.

51. PO Box 1325, Azusa, CA 91072–1325; 626–963–5966; www.nae.net.

52. 1110 Vermont Ave. NW, Suite 1189, Washington, DC 20005; 202–696–8430.

53. 4125 W Newport Ave., Chicago, IL 60641; 877–375–7373; www.touch-stonemag.com.

54. Alphaconferences@aol.com; www.alphausa.org; 866–872–5742.

55. PO Box 1990, San Marcos, CA 92079.

56. www.thejustcause.com.

57. Regeneration.bob@juno.com.

58. 1716 Spruce St., Philadelphia, PA 19103; 215–546–3696.

59. See *The Official Report of the Lambeth Conference 1998* (Harrisburg, PA: Morehouse, 1999).

60. *Daily Christian Advocate* 1, no. 2 (2000): 809.

CHAPTER 11

1. *Commoneo* is to remind, warn, advise, or bring to one's recollection.

2. This final chapter sets forth the reverse side of my argument for doctrinal boundaries in Chapter 9. I now focus on irenics rather than polemics.

3. Vincent's feast day is May 24, the same day as Wesley's Aldersgate experience in 1738, when his heart was "strangely warmed" by the reading of Luther on Romans. Wesley's homily on "The Catholic Spirit" stands intuitively, though not self-consciously, in the Vincentian Tradition.

4. Vincent of Lérins, *Commonitory*, ch. 1, FC 7:268.

5. John 14:26, NEB.

6. Readers who want to follow through on these readings and their implications may consult the works of José Madoz, William O'Conror, N. K. Chadwick, E. Griffe, Thomas Guarino, and A. G. Hamman. For more general related uses of the method see recent works of Walter Cardinal Kasper, Avery Cardinal Dulles, Jaroslav Pelikan, Christopher Seitz, David Steinmetz, Fitzsimmons Allison, Thomas Torrance, and George Lindbeck. It is beyond the range of this study to pursue the relationship between Vincent and John Henry Newman on the development of doctrine, but readers are referred to Newman's *University Sermons* (London: SPCK, 1970); Charles Stephen Dessain, *John Henry Newman* (London: Thomas Nelson), 1966; Nicholas Lash, *Newman on Development* (London: Sheed & Ward), 1975; Emmanuel Sullivan, *Things Old and New: An Ecumenical Reflection on the Theology of John Henry Newman* (London: St. Paul's, 1993); cf. Andrew Greeley, *The Persistence of Religion* (London: SCM Press, 1973); and Yves Congar, *Tradition and Traditions* (London: Burns & Oates, 1966).

7. By the fifth century largely undisputed.

8. Vincent of Lérins, *Commonitory*, ch. 2.

9. Ibid., FC 7:272; cf. NPNF 2 IX:152.

10. Vincent of Lérins, FC 7:271.

11. Vincent recognized that, if the claims of apostolic antiquity were not rightly understood, his own arguments could be used *against* ecumenical consent. For that reason, he set forth historical evidence showing that this method was not new or original to him, but rather had been the established custom and practice from the outset of Christian witness, as indicated by the Council of Jerusalem reported in Acts, and in the tradition from Paul to Nicea to Ephesus.

12. Vincent omitted Augustine's name in speaking of "eminent men," and much has been made of that omission. Vincent's silence does not imply that he disapproved of Augustine's teaching, however. To conclude that it does is to make too much of the argument from silence.

13. A fact that can be easily validated by counting references in the history of exegesis.

14. SCD 165, 69. This list includes all the ecumenical councils and the great "doctors of the church" except Gregory the Great, who had not yet been born.

15. Session I, NPNF 2 14:303.

16. Peter, Athanasius, Theophilus, and Cyril.

17. Vincent of Lérins, *Commonitory*, ch. 7, FC 7:278–280.

18. Gen. 9:22, 23, RSV.

19. Vincent of Lérins, *Commonitory*, ch. 8, FC 7:281–282.

20. John Henry Newman, *An Essay on the Development of Christian Doctrine*, 5.1.1 (London: Sheed & Ward, 1960), 125, translating Vincent of Lérins, *Commonitory*, 29.

21. Col. 4.15–16, italics added, NRSV.

22. Vincent of Lérins, *Commonitory*, ch. 8, FC 7:280.

23. Gal. 1:8–9 RSV; Vincent of Lérins, *Commonitory*, ch. 9, FC 7:282–283.

24. 1 Tim. 5:12.

25. Rom. 16:17, NKJV.

26. 1 Tim. 1:19.

27. Titus 1:10, 11.

28. 1 Tim. 6:4, 5.

29. 2 Tim. 2:16, 17.

30. 1 Tim. 5:13.

31. 2 Tim. 3:6, 7.

32. Vincent of Lérins, *Commonitory*, ch. 21, FC 7:305–307.

33. Ibid., FC 7:305.

34. Ibid.

35. Eccl. 10:8.

36. 1 Tim. 6:20; The Greek original is *kenophonias*; Vincent of Lérins Commoritory, ch. 21, FC 7:306.

37. Prov. 9:14–18, NRSV. How are the faithful to respond when trusted, credentialed, ordained teachers abandon the faith and in fact teach *contrary* to the faith? There are many examples of highly venerated teachers who previously had been orthodox but who made the choice to teach falsely. Having been given authority to teach in the community of faith, having received the community's trust, and having been ordained to its guardianship roles, they fell into disrepute or apostasy.

38. Vincent of Lérins, *Commonitory*, ch. 20, FC 7:303–305.

39. Ibid., FC 7:276.

40. Quoted in ibid., FC 7:277.

41. Cf. Eusebius, CH 7.7, NPNF 2 I:293–297; and Cyprian, *Epistle* 75.7, ANF 5:399.

42. Vincent of Lérins, *Commonitory*, ch. 4, FC 7:272–273.

43. Ibid., FC 7:273.

44. Bishop of Sirmium in Pannonia, deposed 351 C.E.

45. Ibid., ch. 11–12, FC 7:286, 289–290.

46. 1 Cor. 2:8b, NRSV.

47. Vincent of Lérins, *Commonitory,* ch. 12, FC 7:287.

48. Ibid., FC 7:288–290.

49. Ibid., FC 7:300.

50. Ibid., FC 7:301.

51. Ibid., ch. 18, FC 7:302–303.

52. Commentary on Matt. 5:1, quoted in Vincent of Lérins, *Commonitory,* FC 7:302–303.

53. Matt. 13:52, NRSV, italics added.

54. Sermon 74.5; NPNF 1 5:337 (Sermon 24), ACCS NT Matthew Ia, 291.

55. Vincent of Lérins, *Commonitory,* ch. 14, FC 7:293–295.

56. Ibid., ch. 13, FC 7:290–293.

57. Ibid., FC 7:297.

58. Ibid., ch. 14, FC 7:293–295.

59. Ibid., FC 7:298.

60. It has been argued that Vincent himself was uneasy with some of Augustine's views, but there can be no doubt that Vincent and the community at Lérins read Augustine thoroughly, viewed him as authoritative, and quarreled with him only on specific points, not with respect to his method or his authority as an exegete. From the fact that an Augustinian defender, Prosper of Aquitaine, wrote an essay resisting certain points made by Vincent, one cannot conclude that Vincent was generally opposed to Augustine. Such a conclusion requires excessive speculation. In any event, the charge that Vincent was semi-Pelagian (or, more rightly, semi-Augustinian) is not sustainable from his text. See William O'Connor, "Saint Vincent of Lérins and Saint Augustine," *Doctor Communis* 16 (1963):123–257.

INDEX